Tolkien and Wagner
The Ring and *Der Ring*

Christopher MacLachlan

Tolkien and Wagner

The Ring and *Der Ring*

2012

Cormarë Series No. 24

Series Editors: Peter Buchs • Thomas Honegger • Andrew Moglestue • Johanna Schön

Editor responsible for this volume: Thomas Honegger

Library of Congress Cataloging-in-Publication Data

MacLachlan, Christopher:
Tolkien and Wagner
The Ring and *Der Ring*
ISBN 978-3-905703-21-4

Subject headings:
Tolkien, J.R.R. (John Ronald Reuel), 1892-1973
Wagner, Richard, 1813-1883
The Lord of the Rings
Der Ring

Cormarë Series No. 24

First published 2012

© Walking Tree Publishers, Zurich and Jena, 2012

All rights reserved. No portion of this book may be reproduced, by any process or technique, without the express written consent of the publisher

Cover illustration *The Ride of the Valkyries* (1911) by Arthur Rackham

Set in Adobe Garamond Pro and Shannon by Walking Tree Publishers
Printed by Lightning Source in the United Kingdom and United States

Board of Advisors

Academic Advisors

Douglas A. Anderson (independent scholar)

Dieter Bachmann (Universität Zürich)

Patrick Curry (independent scholar)

Michael D.C. Drout (Wheaton College)

Vincent Ferré (Université de Paris 13)

Thomas Fornet-Ponse (Rheinische Friedrich-Wilhelms-Universität Bonn)

Verlyn Flieger (University of Maryland)

Christopher Garbowski (University of Lublin, Poland)

Mark T. Hooker (Indiana University)

Andrew James Johnston (Freie Universität Berlin)

Rainer Nagel (Johannes Gutenberg-Universität Mainz)

Helmut W. Pesch (independent scholar)

Tom Shippey (University of Winchester)

Allan Turner (Friedrich-Schiller-Universität Jena)

Frank Weinreich (independent scholar)

General Readers

Johan Boots

Jean Chausse

Friedhelm Schneidewind

Patrick Van den hole

Johan Vanhecke (Letterenhuis, Antwerp)

About the author

Christopher MacLachlan is a Senior Lecturer in the School of English at the University of St Andrews. His main interests are in Scottish literature and the eighteenth century. He has published articles on many authors, from Robert Burns to Muriel Spark, and edited Matthew Lewis's Gothic novel *The Monk* and R L Stevenson's *Travels with a Donkey* for Penguin Classics.

To the memory of
J Scott Allan,
teacher and friend,
whose generosity fostered
my love of Wagner

Contents

Series editor's preface
Acknowledgments

Chapter One
The resemblance begins   1

Chapter Two
From surface to depth   29

Chapter Three
What is *The Lord of the Rings* about?   65

Chapter Four
The Hobbit as paradigm   89

Chapter Five
Who is Gandalf?   109

Chapter Six
Gandalf and Wotan   123

Chapter Seven
The Ring and *Der Ring*   139

Chapter Eight
An ending   173

Appendix A
Der Ring des Nibelungen: a synopsis   189

Appendix B
The Legend of Sigurd and Gudrún   213

Bibliography   217

Index   223

Series Editor's Preface

Both rings were round, and there the resemblance ceases – this somewhat Gandalf-like comment by Tolkien has been too often misused as an excuse to avoid looking deeper into the relationship between Tolkien and Wagner. It is, of course, no small task to become sufficiently knowledgeable in both Tolkien's and Wagner's works, and the number of people sharing a taste or at least a sufficiently keen interest in the myth-making of these two artists has been rather limited. And yet, 'it never rains but it pours', as we say in Bree, and as chance had it, we are going to publish this year two monographs on this very topic.

Dr. MacLachlan contacted Walking Tree Publishers sometime in late 2010 and submitted a proposal for a book-length study on Tolkien and Wagner, which we were, after it had undergone the usual peer-reviewing process, happy to accept. Later, in March 2011 at the DTG Conference in Potsdam, we were asked by Renée Vink whether we would be interested in a study on Tolkien and Wagner. Needless to say that we were a bit surprised by the existence of two independently conceived and by then already well-advanced monographs on the same topic – the time has obviously been ripe for it! In the end, after having put the two authors into contact and after an extensive comparison of notes, it was decided that the two books were sufficiently different in their approach and of such high quality as to justify publishing them both.

Dr. MacLachlan's study is now in your hands. His insightful analysis of *The Lord of the Rings* (and especially Gandalf) from a Wagnerian point of view provides dozens of eye-openers and has, *inter alia*, the merit of being the first book-length academic (yet highly readable) and extremely knowledgeable study in this hitherto uncharted territory.

Finally, I would like to thank my co-series-editors, the members of the Board of Advisors who evaluated the initial project submission, and the students who served part of their internship as proofreaders and layouters for WTP and wish, in the name of WTP, an enjoyable and stimulating reading!

Thomas Honegger
Jena, January 2012

Acknowledgements

Parts of the third chapter of this book were presented in a paper delivered on 18 February 2011 to the Institute for Theology, Imagination and the Arts in the School of Divinity at the University of St Andrews and I am grateful for comments made during the discussion afterwards. I am also grateful to Renée Vink for her helpful comments and suggestions, all the more generous from somebody working on her own book on a similar subject, *Wagner and Tolkien: Mythmakers*, also published by Walking Tree Publishers.

St Andrews, Scotland, January 2012

CHAPTER ONE

The resemblance begins

Famously, when it was suggested that *The Lord of the Rings* is like *Der Ring des Nibelungen* Tolkien snapped back 'Both rings were round, and there the resemblance ceases' (*Letters*, page 306). Most of his readers and critics have taken him at his word. There are few but passing references to Wagner and his Ring in standard Tolkien criticism. Humphrey Carpenter's *The Letters of J R R Tolkien* (1981) has no reference to Wagner in its index and no index entry for the quotation given above. His biography (1977) has two index references to Wagner. On page 54 Carpenter says the young Tolkien 'delighted his friends with recitations from *Beowulf*, the *Pearl*, and *Sir Gawain and the Green Knight*, and recounted horrific episodes from the Norse *Völsungasaga*, with a passing jibe at Wagner whose interpretations of the myths he held in contempt'. How Carpenter is sure of this he does not say. On page 206 is another rebuttal of the suggestion, this time by Rayner Unwin in his reader's report on *The Lord of the Rings*, that Tolkien's Ring resembles Wagner's, backed up by the general statement that the 'comparison of his Ring with the *Nibelungenlied* and Wagner always annoyed Tolkien'. Carpenter then quotes the 'both rings were round' declaration.

Paul Kocher's *Master of Middle-Earth* (1972), one of the best early assessments of Tolkien's work, has no index entry for either Wagner or his Ring. Neither is there one in Jane Chance Nitzsche's *Tolkien's Art* (1979), although there is one for the *Nibelungenlied*, which is given a passing mention at the beginning of her fifth chapter, 'The Lord of the Rings: Tolkien's Epic'. Patrick Curry, in *Defending Middle-Earth* (1997), has a paragraph on page 48 (his other index entry for Wagner refers to a footnote to this passage) in which he repeats Tolkien's dismissal of a connection between the two Rings, adding that 'there is simply no Wagnerian "Götterdämmerung" in *The Lord of the Rings*'. Perhaps not, although there might be more to say about both *Götterdämmerung* and the end of *The Lord of the Rings*. The *J R R Tolkien Encyclopedia*, edited by Michael D C Drout (2007), has no entry for Wagner or *Der Ring*, although it is mentioned in a phrase that straddles pages 568 and 569 (so that the index gives an inflated idea of the size of this reference) where it is one of several examples of works containing riddle contests. There is no attempt to compare that of Bilbo and Gollum in *The Hobbit* with that of the Wanderer and Mime in *Siegfried*. The other passing reference to *Der Ring des Nibelungen* in the encyclopedia is in the entry on 'Rings' (page 571) where we are told no more than that '[s]ome argue that Tolkien was [...] inspired by Wagner's adaptation of the *Nibelungenlied* though he claimed that outside of the fact that both were round there was no connection'.

There are no index entries for Wagner, *Der Ring des Nibelungen* or the *Nibelungenlied* in Wayne G Hammond and Christina Scull's *Reader's Companion* (2005) to *The Lord of the Rings*, nor in the 'Reader's Guide' of their *J R R Tolkien Companion and Guide* (2006), although there are entries for Wagner in the 'Chronology' volume of that work. Brian Rosebury's *Tolkien: A Cultural Phenomenon* (2003), one of the most independent-minded books on Tolkien, has three references to Wagner but none of them have any real substance. Tom Shippey's second monograph on Tolkien, *J R R Tolkien: Author of the Century* (2000), has no references to Wagner in its index but his first book, *The Road to Middle-earth*, at any rate in its latest, 2005 version, has a paragraph on Tolkien and Wagner in Appendix A (pages 388f). Shippey quotes the dismissal by Tolkien of any resemblance other than roundness between the Rings but adds:

> This is not entirely true. The motifs of the riddle-contest, the cleansing fire, the broken weapon preserved for an heir, all occur in both works, as of course does the theme of 'the Lord of the Ring as the slave of the Ring', *des Ringes Herr als des Ringes Knecht* [...] (page 388)

The German quotation is from Wagner's libretto for *Das Rheingold*, which makes it possible that Shippey has at least looked into Wagner's work. But he goes no further here because his main point is that Wagner is 'the most obvious example' of 'modern attempts to rewrite or interpret old material' which, says Shippey, always irritated Tolkien because 'almost all of [them] he thought led to failures of tone and spirit' (page 388).

Shippey returned to the question of Tolkien and Wagner in a talk he gave at a conference in 2003, reprinted as 'The Problem of the Rings: Tolkien and

Chapter One: The resemblance begins

Wagner' in his essay collection *Roots and Branches* (2007). In some ways this is the fullest academic study of the subject in print hitherto (although it pre-dates the appearance of Tolkien's own previously lost versions of the Norse stories in *The Legend of Sigurd and Gudrún* in 2009). Shippey begins with the 'both rings were round' quotation, commenting that it was 'evidently meant to terminate discussion' (page 97), but he points out that, although Tolkien made dismissive remarks about other things, such as *Macbeth* and allegory, that did not mean that he did not use them himself. Shippey suggests in fact that Tolkien was well acquainted with Wagner's work, including *Der Ring des Nibelungen*, but that 'to Tolkien, Wagner seemed an enthusiastic amateur' (page 98) because he, unlike Tolkien, could not read Old Norse and so could not study the Icelandic sources of the story of the Nibelung's Ring in the original. Nor could Wagner participate in the philological arguments about these sources that were part of Tolkien's professional expertise. Here Shippey is adding to the thesis of his books on Tolkien that he was first and foremost a philologist and his professional life was dedicated to a losing struggle on behalf of his conception of his profession against a growing hostility and, worse, indifference to the proper study of texts and languages, what Tolkien believed was absolutely fundamental to the study of literature, history and culture. It is because of this, according to Shippey, that Tolkien reacted with such feeling against the idea that he owed anything to a dabbling opera composer. Nevertheless, Shippey is fair-minded enough to add that 'just as *The Lord of the Rings* is the most important and influential mediævalist work of the twentieth century, so Wagner's opera cycle was the most important of the nineteenth' (page 98) and that 'the similarities and differences between them deserve to be drawn out'.

Shippey goes on, however, to discuss neither Wagner nor Tolkien but instead the mediæval sources the former used and the latter knew, investigating a problem of the Nibelung narrative caused by gaps and differences among the sources, a problem Wagner had to solve to create his own, coherent version of the story, and a problem, Shippey says, of the kind Tolkien would have found attractive, since he was always drawn to questions of lost meanings. The bulk of Shippey's essay (pages 99 to 107 of a text that runs from page 97 to page 114) is devoted to this discussion (which need not detain us here) before he concludes that 'Wagner deals with all this neatly and expeditiously' (page 108), although it meant reducing two major characters into lesser figures in his version. Then at last Shippey turns directly to the possible influence of Wagner on Tolkien, but again he starts with a convoluted example, arguing that Mime, the unpleasant dwarf in Wagner's *Siegfried*, may have a connection with the dwarf Mim in Tolkien's tale of Túrin, one of his 'lost tales' (a version of which appears in *The Silmarillion* as the twenty-first part of the *Quenta Silmarillion*, 'Of Túrin Turambar'). Plausibly enough Shippey sees this tale as partly a rewriting of the story of Siegfried (most notably because in both stories the hero kills a dragon, and in a similar way) and argues that, although Mim is as unprepossessing as Mime, Tolkien, unlike Wagner, offers some excuse for his malice and treachery, as though correcting the Wagnerian presentation of dwarves as contemptible subhumans.

Shippey's next point is more straightforward and has to do with Wagner's conception of his Ring as central to the story, which is not the case in any of the ancient sources:

> It was Wagner who – one has to concede in very Tolkienian fashion – noted the gaps of the ancient sources and wrote his version of the story determinedly into them. He followed the Ring from the Rhinemaidens to Alberich, to Loge and Wotan, to Fafner, to Siegfried, to Brünnhilde, and back to Siegfried, to Brünnhilde, to the Rhinemaidens. It is a continuing presence in the story, in much the same way, at some time between *The Hobbit* and *The Lord of the Rings*, Tolkien devised a chain of transmission from Sauron to Isildur, to Gollum, to Bilbo, to Frodo, with a final destruction by fire which parallels the return of Wagner's Ring to the Rhinemaidens and its drowning in the flood. (page 112)

Shippey notes that, while Wagner's Ring does not itself make its wearer invisible, it is closely associated with the magic helmet, the Tarnhelm, that does, and that Wagner's Ring is like Tolkien's a Ring of Power that enslaves its owner.

Shippey however goes on to argue that what does not echo in Tolkien is 'the sense that Wagner understands and sympathises with the desire for power' (page 117) and he claims that '[t]here is no-one in [Wagner's] cycle who does *not* want the Ring, and there are no scenes of powerful characters refusing to take it, as there are repeatedly – Gandalf, Aragorn, Galadriel, Faramir – in Tolkien's story' (page 113). This rather overlooks the fact that in Wagner Siegfried gives Brünnhilde the Ring as token of his love (although it is true that he takes it back from her, but he is not himself when he does so, having

Chapter One: The resemblance begins

been given a potion to make him forget that he has ever known her before). More significantly, Shippey also overlooks the fact that at the climax of *Das Rheingold* Wotan is persuaded by Erda to give up the Ring to the giants Fafner and Fasolt to conclude his bargain with them by substituting Alberich's gold for the goddess Freia as their payment for building Valhalla. It is true this is not exactly a refusal to take the Ring like Gandalf's and that almost immediately Wotan begins scheming how to get the Ring back, but he does give it away and in a deep sense it is this action, its consequences and its significance that are at the centre of Wagner's *Ring* just as much as the refusals to take the Ring of Gandalf, Aragorn, Galadriel and Faramir are central to Tolkien's Ring story.

It is at this point in Shippey's article that he brings in the Nazi adoption of Wagner and says 'Wagner and Tolkien were on opposite sides of a great divide created by two world wars and all that went with them' (page 113) and he refers the reader to Tolkien's letter to his son Michael dated 9 June 1941:

> [...] I have in the War a burning private grudge – which would probably make me a better soldier at 49 than I was a 22: against that ruddy little ignoramus Adolf Hitler [...] Ruining, perverting, misapplying, and making for ever accursed, that noble northern spirit, a supreme contribution to Europe, which I have ever loved, and tried to present in its true light. (*Letters*, pages 55f)

Is Shippey correct in taking this to apply to Wagner as well as Hitler? On the other hand, it is not implausible to suppose that Tolkien, a soldier of the First World War, in which he lost close friends, and the father of a combatant in the Second World War, would find it hard to forgive Wagner's German nationalism. As Shippey says, even if it

> might or might not be possible to excuse Wagner for the uses made of his work by the Nazis after he was dead, [...] from Tolkien's perspective, perhaps even more than from ours, the seeds of horror were there in Siegfried's casual and uncondemned brutality, in the picture of a divine/heroic world constantly threatened by cunning, sneaking dwarf-shapes, so easily converted ideologically into *Untermenschen*, sub-humans. (page 113)

But perhaps the vehemence of Tolkien's rejection of an association with Wagner is not unrelated to the fact that his own orcs are even more sub-human and hated than Wagner's dwarves. Shippey, as nervous as most modern critics and readers of the possibility of a connection leading from Tolkien through Wagner to the Nazis, safely concludes that 'if Tolkien did take anything from Wagner, it was perhaps no more than the idea that something could be done with the idea of the Ring of Power, something more, and more laden with significance, than anything in an ancient source, but at the same time and very definitely *not* what Wagner had done with it' (page 113). So that's all right, then; but it rather begs the question what exactly Wagner did with his Ring, and how it was so definitely not what Tolkien did with his.

That is not, however, the end of Shippey's discussion. He has one final, if tentative, thing to say, though it is not very clearly expressed. He begins by pointing out how protective Tolkien was of his own creations, how he felt that 'people should at least ask his permission before using the names and settings which he himself had invented', and yet 'he was well aware that some parts of Middle-earth were not his own invention, were the common property of the ages' (page 113). This looks as though it will develop into a point about Tolkien's bad faith in his acknowledgement of his sources, and perhaps a comment to the effect that his rejection of any debt to Wagner is symptomatic of an embarrassing and embarrassed state of denial about literary indebtedness in general. There is, surely, a general air, in Tolkien's comments on his own work, that it is unique and original. For a man who spent his working life tracing connections between texts and variants, Tolkien was strikingly reluctant to talk about sources and influences on his own work, repeatedly expressing, for example, a dislike of biographical studies as background to the interpretation of literary works. But this is not the point Shippey wants to make. Instead he moves on to the notion that stories have a kind of life of their own, independent of authors, sometimes conveying their essence despite the authors' intentions. 'He thought,' writes Shippey, 'that both Shakespeare and Milton were seriously misguided artistically and politically, but they were great poets, and sometimes – in *Macbeth*, in *Comus* – it seemed as if the language spoke through them, their stories took them over. Possibly the same was true of Wagner' (page 114). For that reason, Shippey suggests, Wagner, whether one likes him and his work or not, might still have to be reckoned with as part of the tradition. This subtle argument certainly says something about Shippey's fair-mindedness, and his fair-mindedness about Wagner, but it releases the dangerous thought that Tolkien too may be another case in which great tales 'speak through and even against their individual authors' (page 114).

It is tempting to think that in making this point Shippey is reacting to his reading of other articles on Tolkien and Wagner, not to say on Tolkien more generally, that seek to preserve what they see as the purity of his meaning from contamination by disturbing influences. As we have seen, much Tolkien criticism ignores the possibility of a connection with Wagner. Some that does consider the comparison worth attention nevertheless comes to comforting conclusions. David Harvey, for example, in his online essay 'One Ring to Rule Them All: A Study of the History, Symbolism and Meaning of the One Ring in J R R Tolkien's Middle-earth' (last updated 20 October 1995), has a section (number 5) on 'Tolkien's Ring and *Der Ring des Nibelungen*' (available online – see the bibliography), consisting mainly of a synopsis of Wagner's *Ring* cycle, that concludes that

> [i]t is quite clear that Tolkien's work owes nothing to *Der Ring des Nibelungen* and it is impossible to draw comparisons between the two works. The few similarities that there are operate as faint and disparate echoes of one another, coming from a distant and common source.

A more sophisticated discussion leading to the same conclusion is Bradley J Birzer's lecture '"Both rings were round, and there the resemblance [c]eases": Tolkien, Wagner, Nationalism, and Modernity' for the Intercollegiate Studies Institute in 2001, published in 2003 and available online (see the bibliography). Birzer explains the background to Tolkien's knowledge of Wagner, noting particularly the influence of C S Lewis. As he says, '[o]f the two major Inklings, Lewis was far more taken with Wagner than was Tolkien' and he goes on:

> Though Tolkien never held Wagner in the same regard as did Lewis, one cannot completely dismiss the comparison between Tolkien and Wagner. At a superficial level, the two ring stories share several things in common: dragons (with vulnerable spots) guarding treasures; important rings that cause evil, directly or indirectly; the broken sword remade; a wandering, grey [*sic*] deity, inspiring men; and the moral and physical stretching of the ring's original possessor. Perhaps most important, Wagner and Tolkien both greatly admired northern courage.

Note the characterisation of these similarities as superficial. This is the only passage in Birzer's lecture dealing directly with the two works and what they might have in common. Most of the rest of his essay deals with what Tolkien said and thought about his work and his ideas, and there is very little about Wagner. Birzer's first move is to claim that even the superficial similarities between the two Ring stories do not prove Tolkien borrowed from Wagner; they only show that both artists drew from the same sources. What's more, Tolkien had many other influences (as though Wagner didn't) and he used his sources differently from Wagner. Birzer names three of Wagner's purposes: nationalism, socialism and 'to show that man could attain his own godhead'. The rest of his lecture is divided into three sections: 'Tolkien vs. nationalism', 'Tolkien vs. socialism' and 'Tolkien vs. Apotheosis'. As these subtitles indicate, Birzer's argument is that Tolkien held views completely opposed to those of Wagner, but hardly anything is said about the latter so that Birzer's reader just has to accept that Wagner's views have nothing to be said for them.

In the first section, on nationalism, for example, Wagner is mentioned in the opening sentence but not referred to again. Instead an outline is given of Tolkien's attempt to reconcile pagan and Christian culture focusing on his study of *Beowulf*, followed by an account of his feelings for England. As Birzer says, Middle-earth represents Europe, and the Shire represents England. 'Tolkien originally hoped that his legendarium would serve as a mythology for England,' Birzer says, but it grew much larger to become 'a myth for the restoration of Christendom'. He quotes from Tolkien's letter to Charlotte and Denis Plimmer of 8 February 1967 in which he writes that in *The Lord of the Rings* 'the progress of the tale ends in what is far more like the re-establishment of an effective Holy Roman Empire with its seat in Rome than anything that would be devised by a "Nordic"' (*Letters*, page 376; the last nine words of this quotation are not used by Birzer but seem worth adding here). This remark of Tolkien's allows Birzer to move on to Lord Acton's essay 'Nationality' (not, as Birzer calls it, 'Nationalism') of 1862 as a demonstration of the dangers of nationalism. He even uses Acton to drag in a reference to Nietzsche, although this must puzzle those who do not know the association of Nietzsche with Wagner, and puzzle even more those who know how that association ended in Nietzsche's denunciations of the composer. It is hard not to think that Birzer is here simply evoking Wagner and Nietzsche as bogeymen, as though there is no need to do more than name them for his readers to react as if in the presence of simple wickedness.

On the other hand, Tolkien's love of England is presented as wholesome and natural. Quoting from an interview of 1966, Birzer moves from Tolkien's 'native feeling and personal wonder about the English countryside' to his 'wonder and delight in the earth as it is, particularly with the natural earth'. Those of us from the northern and western parts of the British Isles are familiar with the way the English regard their national feelings as somehow natural and God-given, indeed so normal and human that they don't count as nationalism as usually understood, more a sort of instinctive rightness of response that other people, not blessed by English birth, can only envy and parody in their own desperate and strident ways. It is odd to find an American sharing this view. Tolkien, with his German surname and South African place of birth, had certain problems about assuming this English birthright, but he managed it. Although his 'earliest memories are of Africa,' he says in the 1966 interview, 'it was alien to me,' and in a letter to his son Michael of 18 March 1941 he writes '[t]hough a Tolkien by name, I am a Suffield [his mother's name] by tastes, talents, and upbringing, and any corner of that county [Worcestershire] (however fair or squalid) is in an indefinable way "home" to me, as no other part of the world is' (*Letters*, page 54). In a set of notes about himself Tolkien made for his American publishers in 1955 he wrote that 'I am indeed in English terms a West-midlander at home only in the counties upon the Welsh Marches; and it is, I believe, as much due to descent as to opportunity that Anglo-Saxon and Western Middle English and alliterative verse have been both a childhood attraction and my main professional sphere' (*Letters*, page 218). Tolkien, with his tweed suits, pipe-smoking, beer-drinking and hearty dislike of the French and fancy foreign ways, came close to a caricature of a certain sort of Englishman (as did C S Lewis, despite his Ulster origins). On the other hand, Tolkien's Roman Catholicism often made him feel outside the central core of Englishness and his identification with his mother, with her English roots, also includes a sense of her as a kind of internal exile because of her conversion to Catholicism against the wishes, and traditions, of her family. In short, Tolkien's nationalism, like all nationalisms (even Wagner's, not to mention Nietzsche's) is neither simple nor straightforward, and although the English often succeed in persuading themselves that theirs is a uniquely gentle and benign form of national feeling, especially compared with their versions of other nationalisms, particularly that of the Germans (or those noisy Americans), it might not be wise to take them always at their own self-evaluation.

For one thing, it might prevent us from looking more closely at Tolkien's feeling for England and asking questions about it. Birzer, as mentioned above, records that Tolkien 'hoped that his legendarium would serve as a mythology for England' but he does not have room to explain what this means. In the long letter of 1951 Tolkien wrote to Milton Waldman, in which he gives a synopsis of *The Lord of the Rings*, and much else, he makes the following self-deprecating remarks about his own mythologising:

> Do not laugh! But once upon a time (my crest has long since fallen) I had a mind to make a body of more or less connected legend, ranging from the large and cosmogonic, to the level of romantic fairy-story [...] which I could dedicate simply to: to England; to my country [...] I would draw some of the great tales in fullness, and leave many only placed in the scheme, and sketched. The cycles should be linked to a majestic whole, and yet leave scope for other minds and hands, wielding paint and music and drama. Absurd. (*Letters*, pages 144f)

We know now, thanks to Christopher Tolkien's labours among his father's papers, that a vast amount of this material was already written and still being produced when Tolkien wrote the letter to Waldman, although his itch to revise and refashion left much of it half-finished or in multiple variants at his death. Tolkien's tone in the extract from the letter to Waldman disguises the scale of his commitment, as great, surely, as Wagner's, to the idea of a new national mythology. No doubt there were times, like that of the writing of the letter, when Tolkien thought it 'absurd', but he would go on devoting time and thought to it to the end of his days. And to start with, at least, the legendarium has a very strong national significance. Birzer says that 'Tolkien often noted that Middle-earth represented Europe' but in fact initially it was more than a representation – it was the place itself. The exact details changed as Tolkien's ideas about it evolved, but many of the place-names of Middle-earth designated real places, particularly in England, and the large island central to much of his mythology, the home of Tolkien's elves, was not a representation of Great Britain but the actual place in a lost past remembered only in dream and legend. As Verlyn Flieger shows, in her book *A Question of Time: J R R Tolkien's Road to Faërie* (1997), Tolkien at least twice, in two unfinished works, *The Lost Road* (1937) and *The Notion Club Papers* (1945-46), tried to write a story of travel through time back to this earlier elvish England. A fundamental part of his mythology was the story of an Anglo-Saxon voyager who found his way to the country of the elves and somehow brought back tales and facts about them, information that formed the basis for English folk-tales. Tolkien's own writings were the imaginative expansion of these scraps and broken memories.

As time went on Tolkien lost faith in the veracity of his legends and dismantled some of the structures that framed them as history rather than fiction. *The Hobbit* and *The Lord of the Rings* can be viewed as a shift out of the legendarium as history towards plain storytelling. Yet even in the 1960s Tolkien was still concerned with the problem of his cosmogony, debating how to reconcile what had been a flat-earth cosmos with a round-earth solar system, because he had come to see this as the more acceptable, since more credible, to modern minds. It may seem 'absurd' that an Oxford professor in the twentieth century should believe in an elaborate mythological system as a true history of his country and its continent in an age before recorded history as it is generally accepted, but in some sense this appears to be the case with Tolkien. One supposes that he could not have believed in it all of the time, and one infers from the changes and rewritings of most of the myths and stories that Tolkien did not always believe they were unalterable facts, but conversely some things persist in more or less the same form in the stories for many, many years, and some basic items have the persistence of conviction. Tolkien repeatedly refers to a recurrent dream of a tidal wave sweeping across the land, a scene that he connected to the myth of Atlantis but, more vigorously, to his own myth of the island of Númenor. So vivid and serious are his references to this event in his mythology that it is not so easy to assert that he did not believe that it happened.

Whatever one concludes about the truth status of Tolkien's myths, there is no doubt that he meant them seriously, to himself first of all but also to his country (even if he was too embarrassed to say so to Waldman without hedging). Why was this? Was he unusual, in England, for instance, in feeling the need to do this during his lifetime? And if there is here, as there surely is, a comparison with other nationalistic inventors of myths, what does that mean in Tolkien's case? Birzer says that Wagner wrote operas based on the pagan northern myths to give the German people 'a nationalist identity'. It was, he writes, 'no accident that Wagner wrote and completed the Ring Opera as Germany and Bismarck struggled to unify and find a common voice', referring to the process of the political unification of Germany in the nineteenth century. Germany, like Italy, was a relative late-comer to this process. Other nations, notably France, Britain and the United States of America, had gone through the nation-forming process in the previous century, acquiring as they did so national flags, anthems, calendar customs and traditions of art, music and literature, amongst other things. Wagner might well have been surprised to have been told that in the twentieth century an English writer would still be engaged in creating a mythology for his country, since he and other German nationalists were sure that what they were doing was only catching up with the English, as well as the French. The Germans felt they had been left behind in nation-building and it is arguable that the intensity of their efforts to catch up was partly responsible for the stridency of some of the results, and the failure to avoid extremes of national fervour that led to unpleasant political consequences. Tolkien's awareness of these was no doubt one reason for the inhibited way he went about constructing his secret mythology, and for his embarrassment about it that leads in later life to his playing down the nationalistic purpose of his legendarium (an attitude his supporters have been happy to share).

There is, however, a clue to the reason for Tolkien's late entry to the national mythology stakes in his allegiance to an English rather than a British nationality. The nation-forming of eighteenth-century Britain was, as Linda Colley shows in her book *Britons: Forging the Nation, 1707-1837* (1992), directed to the idea of Britishness, a concept that would include English, Scots, Welsh and Irish, matching the political union of the four in the United Kingdom. In Tolkien we have an early sign of an English dissatisfaction with the British union of England with what are generally regarded as her Celtic neighbours. In the 1955 notes for his American publisher, Tolkien says of his father's German ancestors that they migrated to England over two hundred years ago 'and became quickly intensely English (not British)' (*Letters*, page 218). Although he then claims that he finds the Welsh language 'specially attractive', he also says that he finds 'both Gaelic and the air of Ireland wholly alien' (page 219). Of Scotland he says no more than that he has often been there, but never north of the River Tay, that is to say, never into the Scottish Highlands, the icons of Scottish identity. In the fiercely anti-American letter of 9 December 1943 that he wrote to his son Christopher, Tolkien states that 'I love England (not Great Britain and certainly not the British Commonwealth (grr!))' (*Letters*, page 65).

Chapter One: The resemblance begins   13

Nationalism is usually defined by distinction from what it is not, from the other, and here it seems clear that the other that Tolkien the Englishman was not was British, that is, the union of English, Scots, Welsh and (some) Irish. It is hard not to conclude that part of the impulse behind his mythology for England was a reaction against what he saw as the overshadowing of the English by the Scots, Welsh and Irish. They had, indeed, been quite successful in establishing for themselves, from the later eighteenth century onwards, strong national images that, although not always matched by political power, had created conspicuous cultural identities for their countries, insisting on them as nations despite union with England (and in the case of Ireland this had led in Tolkien's lifetime to partial disunion with the rest of the United Kingdom). Far from being ahead of Wagner, then, Tolkien was essentially behind him and the Germans in so far as he felt in the 1920s that *his* nation lacked the cultural markers of identity that other nations, even the smaller parts of the United Kingdom, already possessed. And like Wagner he turned to historical sources to construct this national culture, although, feeling that there were few remains of a specifically English historical culture, he was compelled to invent some. Ironically, this put Tolkien in a similar position to one of the pioneers of the Scottish effort to devise a national culture, James Macpherson (1736-96), who astonished the eighteenth century by publishing what he claimed were translations of epic poetry by Ossian, a Scottish Gaelic bard of the Dark Ages. Working at the beginnings of the modern age of textual scholarship (the period when several of the texts Tolkien found most interesting, such as *Beowulf*, were first attracting academic attention), Macpherson over-reached himself in claiming ancient authority for his texts. The Englishman Samuel Johnson was particularly ferocious in denouncing them as forgeries and Macpherson's *Ossian*, though it continued to have influence, both in Britain and beyond, well into the nineteenth century, became an object lesson in how *not* to create a national mythology. Yet the boundaries between archival discovery and reconstruction (or fabrication), between ancient authority and editorial adjustment, remained a tendentious feature of textual studies, especially of early texts and folklore, mirrored in Tolkien's case by the scholarship that has arisen around the establishment of the texts of his legendarium. Fortunately for him, he unlike Macpherson made no claims to be basing his work on real literary remains and concealed the notion that the events he described were historical. This difference between Tolkien and Macpherson is crucial but it is not definitive. There is much else about Tolkien's writings that makes him 'our Ossian', as Christopher Ricks said in the *New York Review of Books* (24 January 1974, page 44), and, like Macpherson, and Wagner, a would-be creator of a national culture.

Tolkien is not however unique in this in England in the first half of the twentieth century, although the parallels are not so much literary as musical. A number of English composers of the period consciously attempted to create a national style, often based on folk music, with settings of English literary texts or musical dramatisations of English historical events, much the same kind of traditional material that interested Tolkien, although in literary rather than musical forms. Sir Edward Elgar, with his cantata *Caractacus* (1898) and his setting of John Henry Newman's religious poem *The Dream of Gerontius* (1900), is an example, and the more interesting here for his musical debts to Wagner. Other examples are Gustav Holst (like Tolkien, an Englishman with a German name), Ralph Vaughan Williams and, of the next generation, Benjamin Britten. An interesting lesser figure, Rutland Boughton (1878-1960), now largely forgotten, combined a style based on English and Celtic tradition with an attempt to establish an annual music festival at Glastonbury that ran from 1914 to 1926 in emulation of Wagner's Bayreuth. Boughton's fairy opera, *The Immortal Hour* (1914), a great success in its time, has a strong resemblance to Tolkien's legends except that it is avowedly Celtic in its sources and inspiration. The lack of any references by Tolkien to this work, given 216 consecutive performances in London in 1922, and 160 more the following year, is somewhat surprising, particularly as the theme of the opera, the marriage of a mortal king to a fairy immortal, is close to the heart of Tolkien's own work. But Tolkien's apparent ignorance of Boughton's attempts to create an English national opera does not weaken the parallel with Tolkien's own nationalist ambitions, and indeed helps to align him with a nationalist movement in English culture in the first half of the twentieth century that, despite what Birzer says, is an echo of the European nationalist cultural projects to which Wagner belongs, along with representatives of other nations, such as Dvořák, Smetana, Grieg and the group of Russian composers including Borodin, Mussorgsky and Rimsky-Korsakov. In fact, in musical terms, English nationalists were indeed the followers of the lead given by German and other Continental composers, and anxious by their own discoveries of genuine English folk music and the composition of works derived from it to refute the nineteenth-century jibe that England was 'das Land ohne Musik', the land without music.

Birzer's second section, 'Tolkien vs. socialism', is as short of references to Wagner as his first, and he makes no effort to explain Wagner's politics. He seems to share the common US prejudice against socialism in any form. Whereas in Europe politicians and political parties labelling themselves socialist have been acceptable enough to form long-lasting governments, in the USA 'socialist' seems to be regarded as an accusation that can destroy a political career. In the presidential election of 2008, and since, the term has been used as an accusation against Barack Obama, and often leads to the assertion that he is not just a socialist but in fact a communist. This is the move that Birzer makes in his essay, swiftly replacing 'socialism' with 'communism' and then going on to explain how the Roman Catholic Church identified the latter as a 'satanic eruption', as he puts it. He then broadens the attack to include 'machine-driven capitalism' (an odd bedfellow for communism) and 'the oppressive democratic bureaucracies of the western world'. To support his view that Tolkien was opposed to all of these he quotes from several of Tolkien's most bitter letters. To his son Christopher Tolkien wrote on 29 November 1943 'I would arrest anybody who uses the word State (in any sense other than the inanimate realm of England and its inhabitants, a thing that has neither power, rights nor mind); and after a chance of recantation, execute them if they remained obstinate!' (*Letters*, page 63). Even if one agrees that the power of the state over the individual in modern times is excessive, and oppressive, summary execution for political differences is an unpleasant idea at the best of times and even more so in 1943, when many thousands, if not millions, were being put to death for political reasons. One is glad of Tolkien's concession of 'a chance of recantation' before the sentence. One might suggest that it is not fair to base ideas of Tolkien's politics on a private letter written during one of the darkest periods of the Second World War. Birzer does not give dates for the quotations from Tolkien he uses in his lecture. He quotes several times from letters of 1943, 1944 and 1945, and also from drafts of letters, probably never sent, of 1956, and makes no comment on the irritable tone of the wartime letters. It is not clear how Birzer regards Tolkien's remarks. Does he mean them simply as evidence of Tolkien's views or does he wish to imply that Tolkien was right, for instance, to sympathise with Franco as a defender of the Church in Spain, and to damn Churchill and Roosevelt as well as Stalin as they met to decide on how to defeat Nazi Germany? Birzer's connecting of Tolkien's anti-communism with that of the Roman Catholic Church leaves the impression that he thinks Tolkien's views rested on more than his own opinions, but when Birzer writes 'Democracy, itself the newly-fashionable word in England during the war, was nothing but a sham, according to Tolkien', it is hard to see where he himself stands, and he leaves the unpleasant feeling that not only does he think Tolkien rejected popular democracy but that he agrees with him. Quoting Tolkien's criticism of democracy along with his remarks about executing those whose politics offend him tends to make Tolkien seem both unpleasant and intolerant and, paradoxically, more like the usual idea of Wagner. Birzer tries to make amends by emphasising Tolkien's environmental concerns (ironically, the same move might be made by defenders of Wagner) and ends the section with a description of the Shire as 'Tolkien's best representation of an ideal agrarian republic', what Birzer concludes is 'essentially an isolationist Jeffersonian society based on a natural aristocracy'. It might be suggested that Wagner knew more about living under an aristocracy than Tolkien ever did, or Birzer does. As with Tolkien's nationalism, Tolkien's politics are left somewhat unexamined by Birzer. His assimilation of the Shire to a Jeffersonian, that is, an American, model is surely self-revealing. It ignores the evident monarchism of the outcome of *The Return of the King*, what Tolkien, to repeat an earlier quotation, described as 'the re-establishment of an effective Holy Roman Empire', a concept that can be most charitably described as wishful thinking, even without repeating Voltaire's remark in his *Essai sur les mœurs et l'esprit des nations* (1756) that the historical original was neither holy, Roman nor an empire.

Birzer's third section, 'Tolkien vs. Apotheosis', is the shortest (three paragraphs only) but just as puzzling as the others. He begins by saying 'Tolkien understood Wagner's apotheosis in the "Twilight of the Gods" as merely a repeat of man's first sin in the Garden of Eden'. One wonders not only how Birzer knows this but also what he means. Presumably by 'Wagner's apotheosis' he does not mean the deification of Wagner himself but Wagner's depiction of the deification of somebody else, although it is hard to see which of the characters in *Götterdämmerung* might be involved. By the end of the opera Siegfried is dead, Brünnhilde has sacrificed herself on his funeral pyre, Hagen has plunged to his death in the Rhine and the river has flooded the hall of the Gibichungs, while Valhalla and the gods within it, including Wotan, have been consumed by fire. What all this signifies is not easy to say briefly but it does not lend itself straightforwardly to an argument for the triumph of anybody, god, human or dwarf. Wagner himself, although only after he had written the libretto and come under the influence of Schopenhauer, tended to view the ending of *Der Ring des Nibelungen* in a very pessimistic light, and the whole work as about tragic failure. Earlier in his lecture Birzer quotes Roger Scruton, the British philosopher, saying that Wagner 'proposed man as his own redeemer and art as the transfiguring rite of passage to a higher world' (from *An Intelligent Person's Guide to Modern Culture* (1998), page 68 of the 2000 edition), but although this is certainly a theme (or pair of themes) in most of Wagner's mature works, from *Tannhäuser* to *Parsifal*, including *Der Ring des Nibelungen*, the treatment of this theme is never simple.

Nevertheless, Birzer presses on with a brief account of Tolkien's ideas about the relationship of the artist as sub-creator to God the Creator, leading up to Tolkien's own conclusion, from his essay *On Fairy-stories*, that conversely the best creative work is God's own story with a happy ending, the Christian Gospel. 'As opposed to the progressive who attempts to remake man in man's image,' writes Birzer, 'the true and Godly sub-Creator creates to glorify and reveal the beauty of God's creation.' This leaves Wagner to bear the blame for nationalism, socialism and apotheosis, and not just for his own time but also, 'as the killing fields of the twentieth century have proven', for ours as well. By the end of the lecture, then, any suggestion that Wagner might have influenced Tolkien has for Birzer become not just unconvincing but downright outrageous, since it would associate Tolkien with all that he thinks is bad about the twentieth century. Somewhat paradoxically, however, Birzer's discussion, particularly in relation to political matters, brings Tolkien into contact with the very issues Birzer wants to isolate Tolkien from, and he opens up the dark possibility that, if it could be shown that Tolkien was after all influenced by Wagner, *The Lord of the Rings* might be something other than the uplifting Christian parable Birzer would like it to be.

And there are people who do insist that Tolkien was indeed influenced by Wagner. One of the most serious and reasonable of these is Edward R Haymes, Professor of German and Comparative Literature at Cleveland State University, who lays out his argument in an essay entitled 'The Two Rings: Tolkien and Wagner', given as a lecture to a Wagner Symposium in 2005 (available online – see the bibliography). Haymes covers a lot of the same ground as Shippey but with an inclination more towards Wagner than Tolkien. He points out that, although an amateur in philological terms, Wagner was steeped in the German and Icelandic sources of the myths he used. Haymes agrees with Shippey that it was Wagner who added to these sources the idea of a Ring of Power, and he explains in detail how Wagner uses that Ring in his opera cycle and parallels this with Tolkien's use of a Ring in his fiction. 'I maintain,' writes Haymes, 'that Tolkien must have absorbed Wagner's notion of the Ring even though he probably knew the Icelandic sources Wagner used better than the composer himself' and he adds that '[t]here are too many aspects of Wagner's specific adaptation of the Ring motif that show up in Tolkien for this to be an accident'. Haymes goes on to add notes on further parallels – the motif of the broken sword reforged, the rejection of modern industrialism, what he calls the triumphal endings of both Ring stories – and concludes:

> If Tolkien had never heard of Wagner: if the *Ring of the Nibelung* had not been a part of every young man's education in the first quarter of the twentieth century; if his best friend [C S Lewis] had not been a powerful Wagnerian; then we might believe that Tolkien had derived some, if not all these aspects from other sources, but the evidence is overwhelming. Tolkien stands convicted of being a closet Wagnerian.

That leaves Haymes with the problem of explaining 'Tolkien's virulent rejection of Wagner as a source'. His answer is to draw a further parallel between the two and suggest that, just as Wagner repeatedly slighted those, like the composer Meyerbeer, who assisted his career and inspired him, denying debts to others, so, Haymes senses, Tolkien showed 'a similar refusal to accept the fact that he had learned much from Wagner's mythopoesis and from his art as a whole'. As suggested above, there is something in this, given Tolkien's reluctance to admit there were influences on his work, but there may however be stronger, less speculative reasons for Tolkien's reluctance to admit to a connection with Wagner, including the historical and biographical circumstances, particularly

Chapter One: The resemblance begins 19

in connection with the two World Wars, noted earlier. More of this will be said below.

Haymes's acceptance that there is a link between Tolkien and Wagner is strongly seconded by another Wagnerian, Alex Ross, the music critic of *The New Yorker*. Writing a review of the first of the Peter Jackson films of *The Lord of the Rings* in December 2003 (the review is online – see the bibliography), Ross asserts that Tolkien 'certainly knew his Wagner' and briefly makes the point that it was Wagner who added the idea of a Ring of Power to the old sources. He suggests that Tolkien was rewriting the Ring story to de-Nazify it:

> You could see *The Lord of the Rings* as a kind of rescue operation, saving the Nordic myths from misuse – perhaps even saving Wagner from himself. Tolkien tried, it seems, to create a kinder, gentler 'Ring', a mythology without malice. The 'world-redeeming deed', in Wagner's phrase, is done by the little hobbits [...]

But Ross thinks that in producing a tamer version of Wagner's myth Tolkien loses some of Wagner's wider and deeper concerns. In effect, he claims that Tolkien, like many people, confused Wagner with the Wagnerian and took the Ring to be 'a bombastic nationalistic saga in which blond-haired heroes triumph over dwarfish, vaguely Jewish enemies', but 'the "Ring" is not at all what it seems' and is 'in fact a prolonged assault on the very idea of worldly power, the cult of the monumental – everything that we think of as "Wagnerian"'. It is Tolkien, not Wagner, who is, in Ross's opinion, politically crude:

> Tolkien believes in the forces of good, in might for right. Wagner dismissed all that – he had an anarchist streak early on – and sees redemption only in love.

Evidently Ross did not pick up Tolkien's description of himself as an anarchist, but he goes on to point out a clear difference between his Ring and Wagner's – that the latter 'can be forged only by one who has forsworn love'. Ross is sardonic about what he calls the 'sexual opacity of Tolkien's saga' and, more seriously, develops the question of what it is that his characters want with the Ring, 'a never-ending nightmare to which people are drawn for no obvious reason'. In contrast, Wagner uses the Ring to show a series of 'intense, confused, all-too-human relationships', culminating in the destruction of Wotan and his world by the 'earthbound passion' of Siegfried and Brünnhilde:

The apparatus of myth itself – the belief in higher and lower powers, hierarchies, orders – crumbles with the walls of Valhalla. Perhaps what angered Tolkien most was that Wagner wrote a sixteen-hour mythic opera and then, at the end, blew up the foundations of myth.

Like Haymes, then, Ross ends by approaching the question of what in Wagner Tolkien reacted against. His assumption that Wagner influenced Tolkien leads to the notion that *The Lord of the Rings* is a rewriting of *Der Ring des Nibelungen* to correct it. Arguing like this in turn suggests ways of reading *The Lord of the Rings* itself, ways that those who follow Tolkien in denying a resemblance to Wagner, or who regard such resemblances as superficial, cannot expect to discover.

Another who believes that Tolkien was not only influenced by Wagner but was also rewriting *Der Ring des Nibelungen* in *The Lord of the Rings* is David P Goldman, who writes under the pseudonym Spengler for *Asia Times Online*. In an essay dated 11 January 2003 entitled 'The "Ring" and the remnants of the West' (available online – see the bibliography) Goldman declares that 'Tolkien has taken back Wagner's *Ring*'. Goldman has clearly read Birzer's piece (he mentions his name but does not give sources) and accepted his version of Wagner as a nationalist, a socialist and an advocate of men like gods:

> Wagner announced the death of the old order of aristocracy and Church, of order and rules. Not only was the old order dying, but also it deserved to die, the victim of its inherent flaws. As the old order died a New Man would replace the servile creatures of the old laws, and a New Art would become the New Man's religion. The New Man would be fearless, sensual, unconstrained, and could make the world according to his will. Wagner's dictum that the sources of Western civilization had failed was not only entirely correct, but also numbingly obvious to anyone who lived through the upheavals of 1848. But how should one respond to this? Wagner had a seductive answer: become your own god!

And how did Tolkien respond to that? Goldman, though noting that Tolkien despised Wagner, lists as many parallels as he can find between his work and the German's and then declares these are far less important than their common starting point, the crisis of the immortals, in Wagner's case, the gods, in Tolkien's, the elves. Where Wagner, according to Goldman, preaches the replacement of the gods by heroic men, Tolkien, who has in mind 'nothing more than the familiar observation that the high culture of the West arose and fell with the aristocracy', recommends that '[o]ne acts with simple English decency and tenacity [...] and accepts one's fate', thus making *The Lord of the Rings* 'an anti-epic [...] whose protagonist is a weak, vulnerable and reluctant hobbit, as opposed to the strong, wound-proof and fearless Siegfried'. The virtues Tolkien sets against Wagner's are 'modesty, forbearance, and renunciation', or, as Ross put it later in 2003, Tolkien 'mutes the romance of mediæval stories and puts us out in self-abnegating, Anglican-modernist T. S. Eliot territory' (whether Ross was deliberately insulting Tolkien's Roman Catholic orthodoxy here is difficult to say, although his remark does draw attention to the essential Englishness of Tolkien's Christianity). Goldman's point is that what *The Lord of the Rings* gives resonance to is 'Anglo-Saxon democracy', and he reads the enthusiasm in the USA for Tolkien, re-ignited by the Peter Jackson films, as typical of 'an anti-empire populated by reluctant heroes who want nothing more than to till their fields and mind their homes, much like Tolkien's Hobbits', although they will respond to pressure 'with a fierceness and cohesion that will surprise [their] adversaries'.

Those who start, then, from the assumption that there is more than a superficial resemblance between the two Rings not only raise interesting questions about Tolkien's achievement but also indicate exciting answers. They succeed in placing Tolkien's work in a cultural and historical context that is broader and more diverse than that given him by the more conservative writers, even Tom Shippey. The association with Wagner, far from degrading or diminishing Tolkien's work, gives it a greater resonance. This could hardly fail to be the case, given Wagner's significance, and notoriety, in Western culture. The nay-sayers who reject a Wagnerian influence seem to deny the potency of that influence, and of Wagner. They would prefer Wagner to be a minor footnote in Tolkien studies, and to regard him as a disreputable side-street in European culture best not entered into. But as Haymes, Ross and Goldman emphasise, Wagner is a central fact of nineteenth- and early twentieth-century culture, unignorable and demanding attention. To try to quarantine Tolkien's work from Wagner's is to make it smaller and less significant, and probably to misunderstand it.

This brings us back to the question of Tolkien's own dismissal of a connection between his Ring and Wagner's. We have already seen Haymes's speculation that this was due to a character trait Tolkien shared with Wagner himself, a refusal to acknowledge influence, and indeed a tendency to deny it. Whether

Tolkien was indeed as self-centred as Wagner, in this or any other respect, is difficult to prove. One hopes not. Tolkien was usually quite free with comments on the writers of fantasy and science fiction whom he had read and enjoyed, such as William Morris, George MacDonald, H G Wells, H Rider Haggard and others. On the other hand, as Shippey points out in his article on Tolkien and Wagner, there were some authors Tolkien expressed his dislike of who would seem nevertheless to have influenced him. Shippey's main example is Shakespeare. In general, Tolkien liked to leave the impression that he had little use for literature produced after Chaucer, and that his own work owed debts to mediæval sources rather than modern ones, if it had any debts at all. His comments on his own writings are remarkably free of remarks on models and parallels. There is of course little enough in his letters about his writings other than the published ones, *The Hobbit* and *The Lord of the Rings*. Perhaps if *The Silmarillion* had appeared in his lifetime he would have had to enter discussions about its literary and other roots. For the most part, however, he comments on his writings in and for themselves. He offers synopses and hints of meanings, and explanations of plots and characters, and sometimes comments on problems in presenting and shaping the material, but mostly this keeps within the limits of analysis and exegesis. He acts as the first textual scholar of his own work, the first editor, rather than as a literary critic, or literary historian in any terms other than those set by the *œuvre* itself. And this is the approach continued by his leading commentators and, of course, by his son Christopher. Tom Shippey, to be fair, does, in his second book, *J R R Tolkien: Author of the Century* (2000), offer to compare Tolkien with other writers of his period, but this is mainly in defence of Tolkien, not to explain him. Other writers on Tolkien seem content to accuse mainstream critics of ignoring their hero and then go on their way. In writing about an author thought to have been cold-shouldered by orthodox literary critics there is some satisfaction in treating him as *sui generis*. For his part, Tolkien may have shared the notion that his work was so different from that of anyone else writing in his time or near it that it was not sensible, or even possible, to discuss parallels and antecedents. After all, it is not an author's obligation to examine his own originality. There is plenty of evidence in Tolkien's letters and the way he presented his work to others (or didn't), even within his own circle, to indicate that he thought of it as odd and special. He was undoubtedly secretive about it, and sometimes embarrassed. One side of this might be irritation at the suggestion that he owed it all fundamentally to the example of somebody else. More on this will be found in the last chapter of this book.

It might however have been more than embarrassment that made him deny a connection with Wagner, and here we return to the issue raised in discussing Edward R Haymes's theory as to why Tolkien denied a debt to Wagner. Christine Chism, in her essay 'Middle-earth, the Middle Ages and the Aryan nation: myth and history in World War II' (in *Tolkien the Medievalist*, edited by Jane Chance, 2003) argues strongly that, faced with what Hitler and the Nazis had done with Wagner's mythology, Tolkien had to find a way to justify his own use of material derived from similar 'Germanic' sources. However one views her argument (and it seems to me she too readily succumbs to conflating Wagner with Siegfried, and thence with Hitler), she is surely right to dwell on Tolkien's horror and disgust at what the Nazis had done to the mediæval northern literature and culture he had loved since his boyhood and made the focus of his academic life, and willy-nilly Wagner was implicated in this. Chism's conclusion, that *The Lord of the Rings* is Tolkien's refutation of the politicisation of Nordic mythology that glamourised the Third Reich, is skilfully made and aligns her with those we have already considered who see Tolkien's work as a rewriting of the Nibelung myth and as an anti-epic. Her most challenging suggestion, however, is that in fashioning such a rebuttal of the harnessing of myth to create modern totalitarianist art Tolkien left himself 'alone and palely loitering', like the voice of his late poem 'The Sea-Bell', bereft of the conviction necessary to continue writing his own mythology. 'Tolkien's war-driven, self-questioning investigation of the uses of mythology', Chism writes, 'had brought him to a point with no energy to move forward and yet had worn away at the enabling presumptions for going back' (page 88), where 'going back' included resumption of the work of completing *The Silmarillion*. For Tolkien, rejecting an association with Wagner was not just a reaction against any connection with the artist known to be admired by Hitler and used by the Nazis, although that surely comes into it, but more deeply a resentment born out of a conscious and artistic struggle against the meaning of Wagner's work in the twentieth century, a struggle that forced Tolkien, perhaps against his will as well as his inclinations, to acknowledge the dangers of mythology and the need to renounce it. Yet while this may be the case it does not make it impossible that it was a misunderstanding of Wagner, however correct it was about Hitler, and it does not rule out the likelihood of Wagner's influence on Tolkien. As Chism says, 'Wagner is even more useful as a source for Tolkien to work against' (page 76). Despite her evident dislike of Wagner, and her desire to give Tolkien the last word against him, Chism does almost as much to show that there is a case for examining Tolkien's debt to Wagner as any of those, such as Haymes, Ross or Goldman, who take it as obvious.

The exact evidence for Tolkien's knowledge of Wagner's work, and specifically of *Der Ring des Nibelungen*, is quite restricted. As Haymes says, 'Tolkien's biographers have been complicit in covering up any real connection' between him and Wagner. He goes on: 'I have read – but been unable to confirm in primary sources – that [C S] Lewis and Tolkien regularly attended performances of the Ring in London, a fact that Tolkien and his biographers generally "forget".' The main source seems to be Humphrey Carpenter's 1978 book *The Inklings*, which on page 56 records two events from the early 1930s. According to the recollections of Tolkien's daughter Priscilla, Tolkien and Lewis once attended a performance of one of the Ring operas at Covent Garden wearing everyday suits rather than the evening dress customary in the part of the theatre where they sat. They apparently had not had time to change. Though this story is a second-hand one, based on the memory of someone who was not present, it is tempting to draw some conclusions from it, such as that Tolkien and Lewis went to hear Wagner in London on other occasions when they *were* properly dressed for the occasion. Derek Brewer says, albeit somewhat tentatively, that he thought Tolkien went with Lewis to hear Wagner annually in the 1930s. Another conclusion one might draw from Priscilla Tolkien's story is that her father was, like Lewis, so keen to see Wagner that he put up with the embarrassment of not being correctly attired and, if indeed this was because of having to rush (from Oxford?) to London for the performance, that also suggests a readiness to put up with some inconvenience in the cause of attending a Wagner performance. But this is speculation for want of stronger evidence about Tolkien's opera habits in the 1930s (although on the other hand it is no more speculative than the assumption made by writers hostile to Wagner that Tolkien took no active interest in his work and had no liking for or deep knowledge of it).

Chapter One: The resemblance begins

The other piece of evidence for Tolkien's knowledge of Wagner is stronger. It seems clear from letters and diaries that C S Lewis had decided to lead a group of his friends to London to see the whole of Wagner's Ring cycle. For some reason, however, he delegated the task of buying the tickets to another member of the party, that person forgot to do so and the outing did not take place. It appears, nevertheless, that in preparation Tolkien, Lewis and his brother Warren began studying the libretto of *Der Ring des Nibelungen*, to begin with, at least, in the original German. They appear to have begun with the second part of the cycle, *Die Walküre*, but the story goes that Warren Lewis's German proved not up to the task and he was forced to read from an English translation. There seems no doubt, however, that the three of them did work their way through the words of Wagner's opera, although there is no mention of their having done the same for the other three parts of the cycle. But to study even one part in this way is extraordinary and shows a strong commitment to trying to get the best out of attending a performance. Nowadays, with the availability of several complete recordings of Wagner's cycle, usually supplied with a libretto, the Wagner enthusiast can easily listen to and follow the words, with a parallel English translation to hand as well. In the 1930s that was less possible and one imagines that only really committed Wagnerites invested the time and effort required to grapple with Wagner's text on its own. Tolkien and Lewis were extending to Wagner their own practice of reading literary works, especially the Icelandic tales and sagas, in the original language, the *raison d'être* of Tolkien's earlier literary club at Oxford, the Kolbitars, predecessors of the more famous Inklings.

It is perhaps necessary to point out that the text of *Die Walküre*, like the rest of *Der Ring des Nibelungen*, is far from simple linguistically. Wagner devised for his Nibelung cycle a prosody based (very roughly, Tolkien would say) on mediæval alliterative verse, such as that of the Icelandic Edda poems and the Old English epic poem, *Beowulf*. Wagner also employs a great many archaicisms and revived words to give his characters a diction suited to the ancient heroic world he is portraying (in this of course his practice is similar to that of Tolkien in his Middle-earth fiction). Compared even with Wagner's other operas, mostly written in rhyming verse using a poetic diction that aspires to mediævalism, *Der Ring des Nibelungen* is couched in a language that is peculiar in both senses of the term. It is therefore no surprise that Warren Lewis, lacking the philological training of Tolkien and the linguistic and literary background of his brother, found it hard to cope. Many who enjoy the music and believe they know what the operas are about would find it difficult to say what Wagner's words actually mean, preferring sound to sense, except for key terms that stand out in the aural flow (such as 'Ring', 'Schwert', 'Speer', 'Wurm' and so on). It is a mark of the thoroughness with which Tolkien approached *Die Walküre* that he joined the Lewises in studying the libretto word for word in the original, no doubt translating as they went, even when not helping Warnie to follow it. Alas, as with the theatre visits, we can only speculate about other examples of such thoroughness. There is no evidence that the three read other Wagner texts together. Perhaps Warnie's difficulties meant the experiment with *Die Walküre* could not be repeated with *Das Rheingold*, *Siegfried* and *Götterdämmerung*. Perhaps instead Tolkien read the libretti of them on his own, which he was no doubt perfectly capable of doing, and so no trace of this has been left in the memoirs or memories of others. Be that as it may, the likelihood that he worked carefully, accompanied by C S Lewis, through the text of *Die Walküre* is in itself highly significant, for in many ways that opera is at the heart of Wagner's Ring cycle. Although it is not where Wagner began it, and nor is it of course the end, *Die Walküre* focuses on the central problem of the story, the relations between the gods, especially Wotan, and men, in particular the hero Siegmund, father of the more famous, dragon-slaying Siegfried. The long debates in *Die Walküre*, particularly those between Wotan and his wife Fricka, and between Wotan and his daughter Brünnhilde, the valkyrie of the opera's title, dwell on the issues of responsibility and leadership, sacrifice and destiny, that are the deeper themes of Wagner's work, and, as I shall argue, of Tolkien's, too. Here is where Wagner really could have influenced Tolkien. Ironically, *Die Walküre* is the one part of *Der Ring des Nibelungen* in which the Ring itself never physically appears.

Before tackling these deeper connections between *Der Ring des Nibelungen* and *The Lord of the Rings*, however, let us first look at the more superficial resemblances, the similarities that have immediately struck those who know both works. From these can be developed deeper connections, although to bring these out fully needs some preparatory discussion of Tolkien's ideas about literature and of the book that precedes *The Lord of the Rings*, *The Hobbit*. But rather than postpone discussion of the way *The Lord of the Rings* and *Der Ring des Nibelungen* resemble each other until these matters have been dealt with, let us turn to a preliminary comparison of the two.

CHAPTER TWO

From surface to depth

For anyone who knows *Der Ring des Nibelungen* (if you do not then please see Appendix A), it is hard not to see a number of correspondences and parallels with *The Lord of the Rings*. Even Bradley J Birzer, who as we have seen denies that Tolkien owes any real debt to Wagner, has a short list of features common to *Der Ring des Nibelungen* and *The Lord of the Rings*, but David P Goldman, writing under the pseudonym Spengler in the online *Asian Times*, produces a table in his article of 11 January 2003 that claims to list no fewer than seventeen parallels between Wagner and Tolkien:

Wagner	Tolkien
Alberich forges a Ring of Power	Sauron forges a Ring of Power
Wotan needs the giants to build Valhalla	The Elves need Sauron to forge their Rings of Power
The Ring gives the bearer world domination	The Ring gives the bearer world domination
Wotan uses the Ring to pay the giants	Sauron betrays the Elves
The Ring is cursed and betrays its bearer	The Ring is evil and betrays its bearer
Fafner kills brother Fasolt to get the Ring	Smeagol kills friend Deagol for the Ring
Fafner hides in a cave for centuries	Smeagol/Gollum hides in a cave for centuries
Siegfried inherits the shards of his father's sword	Aragorn inherits the shards of his father's sword
Brünnhilde gives up immortality for Siegfried	Arwen gives up immortality for Aragorn
Wotan plays 'riddles' for the life of Mime	Gollum plays 'riddles' for the life of Bilbo
A dragon guards the Nibelungs' hoard	A dragon guards the dwarves' hoard

Wagner	Tolkien
The gods renounce the world and await the end	The Elves renounce the world and prepare to depart
The Ring is returned to its origin, the River Rhine	The Ring is returned to its origin, Mount Doom
Hagen falls into the river	Gollum falls into the volcano
The immortals burn in Valhalla	The immortals leave Middle-earth
A new era emerges in the world	A new era emerges in the world
Men are left to their own devices	Men are left to their own devices

One way to begin considering the detailed comparison between the two works is by analysing this list, although some of the items will prove to be more convincing than others, and a few are not convincing at all. Making such a comparison will, if nothing else, convey to the reader reminders of what happens in both Wagner and Tolkien. The list roughly follows the sequence of events in *Der Ring des Nibelungen*.

1. Alberich forges a Ring of Power: Sauron forges a Ring of Power

Both Rings, in other words, are created by evil beings. They are tainted by this from their beginnings. Alberich has stolen the gold to make the Ring from the Rhine, having renounced love in order to gain wealth and power. He was partly driven to this by the rejection of his amorous advances by the Rhinemaidens, the guardians of the gold, who also foolishly told him how to steal it, and on what condition. However else one reads this (many commentators interpret Alberich as a representative of those who dismiss or suppress their human feelings in order to gain wealth and the power it brings), Alberich's making of the Ring of Power is an act of greed and of desire for a relationship with his fellow-creatures based on domination and control. He is the epitome of the Machiavellian dictum that it is better for a ruler to be feared than loved. Much the same can be said of Sauron, although typically Tolkien omits any possible sexual dysfunction as part of Sauron's motives for seeking domination. 'Presumably', as Alex Ross says, 'Sauron gave up carnal pleasure when he became an all-seeing eye at the top of a tower, but it's hard to say for certain. Maybe he gets a kick out of the

Chapter Two: From surface to depth 31

all-seeing bit.' Sauron, we are told in *The Silmarillion*, forged the One Ring to control all the other Rings of Power that he had helped the elves to create: 'And while he wore the One Ring he could perceive all the things that were done by means of the lesser rings, and he could see and govern the very thoughts of those that wore them' (page 288). Perhaps Ross's joke about voyeurism is not so wide of the mark after all. This makes Sauron like one of Wagner's other villains, the magician Klingsor in *Parsifal*, who observes the approach of the hero to his castle through a magic mirror, a sort of fantasy surveillance camera that allows Klingsor to spy on all who invade his premises. There is, however, no evidence that Tolkien was familiar with *Parsifal*, even although it is, along with *Tannhäuser*, an opera full of Christian symbolism and its focus on the myth of the Holy Grail might seem of interest to a mediæval scholar like Tolkien. On the other hand, Tolkien shows little interest in the Grail Legend, and seems to have believed Arthurian legends were either too Celtic, or too Frenchified, for his Anglo-Saxon taste.

A necessary point to make here (at the risk of boring the reader with its reiteration) is that, as Tom Shippey says, the idea of a Ring of Power seems to be Wagner's invention. The magic ring in the Edda poems and the Volsung saga is a feeble device compared to Wagner's Ring, with its power to bend others to the holder's will, and to corrupt that will in turn.

2. Wotan needs the giants to build Valhalla: The Elves need Sauron to forge their Rings of Power

This seems a weak parallel to draw and in fact one not very clearly drawn at all. Wotan's employment of the giants Fafner and Fasolt is a contract he enters into, whereas the elves are seduced by Sauron into collaborating with him in the creation of a set of rings. Sauron exploits the elves' pride in their ability to make beautiful things and their lust for jewels of high price. Wotan merely employs the brute strength of the giants. If anything, Wotan is more like Sauron than the elves, since he makes his contract with the giants to give them the goddess Freia as their payment intending to avoid fulfilling it, since the departure of Freia, who supplies the apples of youth to the other gods, will mean that they age and die. Like Sauron, he is a cheat, although he acknowledges that he is bound by his promises, recorded as runes on his spear, the symbol of his power. He has been persuaded to equivocate with the giants by Loge, the trickster god of fire, who has led Wotan to think he can come up with an alternative payment for the giants that they will take instead of Freia. Arguably, Loge is the Sauron figure here, playing off the others, making them follow his agenda without revealing it. Wagner keeps close to the Icelandic sources in his characterisation of Loge, whose equivalent in Norse mythology, Loki, is an ambiguous figure. Although one of the immortals, Loki is not always on the side of the other gods. In some stories he helps Odin and Thor, in others he tricks or betrays them. He is never to be trusted, just like fire itself. Sauron's close association with fire suggests a link with Loki, as does his status as an outcast from the society of the other immortals, like his master Morgoth. In one of many instances of doubling in Tolkien's legendarium, both Morgoth and Sauron play the part of fallen angels, adversaries of the good of which they were originally a part before pride overcame their allegiance to truth and to the will of the divine power. Loge, though not really a Satanic figure, is shown by Wagner to be detached from the other gods, and unimpressed by them, even Wotan. At the end of *Das Rheingold*, as Wotan leads the other gods across the rainbow bridge into Valhalla, Loge hangs back and lets them go without him, commenting that the gods are hurrying to their end. The pompous noise of the ending of this first part of *Der Ring des Nibelungen*, often heard in the concert hall as 'The Entry of the Gods to Valhalla', should seem undercut in the opera house by the figure of Loge, obstinately declining to join in. The audience needs to anticipate the role of fire in the destruction of the gods and of Valhalla itself at the end of the cycle.

Loge's answer to the question of what Wotan can give the giants instead of Freia is Alberich's gold, with or without his Ring, the Nibelung's Ring. Loge correctly guesses that Fafner for one has more lust for gold than for a goddess (Fasolt is less easy to convince, but is also easily bullied by his brother). Loge's cynical view of the giants is like Sauron's of the elves, and of many others. There are limits to Sauron's powers of persuasion, however. As Tolkien shows, the northern dwarves, despite their love of gold and jewels, are not persuaded to join Sauron. Sauron and Loge, however, both rely on the calculation that people have their price and their weaknesses and that it is upon the exploitation of these that power is built. While Wagner tempts the audience to see Loge's refusal to participate in the delusions of grandeur of Wotan and the other gods as clear-sighted and realistic, he also means them to reflect that the fire god is, ironically, somewhat cold-hearted. He is clever but selfish and, although selfishness is also a fault of other characters in *Das Rheingold*, including Wotan, Wagner conveys to us the possibility that Wotan in particular will grow out of his selfishness where Loge will not. The key moment is when the mysterious prophetess-goddess Erda persuades Wotan that he must give up the Ring to the giants. Though he does so with an ill grace, and very soon begins plotting how to retrieve it, he does manage to step back from his immediate desires far enough to yield up the Ring at least temporarily. This flexibility of purpose promises much for the future.

Loge, on the other hand, when he breaks away from the other gods, says that he does so in order to retreat into what he has been before, and indeed he never personally reappears in *Der Ring des Nibelungen*, returning only as fire itself, without the voice or mind of an individual. When Wotan summons Loge at the end of *Die Walküre* to surround the crag on which the sleeping Brünnhilde will lie until a hero wakes her, he speaks of calling Loge in the form in which Wotan first found him, implying that the fire god has regressed into a primordial state. Such regression is paralleled in the story of Sauron, who after his earlier defeats had to abandon physical form and become a disembodied spirit, a fact about Sauron that colours our impression of him as not a full being at all. Notably, of course, he never appears in *propria persona* in *The Lord of the Rings*. He is nothing but a seeing eye, or a mind-filling voice. In fact, the reader's idea of Sauron is created obliquely, by description of his minions and his habitat – dark, desolate and full, be it noted, of fire.

So if we cannot make much of Goldman's parallel between Wotan's need for the giants and the elves' need of Sauron, is there anything to be said about the god's reliance on the giants? The fundamental and crucial point here surely is the fact of reliance itself, and here there is a parallel with Sauron certainly, but also with other key figures in *The Lord of the Rings*. The obvious point that Wagner makes in *Das Rheingold* is that the gods are neither all-powerful nor all-sufficient, and they depend not only on each other (as in the case of Freia's apples) but also on non-divine beings, such as the giants. To accomplish his aims, Wotan must employ others. There is a parallel here with Sauron, who cannot wield power without having those who wield it in his name. There is a difference, too, however, in so far as Sauron seems able only to recruit followers by compulsion or trickery or crude rewards of a share of his power. Wotan's power rests on his spear and the runes carved on it, runes recording contracts and agreements, runes of law. Wotan has himself set up an authority greater than himself, an abstract concept of justice, consistency and open decision-making to which he has agreed to bind himself in order that others will do so too. True, he finds in *Das Rheingold* that he has bound himself into a contract with the giants that he regrets and would like to get out of, but significantly he is reluctant just to break it (that would mean breaking his spear), because then he would fall back into a chaos of unreliable relationships and unenforceable promises. In *Das Rheingold* Wotan faces the price of trying to set up an ordered society, one that relies on something other than might and sheer power but instead depends on negotiation and persuasion and agreement. The symbol of the new society is not just Wotan's spear but Valhalla itself, a permanent home for the gods, a physical manifestation of an ordered society, with the gods at the top, surveying the world and engaged in imposing justice upon it. The geography of *Das Rheingold*, with its uninterrupting changes of scene between levels of the world – the depths of the Rhine, the mountain-tops near Valhalla, the caves of the Nibelung dwarves – adds to Wagner's picture of a layered society held together by lofty rulers. It is an image not far from that of Middle-earth, although Tolkien offers not just rulers in high places and subhumans underground but other geographical metaphors of social layering, such as the contrasts between Minas Tirith, Edoras and Hobbiton.

Wotan, then, needs the giants to build Valhalla because he cannot do everything himself. He will go on needing others throughout the cycle, and his real problems stem from the conditions under which his needs can be met and the way those in turn affect his aims. Though he may begin by believing in his own might and right, the bulk of *Der Ring des Nibelungen* is about how those beliefs must change, and the paradox that in the end Wotan's will is not enough and his might is a weakness, not a strength. He will end not as the master but as the servant, not the giver but the supplicant. Buried in Wotan's contract with the giants is the whole problem of how power is executed in an interdependent community, a problem made more complicated than easy by disparities of

Chapter Two: From surface to depth   35

strength, influence and intelligence amongst individuals in that community. That is a major theme of *The Lord of the Rings* too.

3. The Ring gives the bearer world domination

As we have seen, most of those who discuss Tolkien's debts to Wagner acknowledge that in this respect the German was an innovator and the Englishman in some sense follows him. One could cavil about this, arguing that Tolkien could have come up with the idea independently or that it is not so unusual that he could only have got it from Wagner, but the difficulty with that line of argument is the sheer importance of Wagner and his cultural impact in his time and through at least the first half of the twentieth century. Goldman puts this with his usual rhetorical flash:

> It is hard for us today to imagine what a cult raised itself around Wagner after the 1876 premiere of his *Ring cycle*. Compared to it the combined fervor for Elvis, the Beatles, Madonna and Michael Jackson seems like a band concert in the park.

This is, if anything, an understatement, since it presents Wagner as if he were merely a popular musical entertainer when in fact he was regarded, and regarded himself, as much, much more than that. His music, in a sense, was only the medium by which he broadcast a new set of ideas about religion, politics, culture, human nature and society. As Goldman adds, '[p]erfectly sensible people attended a Wagner opera and declared that their lives had changed'. Artists, philosophers and social thinkers seriously considered Wagner as life-changing. The list of British writers influenced by Wagner is alone long and impressive, and similar lists can be completed for other countries, and other kinds of artists and thinkers. Much of this information, of course, was put into the shade by Nazism. Wagnerism never quite became a love that dare not speak its name, but critics and biographers of the second half of the twentieth century were reluctant to make much of it in the lives and works of their subjects, and popular readers rarely know of Wagner's influence on well-known authors (C S Lewis is a case in point).

It is however inconceivable that Tolkien had not heard of Wagner's Ring and its gift of world domination. When he began work on the sequel to *The Hobbit* and gradually came to realise that it would have to grow out of the one residual mystery Bilbo's story had left him, the little ring of invisibility he had picked up in a tunnel under the Misty Mountains, Tolkien must have known that making that ring a Ring of Power was to follow in Wagner's path. And he must have known it was *Wagner's* path, if only because he was a friend of C S Lewis. This is what makes Tolkien's tetchy remark that 'both rings are round and there the resemblance ceases' so incredible. It is hard to resist the claim that the tetchiness here is a consequence, not of Tolkien's irritation with the Swedish editor whose introduction to his translation of *The Lord of the Rings* was the object of his wrath, but of the consciousness of his bad faith in denying a resemblance between the Rings that he knew extended well beyond their roundness.

But what is there to say about the power of world domination? In both works this is always strangely potential rather than actual. Alberich uses his Ring to compel his fellow-Nibelungs to bring him a hoard of gold and his brother Mime to make for him the magic Tarnhelm that lets its wearer change his shape (the Tarnhelm in fact seems much closer to Bilbo's original ring in its functions than the Nibelung's Ring itself), but once the Ring is stolen from Alberich and then passed by Wotan, at Erda's urging, to Fafner it virtually ceases to operate as a means of domination. Fafner takes it and the rest of the hoard to a cave in the forest, turns himself into a dragon and sleeps on the Ring and the gold for years, doing nothing with them. Meanwhile, Alberich and Wotan, and in time Mime, try to think of a way of retrieving the Ring, but the dwarves are too weak to kill its guardian, and the god, however ready he was to slip out of the strict terms of his original contract with the giants, feels bound by his own laws not to break the contract completely by stealing from Fafner what he agreed to pay him for building Valhalla.

And so, while the Ring lies unused in the dragon's cave, in the world outside it exists as a threat, an ultimate power goal, a political concept around which Wotan, Alberich and Mime circle. Much the same is true even after Siegfried has slain the dragon and taken the Ring for himself, with the exception that he eliminates Mime from the group seeking its power. Siegfried, unconcerned with the idea of world domination (along with most other ideas), shows no inclination to use the Ring and instead gives it to Brünnhilde as a love-token. She in turn accepts it as such and refuses her sister Waltraute's plea that she should save the gods by giving the Ring back to the Rhinemaidens, although

Chapter Two: From surface to depth 37

in the end that is what she will do, but only after the Ring has become a token of exchange in the sordid sexual politics of the Gibichung court, involving Siegfried's betrayal of Brünnhilde to both Gunther and Gutrune, through the influence of Alberich's son Hagen. Long before this Wotan has renounced his desire to possess the Ring and the world domination it promises and by the end only Alberich and Hagen seem to be trying to obtain the Ring for actual use. In Hagen's case this attempt is what drives his plotting against Siegfried that leads to the final catastrophe, and Brünnhilde's sacrifice of both herself and the Ring. The last seen of Hagen is as he dives into the floodwaters of the Rhine in a despairing attempt to rescue the Ring from the Rhinemaidens.

Not world domination but the *thought* of it, then, is what operates in Wagner's *Der Ring des Nibelungen*, though only a few of the characters seem to have this thought. Those that do instigate courses of action that then drag in the rest, driving the world to cataclysm and, incidentally, their own destruction (except for Alberich: is his survival just a loose end, or did Wagner mean something by leaving the one who first made the Ring and cursed it unaccounted for at the close?). To compare great things with small, the Ring of the Nibelungs is like the million pound note in the 1893 story by Mark Twain ('The £1,000,000 Bank-Note' in *The £1,000,000 Bank-Note and Other New Stories*, New York, 1893): its reputation is so powerful that the thing itself does not need to be put to use. The bearer of the note, like the bearer of the Ring, receives special treatment even if he makes no use of it.

Tolkien's Ring has a similar notoriety. Bilbo uses it in *The Hobbit* to make himself invisible, not knowing that that is not its only power (at the time he wrote *The Hobbit*, Tolkien was no better informed). He uses it for this purpose again in *The Lord of the Rings*, and so do Frodo and Sam, although with more awareness that such use is dangerous, but that is all the Ring is used for. We learn that the employment of it attracts the attention of Sauron and his Ringwraiths, but although that may be a function of the Ring itself it seems no help to world domination by the bearer, but rather the reverse, since it exposes him to his enemies, as Frodo finds on Amon Hen. Other properties attributed to the Ring, such as its tendency to get lost when it suits it, and to weaken the bearer, do not seem helpful either. Nobody in either *The Hobbit* or *The Lord of the Rings* is seen using the Ring for what is said to be its greatest power, to compel others to do the Ring-bearer's will and so assist him to world domination, although we are often told that, should Sauron possess the Ring, he would take over the world, and some characters, notably Boromir and Saruman, clearly believe that if they had the Ring they would be able to assert huge political and military power. As Christine Chism says, the Ring is 'that weirdly empty, weirdly powerful object around which the narrative assembles itself' (page 64): 'In itself it is a mere form, or Form itself, abstracted from context, content, and narrative and refined to a blank tyranny' (page 79). One can say the same about Wagner's Ring. Both Wagner and Tolkien seem to have realised that world domination as a concept is credible but not feasible. The will to achieve, and the attempt to secure, the means to do so are real and dangerous enough, but the thing itself exists more as a threat or a nightmare.

In all the attempts, which Tolkien himself loathed, to identify his Ring with some particular weapon of mass destruction or other tool of world domination, this aspect of his story seems to have been overlooked. Like Wagner, he is not writing about what the Ring itself does so much as about what the thought of it does, what the possibility of massive and unanswerable power does to individuals and through them to their communities, and the communities around them. The Ring brings into existence the concept of world domination, in Tolkien as well as in Wagner, and here we can surely offer an historical interpretation. Wagner was born in Leipzig almost in the midst of one of the largest battles in the Napoleonic Wars, when troops from all the major European nations and most of the smaller ones clashed over several days on a scale that prefigures the warfare of the later nineteenth century, and early stages of the Great War itself. This was in 1813, a year after Napoleon's failure in Russia, when his empire both reached its height and its most prodigious extent and also tipped over into the decline that the defeat at Leipzig confirmed would continue. Yet Napoleon, for all his failure, raised the possibility of domination of Europe, and then of the world, by one man leading a whole nation and its allies. Only after Napoleon was the idea of world domination conceivable. It would haunt Europe until at least 1945 and Tolkien would write *The Lord of the Rings* in the shadow cast by the most dangerous of Napoleon's emulators. Wagner gets the blame for giving Hitler the idea of world domination but it might be argued that he only made myth out of Napoleonic history and gave artistic expression to a fact about the nineteenth century. It could be argued that Wagner also articulated the objections to Bonapartism, although it is doubtful if Hitler saw them. World domination is a fact not in the sense of being a thing or an event but as a concept, a threat, a willed idea. As such it clearly drives the processes leading to the outbreak of World War I as surely as railway timetables or the naval arms race. Whatever other reasons were given for fighting that war and the next, underlying them all was the fear that it was possible for one nation to achieve domination in Europe, and hence in the whole world. It is significant that Tolkien emerged from his experience of World War I writing myths of huge conflicts between vast forces of elves and orcs, over continent-sized territories, in which the prize is total destruction of the enemy and total domination of Middle-earth. Before he wrote *The Lord of the Rings* Tolkien had already brooded for twenty years or more on tales, later published in *The Silmarillion*, of world-historical conflicts. Underlying this was the geo-politics of the post-Napoleonic era.

Wagner had a more provincial experience of these matters. Though he lived to see the unification of Germany into a new Reich under a Kaiser, he spent his formative years mostly in the politics of Saxony and Bavaria. It is a tribute to his imagination that he transcended these in *Der Ring des Nibelungen*. His earlier operas had concerned themselves with purely German political dreams, except for his first success, *Rienzi*, based on a truly Napoleonic figure and, incidentally, the Wagner opera that some say most enthused Hitler.

4. Wotan uses the Ring to pay the giants: Sauron betrays the Elves

This does not look like a parallel at all unless we take the statement about Wotan as implying, as we have described, that he reneged on the letter of his contract with the giants by substituting Alberich's gold, and the Ring, for the goddess Freia as payment for building Valhalla. In that rather narrow sense Wotan might be said to have betrayed the giants and this could be said to be made worse by the fact that, before he gave them the Ring, Alberich cursed it. Almost immediately Fafner and Fasolt quarrel over who should have the Ring, leading to Fafner's murder of his brother for its sake. As the orchestra forcefully reminds us, by loudly playing Alberich's curse music, this is the first occasion on which his curse operates. Sauron betrays the elves in a more direct way, by pretending to be on their side while still serving his evil master Morgoth and doing his best to bring about their downfall. He helps them to make the rings by which he aims to control them with his own master-ring.

Actually, the people Wotan really betrays are the Rhinemaidens, the rightful owners of the gold from which Alberich makes the Ring. When Wotan asks Loge what he has found to give the giants instead of Freia, Loge at first says he has found nothing. The other gods turn on him for this and accuse him of malice in raising false expectations. They begin to blame him for the entering into the contract with the giants that seems to be leading them into disaster. Then, as it were changing the subject, Loge tells the gods about the plight of the Rhinemaidens, their gold stolen from them by an ugly dwarf who has fashioned it into a Ring of Power and who now lords it in his underworld. Wotan, in deciding to seek out Alberich and confront his thievery, is rather non-committal about his intentions and whether or not he will confiscate the dwarf's gold in order to return it to the Rhine. In the end he decides he has greater need of it to pay off the giants than to restore it to the Rhinemaidens. When, at the end of *Das Rheingold*, the Rhinemaidens are heard crying out for justice and their gold, Wotan curses them and delegates to Loge the task of silencing their complaints, while he leads the divine party over the rainbow bridge into their new home, Valhalla. It is hard to see, however, how this makes Wotan like Sauron. If anything, it makes him like Saruman and Denethor, two figures who are ready to act according to their own interests at the expense of others, and who take refuge in equivocation and unspoken aims. But this is only to say that in both Wagner and Tolkien there are situations where characters make choices that favour themselves, not others, and sometimes have to prevaricate to do so. One hardly can suppose Tolkien took this from Wagner.

The issue, however, may be not the betrayers, but the betrayed. The giants, the Rhinemaidens and the elves have this in common, that they are all beings from an earlier, pre-human state of the world. They represent a state of beginning, or at least a more primitive state, and their treatment by Wotan and Sauron marks the beginning of the end of their former existence and the coming of a new age, an age in which men – human beings – will occupy centre stage. The Rhinemaidens are the first beings to emerge from the primordial soup of E-flat arpeggios that begins *Der Ring des Nibelungen* and they present themselves as carefree and frolicsome. Their innocence is rudely exploited by Alberich but

Chapter Two: From surface to depth

they remain unsophisticated in their pleas to Wotan for the return of their gold. By the time he hears these pleas, however, the world has moved on into the ambiguous society of Wotan and Loge. The giants are also simple creatures, as their blunt music shows. They seem not to have suspected that Wotan's promise to give them the beautiful Freia is unlikely to come true, and however their scenes are staged there ought to be something grotesque about the incongruity of the idea of a sexual relationship between not one but two giants and a female goddess. Although Fasolt dimly regrets replacing Freia with the gold as payment, he is unable to turn his sense of disappointment into a protest or to use it to begin to understand what is happening. His clumsy attempt to assert his claim on the Ring only leads to his death at his brother's hand. Fafner, for his part, is so lacking in imagination and insight that all he does with his prize is sleep on it and turn into a slothful dragon. Like the Rhinemaidens, then, the giants represent a simple-minded world that is rapidly outpaced by events.

Tolkien's elves are not so naive. In some respects their fault is the opposite, an over-sophistication, a pride in their own cleverness, that lays them open to the wiles of Sauron. But in a way they are as limited as the Rhinemaidens and the giants by a simplicity of outlook, based on confidence about who they are and what they do in the world. Most significantly, the elves expect the world to run more or less as it always has. This is a consequence of their immortality. As ageless beings who live through long centuries, they tend to see not change but repetition and continuity in the world. The result is that they lack ambition and fail to recognise it in others. Their effort goes into refining the conditions of existence and so they direct their energies into art, a sphere of beauty and permanence lying outside time and change. They do engage in wars and politics but the chief object of these is the recovery of the silmarils, supreme works of art whose recapture from Morgoth would restore the *status quo ante*, and take Middle-earth back to an earlier stage. When they despair of that idea their reaction is to retreat from the world and literally depart from it into the mists of the West. Though they have managed to summon the energy to wage war on Morgoth and Sauron in the past, in *The Lord of the Rings* they have lost the will to defend themselves except by passive magic barriers around their enclaves in Rivendell and Lothlórien. Like the Rhinemaidens and the giants, they are left behind by events.

If we seek the origins of *The Lord of the Rings* in *The Silmarillion* and the Tolkien legendarium as a whole, we find resemblances to the origins of events in Wagner's cycle. Tolkien couched his creation myth in a quasi-Biblical genesis out of the mind of the one true god of his system. Significantly, however, he described the act of creation as a musical performance. The deity sang a theme and his 'demiurges' took it up with variations, establishing the patterns that materialised as the world and its history. There is a clear parallel with the opening of *Das Rheingold*, which begins on a basic deep note, out of which rise harmonics that multiply and combine, with a quickening tempo, until, as the music rises to a climax, the voices of the first beings, the daughters of the Rhine, break into wordless song. But just as the creation music in Tolkien is disrupted and then diverted into new paths by the intrusive voice of the demigod Melkor, who refuses to follow the divine score and insists on improvising his own themes, and discords, so the music of the Rhinemaidens is interrupted by the egotistical dwarf Alberich, and thus begins the story. In Wagner, of course, the process happens once and for all (and briefly, for despite its size *Der Ring des Nibelungen* is not interminable). Tolkien, with no need to worry about possible performances or even possible publication of his work, could give himself æons of time and thousands of words to draw out the implications of the music of time. He indulged himself in a series of narratives illustrating the disruption of harmony by selfishness and ambition, and Sauron's attempt to take over Middle-earth in *The Lord of the Rings* is only the latest of these in his mythology. Yet in essence Tolkien does what Wagner does: he begins from harmony and shows how time and change, embodied in ambition, disrupt it, leading to conflict and historical change. It is the process shown at the beginning of *The Hobbit* and of *The Lord of the Rings*. Into the pastoral innocence of the Shire breaks another world. In both the immediate agent of change is not Sauron but Gandalf. He it is who forces Bilbo and Frodo to leave their comfortable, static lives and become involved in the ways of the world. In *The Hobbit* this actually involves a contract. Perhaps Goldman's mistake is really his comparison between Wotan and Sauron as betrayers when in fact the comparison should be between Wotan and Gandalf.

5. The Ring is cursed and betrays its bearer: The Ring is evil and betrays its bearer

This may seem a small point of resemblance but it is in fact most significant. It is not just that the Rings are dangerous to other people (because they are Rings of Power) but also that they are dangerous to the bearers. This is surely as much Wagner's invention as the idea of a ring that gives world domination. One might seek for folk-tales about magic weapons or objects that are dangerous to their users, or stories in which magic abilities such as invisibility turn out to be more risky than they are worth. H G Wells's Invisible Man could be adduced here, and could be an influence on Tolkien, although, despite the fact that Tolkien was a reader of science fiction (see his references to *The Time Machine* in 'On Fairy-stories'), he has left no evidence of any debt to Wells. But much the same argument applies here as earlier in discussing the Ring as an implement of power. To paraphrase the quotation from Edward R Haymes used earlier, since Tolkien clearly knew about Wagner and could hardly help knowing about *Der Ring des Nibelungen* because, for one thing, he was a friend of C S Lewis, it is much easier to suppose that he took the idea of a ring that harmed its owner from Wagner than from elsewhere.

There seems to be a superficial difference between the Rings, as Goldman's phrasing indicates, in so far as Wagner's is made dangerous by the curse Alberich places on it when it is wrested from him by Wotan, whereas Tolkien's Ring is originally and essentially evil by virtue of its manufacture by the evil Sauron. Indeed, Tolkien says that Sauron put a part of himself into the Ring, so that it is made of the same stuff. Remembering, however, that Tolkien's explanations of the origin and nature of his Ring are all *post hoc*, invented after the first version of *The Hobbit* in an effort to fit that story into the legendarium and make Bilbo's Ring the fulcrum for the sequel, it is worth observing that in terms of narrative origin Bilbo's Ring is also cursed by its 'first' owner, Gollum, as it moves out of his possession into that of his adversary. Perhaps it is not true to say that Gollum curses the Ring as such, but he certainly surrounds it with curses, and curses him who now has it. And just as Wotan, to find the Ring, had to travel deep underground into Alberich's realm, so Bilbo encounters Gollum the Ringbearer deep underneath the mountains. There are a number of parallels between Alberich and Gollum. They are both subterranean beings, they both at one time possess a Ring of Power, which they use for quite mundane ends (the acquisition of gold or fish), and they both lose their Rings to beings from the upper world. They both curse the takers of their Rings as thieves and they both follow them around trying to get back what they regard as theirs. Gollum's pursuit of Frodo in *The Lord of the Rings* is matched by Alberich's appearance outside Fafner's hole in *Siegfried*, where Wotan encounters him, and his appearance in *Götterdämmerung*, as a spectral figure whispering reminders of the task of recovering the Ring into the ear of his son Hagen. We are left to imagine how the loss of the Ring has ruined Alberich's existence, just as it ruins Gollum's, turning them both into obsessed wanderers, always drawn to where the Ring may be, and unable to think about much except their sense of wrong, their vengeance and their loss. Although technically in Tolkien the Ring is Sauron's, for readers of *The Hobbit* and *The Lord of the Rings* it is surely as much, if not more, Gollum's, or was until he lost it.

It is hardly necessary to trace the effect of each Ring on its later bearers. Wotan, momentarily, refuses to give it up and is only just saved from the Ring and himself by Erda, the voice of a deeper wisdom that he must acknowledge; Fafner, reduced to dragon sloth, is killed for the Ring; so are Mime and Siegfried; and Hagen kills himself for it. Bilbo and Frodo both suffer ill effects and a final sense of displacement from their lives, and Gollum loses his life in a last act of possession of the Ring. Only Sam seems to survive wearing it, perhaps because he did so for a relatively short time. On the other hand, it could be argued that he is never quite the same person after he has worn the Ring, and his later career as a leader of the hobbits in the Shire might be taken as a sign that, having sustained the burden of the Ring for no more than a few hours, he became a more serious and responsible person thereafter, and even a more ambitious one.

Tolkien's Ring brings out the worst in people. Even if only temporarily, it makes Bilbo and Frodo greedy and selfish. Its long-term effects are evident in Gollum, and Tolkien skilfully gives us some indication of what Gollum used to be to show how he has decayed under the Ring's influence. Even some who never own the Ring, such as Boromir, are made narrow-minded and perverse by it. Wagner shows similar effects from the influence of his Ring. Those who criticise the characterisation of Mime should consider how his obsession with gaining the Ring has made him, like Gollum, a whining, obsessive liar. Alberich

Chapter Two: From surface to depth 45

is similarly ruined by ring-obsession, and his son Hagen glories in his lack of feeling for others. Siegfried, like Fafner, is, in *Götterdämmerung*, reduced to a sensual stupidity, though this is partly also caused by the forgetfulness Hagen's potion has induced in him. When Siegfried has the chance to return the Ring to the Rhinemaidens he rejects it for the quixotic reason that they urge him to yield it because of its dangers and he is too brave to give in to threats. For this presumption he is stabbed in the back by Hagen. He is like Isildur, who relied on his own abilities and neglected proper precautions, so that he ended up ambushed by orcs and killed by them as he escaped, when the Ring, abandoning him as a failure, slipped from his finger, so that he became visible to the orc archers. Siegfried's betrayal is managed in a different way and does not involve the fickleness of the Ring, but there is a parallel in the fact that immediately before his death he is revealed to the Gibichungs for what he is, the first lover of Brünnhilde. Hagen, by inducing Siegfried to tell his life story, and slipping him an antidote to the forgetfulness potion as he comes to the episode of his awakening of Brünnhilde on her rock, discloses to Gunther and the others Siegfried's prior claim on the valkyrie and creates the excuse to kill him.

6. Fafner kills brother Fasolt to get the Ring: Smeagol kills friend Deagol for the Ring

It is indisputable that at an early stage of both stories internecine murder takes place. In Wagner's case the murder is of brother by brother. In Tolkien the killer and victim are not said to be related but their names, Smeagol and Deagol, chime together in a way that suggests some sort of kinship, just as Fafner and Fasolt, in sharing initial syllables, sound like brothers (Wagner indeed changed the name of Fafner's brother in the Norse sources to get this effect). In any case, the point is that close ties mean nothing in the face of the Rings' temptation. Wagner uses the murder to show immediately the effect of Alberich's curse on his Ring and so sets a pattern for the rest of the tale. In Tolkien, as mentioned above, much of the prehistory of the Ring before it appeared in *The Hobbit* was developed after that book was first published, in a complex process of imagining its origins. Taken chronologically, Sauron is where the story begins, and then there is the story of Isildur, but, as mentioned above, readers may easily perceive the Ring as Gollum's, and so the story of its finding by Deagol and the seizing of it from him by Smeagol/Gollum is at any rate a second beginning for the Ring and, because it is a story nearer to the events of *The Hobbit* and *The Lord of the Rings*, may well leave an impression of inaugural force more striking than the somewhat bald and colourless information that the Ring was really made by Sauron.

7. Fafner hides in a cave for centuries: Smeagol/Gollum hides in a cave for centuries

Once possessed of the Ring, Fafner, as noted above, does nothing with it. It is merely part of his hoard. Gollum perhaps does more with his Ring, but not a great deal more, and eventually it, like Fafner's Ring, is buried underground, used only by Gollum so that he can evade goblins in the tunnels under the mountains, and since these tunnels are quite dark it hardly seems an essential piece of equipment. The Ring is said to have had an effect on Gollum, turning him from Smeagol into the sub-hobbit creature he is by the time Bilbo meets him. His fate is similar to Fafner's. The giant's transformation into a slothful dragon is a degeneration that parallels that of Smeagol into Gollum.

In both stories the period of idleness and neglect of the Ring has the same effect. The failures of Fafner and Gollum to realise the potential of the powerful object they have acquired foreshadows the exploitation of that potential. Paradoxically, the Rings seem more powerful for *not* having been used for so long. The fears and speculations of those who do not have them but desire them, or dread that others will gain them, make the Rings the centres of anxiety as well as of plotting and manœuvring. As Christine Chism says, 'the Ring is a productive mystery, opening a space for the generation of story' (page 79). She tries to claim that this is true only of Tolkien's Ring. 'Alberich's ring begets gold; Tolkien's begets stories', she writes, but this misses the way Wagner too weaves narratives around his Ring. For some, indeed, the propensity of Wagner's characters to settle down and tell once more their version of the story so far is one of the less exciting aspects of *Der Ring des Nibelungen*, but these narratives, by Wotan, Mime, again by Wotan as the Wanderer, and by others, build, like Tolkien's references in *The Lord of the Rings* to his legendarium, the complex entity of the Ring and its associations, despite its virtual absence from the plot for long periods, and its relative inactivity when it is present.

But in a simple sense the hiding of the Ring in a dark cave for centuries is expressive of its nature. It is secretive and unknown, a thing of darkness. Fearsome as that is, bringing it to light is probably more dangerous, for once out of its hole who knows what it might do?

8. Siegfried inherits the shards of his father's sword: Aragorn inherits the shards of his father's sword

The motif of the sword-splinters is present in the Icelandic sources Wagner used and Tolkien knew and so the latter could claim he was not simply following the former here, but the fact remains that the reforging of the sword Nothung by Siegfried is such a dominant feature of the first act of the opera named after the hero that Tolkien could hardly expect to use the device of the broken sword without evoking a comparison with Wagner. However much he or his apologists protest, the most prominent use of this motif is Wagner's and Tolkien cannot have failed to know this. Wagner's use is also of course the most dramatic, since he builds the climax of the first act of *Siegfried* around the hero's forging of his own sword out of the fragments left by his father. Mime the dwarf, despite his skills as a metalworker, is unable to refashion the sword. Many critics take this to be an image of Wagner's own artistic pride, a picture of how he, defying the critics and those hidebound by operatic and musical convention, created a powerful new work using revolutionary new harmonies and dramaturgy, what Wagner himself claimed was the art work of the future. Perhaps deliberately, Tolkien avoids all this. Aragorn's sword, which belonged to his forefather (and not father) Elendil, is remade for him by the elves, virtually their only contribution to the war against Sauron and the return of the king, and this is related in a bare couple of sentences in *The Lord of the Rings*, as if to rebuke Wagner for making such a song and dance about the business of sword-making.

Originally, Aragorn's sword is said to be dwarf-made. It was broken by his ancestor Elendil in combat with Sauron himself but enough of the blade was left attached to the hilt to let Elendil's son Isildur hack off the finger on which Sauron wore the Ring. This amputation caused the immediate loss of Sauron's power that led to his defeat and the subsequent possession of the Ring by Isildur himself, with fatal consequences. The story of Aragorn's sword, then, is one of the finest examples of Tolkien's narrative method, loading an object with a complex and vital history. The reforging of this sword to do battle again against the forces of Sauron is clearly an act of heroic proportions, and predictive of another victorious outcome. Siegfried's sword has a far less auspicious history. How it was first made Wagner does not relate. It comes into his story at the time of the forced wedding of Sieglinde, Siegmund's twin sister and Siegfried's mother, to Hunding. At the marriage feast in his house, which is built around a massive ash-tree, a stranger, in a grey cloak and wearing a wide-brimmed hat drawn down over his face, enters and plunges the sword hilt-deep into the trunk of the tree. None can withdraw it until Siegmund, fleeing weaponless from his enemies, stumbles into Hunding's house. He is instantly drawn to Sieglinde, and she to him, though neither at first recognises the other, so long have they been parted. When Hunding declares that Siegmund can stay the night in his house as a guest but must in the morning face him as an enemy, weaponless or not, Sieglinde privately reveals to her brother that the sword is there for a man who needs it. While Hunding sleeps, Siegmund draws the sword from the tree and brother and sister, now united, and indeed lovers, escape, pursued by Hunding and his followers. Wotan, at first inclined to assist the twins, is reluctantly persuaded by his wife Fricka that their incest is intolerable. He intervenes when Siegmund fights Hunding, interposing his spear so that the sword shatters upon it. Brünnhilde, defying her father's express wish, though not, she believes, his true desire, rescues the fragments of the sword and Sieglinde, too, and takes them to refuge from Wotan's wrath, which she herself confronts and by which she is condemned. Sieglinde is found by Mime in the forest. She dies giving birth to Siegfried and the dwarf takes the babe and the sword fragments into his care.

In Wagner, then, the sword is an ambivalent gift of the god Wotan to the heroes he hopes will recover the Ring. The idea of it occurs to Wotan at the end of *Das Rheingold*, just before the entry to Valhalla, and represents Wotan's first thoughts on how to undo the problems caused by the contract with the giants, Alberich's theft of the Rhinegold and his curse on the Ring he made from it. The sword then is as much a tool as a weapon and this causes further problems, for Wotan and for those who wield the blade. It is matched by Wotan's spear, the symbol of his adherence to legality, to order and agreements. Siegmund and Sieglinde violate the laws of marriage and so the sword must break on the spear, or Wotan's authority is lost. Later, after Siegfried has reforged it, and Wotan challenges him at the foot of the mountain on which Brünnhilde sleeps, the sword will in turn break the spear, as Siegfried's impetuosity and refusal to be bound by precedent thrusts aside the whole structure of Wotan's jurisdiction.

The sword has, however, another part to play. When Siegfried, disguised as Gunther, claims Brünnhilde as Gunther's bride, he tries to keep faith with Gunther by placing the sword as a symbolic barrier between him and Brünnhilde in their bed. When later she accuses him of seducing her (because he, not Gunther, wears the Ring, which Siegfried took from her at that time on her mountain), Siegfried swears that the sword separated them. Brünnhilde, however, remembering, unlike Siegfried, their true first marriage, counterswears that when they went to bed the sword hung on the wall. The sword, then, becomes it its turn a symbol of what is right and what is wrong.

As such it seems to operate very much in a sexual context. Quite apart from any pre-Freudian phallic implications, the sword in *Der Ring des Nibelungen* is prominent, as we have seen, in the coming together of the two most important pairs of lovers in the story, Siegmund and Sieglinde, and their son, Siegfried, and Brünnhilde (actually Siegmund's half-sister, since Wotan is father to both, and therefore, as Anna Russell amusingly pointed out, Siegfried's aunt, like the rest of the valkyries). Nothing of this appears in Tolkien, although interestingly Peter Jackson's film version associates the remaking of Aragorn's sword with Elrond, the father of Arwen, Aragorn's beloved. There is a suggestion that either the sword is her gift to him or that it is Elrond's and intended as a substitute for his daughter, since if she marries Aragorn she will have to choose to become human and leave her father, and his kind, for ever (in effect, a choice Wotan forces on Brünnhilde in *Die Walküre*). Whether or not Wagner is the cause, Jackson seems ready to connect the sword with the dilemmas of family relations and the choices of lovers. In contrast, Tolkien himself makes very little of the reforging of Aragorn's sword and the weapon itself loses significance thereafter.

9. Brünnhilde gives up immortality for Siegfried: Arwen gives up immortality for Aragorn.

It is not quite correct to say Brünnhilde gives up her immortality. Wotan punishes her for her disobedience in trying to protect Siegmund against him and for rescuing Sieglinde by condemning the valkyrie to sleep on an exposed mountain-top until awoken by the first man who comes along; then she shall be his mortal wife. Brünnhilde has no choice in this, but she does plead that the man who is to become her husband should be a hero, and Wotan agrees that, to ensure this, the mountain-top shall be surrounded by fire through which only a hero will be brave enough to make his way to the sleeping bride. The orchestra tells us that this hero will be Siegfried. Whether Brünnhilde guesses this is not clear but she accepts her fate and, although, when she is awakened by Siegfried, she for a moment wavers and tries to assert her divinity, love soon overcomes her regrets for her former existence and she commits herself to the hero.

Arwen's story is far less developed in *The Lord of the Rings*. It exists mainly in an appendix. Yet it is strongly related to the core of Tolkien's legends because the story of Arwen's sacrifice of her elvish immortality for love of the human Aragorn is a parallel to the story of Beren and Lúthien. He is the man who fell in love with the elf-maiden Lúthien, who, before Arwen, was also willing to accept mortality to share life with a human. Beren is one of the heroes of *The Silmarillion*, in fact the only person to recover one of the lost silmarils from Morgoth, although he needs the help of Lúthien to do so. Their story is one of those that Tolkien worked on for most of his life and it is central not only to his mythology but also to his own life. He had the name Lúthien, as is well known, placed on the gravestone of his wife Edith and at his own death the name Beren was added for him. The first encounter of Beren and Lúthien, Tolkien confirmed (see his letter to Christopher Tolkien, 11 July 1972), was based on an incident from his early life with Edith, a memory of her dancing amongst wild flowers. In the stories of Lúthien's and Arwen's sacrifice of their elvishness for the sake of mere mortal husbands it is surely right to see Tolkien's own sense that in marrying him Edith had sacrificed something pure and precious beyond the nature of the ordinary male. There is in this much of Tolkien's idealisation of women, his setting them on pedestals above the sordid world that men must deal with. It is notable how three of the four major female characters in *The*

Chapter Two: From surface to depth 51

Lord of the Rings, Goldberry, Arwen and Galadriel (Éowyn is the exception), all live in protected enclaves, apart from the warfare and treachery of the world into which the men and hobbits must go.

In his own way Wagner is also an idealist about women. Though far less prudish than Tolkien in obvious respects, Wagner also sees women as redeemers of the world and of men. Sieglinde brings Siegmund his father's sword and she survives her brother's death to bring their son into the world. Brünnhilde is the one who defies Wotan to bring this about, she is the one who inspired Siegmund to do his duty by Sieglinde, and Sieglinde not to despair. It is Brünnhilde who does her best to educate Siegfried. She resists the easy option of giving up the Ring to Waltraute and, although she is misled by Hagen into plotting against Siegfried, she rises above the tragic consequences in the redemptive climax of the end of *Götterdämmerung*. If only the men could be as heroic as her, and as ready to set aside divine pretensions, the world would be a better place.

It is true that Gutrune is a weak character, like Freia in *Das Rheingold* a pawn in the interchanges among men. Fricka too seems at first a conventional type, and in *Die Walküre* her role seems to be as the nagging wife, but Wagner's music for her when she insists on upholding the rights of marriage and demands that Wotan abandon the incestuous Siegmund and Sieglinde gives her a strong moral presence. She represents another sort of idealism but still a womanly one. The fifth female figure in *Der Ring des Nibelungen*, Erda, is the most shadowy and also the most unworldly, and perhaps for that reason she is an idealistic representation, too. Her name, of course, makes her the voice of the earth itself, and her role in *Das Rheingold* as the admonitory voice of deeper wisdom to Wotan gives her a matriarchal authority. She then becomes an actual mother when Wotan fathers the valkyries on her, but when he rouses her at the start of the third act of *Siegfried*, with the hero on his way to wake Brünnhilde, Erda proves unable to help him or advise him, and he ends by telling her what she should know, that the end of the gods is near. The bypassing of ancient womanly wisdom is repeated in the Prologue to *Götterdämmerung* when the Norns falter in the task of weaving the web of fate and the coils disintegrate. Symbolically, the next voice we hear is that of Brünnhilde urging Siegfried on to new deeds.

Women in Wagner's works have more agency and more responsibility, for themselves and others, than in Tolkien's, but they are also used to stand for high ideals. They inspire and redeem, and are ready to sacrifice themselves for men, especially for love. This is a frequent theme in Wagner's work, prominent in *Der Fliegende Holländer*, *Tannhäuser*, *Lohengrin* and *Der Ring des Nibelungen*, and not absent from *Tristan und Isolde* and *Parsifal*. Wagner thought he was dramatising an age-old theme, one he could trace to his mediæval sources, but in fact it was a theme expanded and intensified by Romanticism. Tolkien may have thought that he too was presenting his idealised females in a mediæval traditional manner and he reinforced this with his references to the concept of the Virgin Mary as the Roman Catholic Church has developed her, that is, as the type of the divine female he believed art should describe. But his idealisation of women is also in the same Romantic tradition as Wagner's.

10. Wotan plays 'riddles' for the life of Mime: Gollum plays 'riddles' for the life of Bilbo.

This seems out of place in Goldman's list because it draws a comparison between *Der Ring des Nibelungen* and *The Hobbit*, not *The Lord of the Rings*. It comes at this point in his list because he is roughly following the order of events in Wagner's work, not Tolkien's.

Apart from the fact that again Tolkien could try to claim that he was following the precedent of mediæval sources, such as Anglo-Saxon riddles, of which some of those used in *The Hobbit* are variants, or question-and-answer poems in the *Poetic Edda*, there seems little to add here. Both Wagner and Tolkien do have riddle contests and in both the snivelling unpleasant character loses. Wagner's has the advantage that it uses riddles about the plot of his work where Tolkien's are just riddles (because when he wrote it he had no notion of the sequel to *The Hobbit*). Both, however, end with a riddle that the loser cannot answer although that answer is of vital importance to him. Mime can give all the information Wotan requires about the past but cannot say who will forge the sword for Siegfried; Gollum guesses all Bilbo's riddles but cannot say that what he has in his pocket is the Ring.

Chapter Two: From surface to depth   53

11. A dragon guards the Nibelungs' hoard: A dragon guards the dwarves' hoard.

Again the comparison here is, as in the previous example, between *Der Ring des Nibelungen* and *The Hobbit*, not *The Lord of the Rings*. This is one case where Tolkien cannot be held to be imitating Wagner since European dragons traditionally guard hoards of gold and other valuables. Wagner is no more the inventor of this than Tolkien, or the authors of the Icelandic poems or *Beowulf*.

12. The gods renounce the world and await the end: The Elves renounce the world and prepare to depart.

This brings us to the meanings in the endings of both works and really needs to be taken along with the last three of Goldman's parallels:

15. The immortals burn in Valhalla: The immortals leave Middle-earth.

16. A new era emerges in the world.

17. Men are left to their own devices.

The outcome of Wagner's *Der Ring des Nibelungen* is often misunderstood, more especially since its subversion by Hitler, and the uncritical acceptance of the Nazi reading of *Götterdämmerung* by popular historians and television documentary makers, so fond of accompanying newsreel of the fall of the Third Reich with Wagnerian music, especially Siegfried's funeral march. This assumes that the point of Wagner's climax to his cycle is the tragic loss of the gods, and that in some sense the gods represent heroic humanity. Bradley J Birzer, as we have seen, believes Wagner apotheosises (as he tries to put it) human beings. Goldman takes the same view. There is some excuse for this because of the dramatic prominence in *Götterdämmerung* of the death and funeral of the human hero Siegfried, coincident as it is, more or less, with the destruction of Valhalla and the self-sacrifice of the ex-valkyrie Brünnhilde. In addition, the grandeur of Wagner's music for Valhalla and the solemnity with which it is combined with that representing Siegfried, Brünnhilde and their relationship at the end of the cycle can make it difficult to see differences in the treatment and meaning of their destruction. Music is perhaps not very good for discriminating between mourning something which, though grand, is now outdated, and somebody who, although a failure, represented a real hope for mankind. Tolkien, too, has trouble with regret for something that nevertheless must end.

Wagner's meaning is of course ill-served by extracting the valediction to Siegfried and to the gods from the end of his cycle without attention to what he has to say about the end of the gods earlier. The idea of the end of the gods, of Götterdämmerung, enters as early as the final scene of *Das Rheingold*, in the oracular words of Erda's warning to Wotan. Almost from the start, we should be aware that the existence of the gods is at stake and is likely to pass away. Wotan will at first resist his fate and, deciding that the Ring will give him the power to prevent his own decline, he begins devising a plan to secure it, but he will come to see this as futile, and that he has himself set going the train of events leading to the twilight of the gods. His choice is between raging against this and vainly trying to prevent it, and accepting it and fading away in a dignified manner. He just about manages the latter, although in his confrontation with Siegfried below Brünnhilde's crag he loses control enough to provoke a fight that he inevitably loses. But a large part of the meaning of the whole work is Wotan's acceptance that the gods' day is done and that of men has dawned.

Far from glorifying the gods, then, *Der Ring des Nibelungen* is about their inevitable decay. This should be clear enough from the events in the story, particularly of the two central operas. In *Die Walküre* Wotan's half-baked plan to use a human proxy to retrieve the Ring from Fafner is frustrated by his own rules, and the rebellion of his daughter against them forces him to banish her. In *Siegfried* Wotan does his best to play the part of the disinterested observer, teasing Mime and Alberich with the possibility he might help them to the Ring while leaving Siegfried to take it for himself. His detachment falters at the end, as we have just noted, sufficiently for him to be dismissed by Siegfried, and then he retires to await Götterdämmerung in Valhalla. He is only indirectly responsible for the valkyrie Waltraute's mission to her sister Brünnhilde to plead with her to save the gods by returning the Ring to the Rhine. Waltraute overhears Wotan muttering about this but takes it upon herself, without orders from her father, to try to bring it about.

Central to Wotan's final attitude is his second meeting with Erda, just before his confrontation with Siegfried. Ostensibly he rouses the Wala to ask her ad-

Chapter Two: From surface to depth

vice but he must know that events have moved beyond her scope. He ends by telling *her* what will happen, how the era of the gods will end. She is confused and inarticulate, fearful of his grim gaiety in accepting fate. She slips back into being the sub-rational, unconscious earth-force she stands for, just as Loge has degenerated back into the unselfed fire that is his essence. Wagner, having begun his cycle with an image of creation in *Das Rheingold*, followed by a theft of knowledge that begins pre-history, has managed to move to the final phases of his cosmology, when the gods cease to walk the earth and become the stuff of myth and legend.

On the political level, however, Wotan's ending is a commentary on the problem of power. He is, with his spear, the embodiment of laws and contracts. He represents the effort to create order in the world by prescriptive force and his actions in *Das Rheingold* and *Die Walküre* show him attempting to rule the world from above. He does so, as he believes, for its own good. He has sacrificed some of his own personal power and accepted a restriction of his will by the needs of others. This is one of the meanings of his exchange of an eye for wisdom, for the opportunity to drink from the waters flowing from the World Ash-tree, a stem of which he made into his spear. Not only does his single eye mean that he sees things without duplicity, but it also marks his pledge that he sees with more than just an eye. But this is, in the end, not enough. In the end, having one eye is still a defect, and still means he has only his point of view. There is no way to convince those he wishes to lead that his power is always benign and at their service. Benevolent dictatorship is still dictatorship, and order imposed, no matter how justified or justifiable, is still an outside force. Wotan comes to realise that he is, as they say, part of the problem, not the solution. If the world is to become a better place it cannot do so by order, not even of the most well-meaning kind. People have to embrace change themselves. That is why the gods must end.

Wotan's choice is made more poignant because he resigns his responsibility apparently in favour of Siegfried. Despite the musical excitement with which Wagner surrounds him, and the descriptions of him as the greatest hero who ever existed, no serious commentators in modern times can find in Siegfried anything much to admire, and many openly despise him. One might have to accept that Wagner was just wrong and that therefore *Der Ring des Nibelungen* has a large hole in it where a positive image of man should be. Some commentators have tried to fill the gap by setting Siegfried aside and concentrating on Brünnhilde as the true representative of the human, trying to ignore her pre-human valkyrie existence. There is much to be said for this. Certainly it is Brünnhilde who dominates the final scene of the work and she it is who displays nobility, magnanimity and a truly human acceptance of life and death. But she also loves Siegfried, praises him and mourns him. Perhaps the way out is to ignore Wagner's own Siegfried worship and trust the tale, not the teller. Siegfried is the flawed character the critics scorn but he is all too human because of that. He is, of course, in an impossible position. Wotan created and trained his father Siegmund for the mission to retrieve the Ring and then found he could fool nobody into thinking Siegmund was anything but his stooge. Thus Siegfried has to be ignorant and undirected, innocent of divine interference, and in fact brought up in a way far removed from that of his father, and the influence of his grandfather. The consequence is inevitable and inevitably unattractive. Whether he meant it consciously or not, Wagner makes Siegfried a nineteenth-century counterpart to the eighteenth-century delusion known as the Noble Savage. Wagner reverts to a seventeenth-century view of uncivilised man as nasty and brutish and with a short life. Nevertheless, he is the man to kill the dragon and without him the Ring would not have been recovered and eventually destroyed. Whatever illusions Wagner had about his hero, his work of art has a clear and uncomfortable view of what it would take for a man to rid the world of the primal curse of interfering godhead and begin human history.

Tolkien, in comparison, treats the same questions in a fashion that largely avoids disturbing his readers and many probably miss what is really going on with his elves, if they have not read deeper into the legendarium (a thing that was impossible to do until many years after Tolkien's death). Tolkien's mythological history consists of the rise and decline of successive groups of beings before the arrival of humanity, the first and only group that is mortal. The other groups therefore overlap in time so that, although the myths, arranged in chronological order, as in the published *Silmarillion*, move their focus from the one god to the lesser demigods to the elves and dwarves and eventually to men, technically they all end up existing and interacting together, as we see in *The Lord of the Rings*, set in the Third Age of Middle-earth, when all the various beings (including hobbits, very much an afterthought) have come into being. In narrative terms, however, dominance belongs to the species of the moment, so that the early tales in the sequence are about the world of god-like beings, a quarrelling pantheon not much unlike those of Greek and Scandinavian mythology, and then the stories become the history of the wars of the elves, with themselves and with their dark opposites, the orcs (and sundry other evil creatures, including dragons; there are also the dwarves, who are both a digression and a diversion from the history of the elves, and provide a parallel story before they become caught up as adversaries and sometimes as allies in the elvish story). Then men begin to appear on the scene, interfering in the lives of elvish kingdoms and sometimes allying with them in their wars, and sometimes siding with their enemies. As the legends develop they move towards the dominance of men in the world and the fading of the elves out of it. Tolkien in fact meant this, at times literally, as an explanation of European, and particularly English, folk culture. Elves are real, and were real in the past, but pushed aside by men. They became mythological and turned into the stuff of fairy tales, which are pale, debased echoes of the real relations between elves and humans, containing all that is left to human knowledge of the history of the ages when elves flourished in Middle-earth. Tolkien's unfinished time-travel novels show him trying to devise ways by which the history of the elves might be handed down to the present day.

The fading of the elves, however, is a core element in their nature and history, and it arises out of their most fundamental attribute, their immortality. Paradoxically, it is because their lives have no termination that they lose the will to exist and fade away. Ultimately, they cease to care. They suffer a kind of culture shock when they get to know mortal men and discover that, by their standards, these short-lived beings are more active and vigorous than they are. Men must be active and use the time they have. Even unwise or unsuccessful action is preferable to inactivity. In a way the elves have too much time to consider what to do and spend so much time weighing up the possibilities and consequences that opportunities slip by and a kind of order based on what has always happened imposes itself, resisting change. With their short lives men also have short memories, and in any case do not have time to enquire into or learn what has gone before them, whereas for the elves everything claiming to be new has deep roots in the past that shape the response to the present, and the future. Unlike Wotan, the elves are not exactly active in imposing their order on the world but their world-view imposes itself on them by virtue of their memories and sense of themselves in time. To them men are like Siegfried to Wotan: brash, unreflective, short-term activists who make things happen and so change the nature of history. Like Wotan, the elves come to accept that this is as it should be and the future belongs not to them but to restless mankind. And so they begin drifting away from Middle-earth. Because of the differences of form between drama and fiction, Tolkien makes the departure of the elves not a grand climax like the burning of Valhalla but a long, melancholy withdrawing. Bands of elves travel through the woods at night towards the Grey Havens, where they will take ship to the Lands of the West. These scenes are the closest *The Lord of the Rings* gets to the spirit of the Celtic Twilight art and literature of the late nineteenth century, a cultural movement not now much admired but potent in its day. Some of Tolkien's earliest verse, for example, the poem 'Goblin Feet', belongs to this movement (see Dimitra Fimi's book *Tolkien, Race and Cultural History*). Significantly this poem was largely repudiated by him later, or revised to make it seem more in keeping with his later mythologising. It is however hard to deny that the islands of the west to which the elves depart are parallels to the Celtic stories of Arthur's Avalon and Tír nan Óg, even if Tolkien's public comments on such Celtic mythology, like his references to Wagner, fall short of acknowledging any debt.

If, however, Goldman is right to see parallels between *Götterdämmerung* and the departure of the elves from Middle-earth, he has nevertheless noticed only part of the story, for there are other immortals who depart at the end of Tolkien's Third Age. A much more direct parallel to the supersession of Wotan in Wagner's cycle is that of Gandalf in Tolkien's. The wizard is the clearest counterpart to the god. He, like Wotan, though powerful in himself, chooses mortals to carry out his plans and tries to direct them. In so doing Gandalf, like Wotan, discovers that he cannot command compliance but must negotiate it, and in crucial matters he must often rely on human initiative, or let matters run their course. Tolkien is less harsh on his supernatural organiser than Wagner, and he does not give Gandalf Wotan's awareness of his own doom, but he does show Gandalf taken from the central role by a fatal confrontation (although he also brings him back later). Gandalf facing the balrog in fire and darkness in Moria is a scene reminiscent of Wotan's facing Siegfried beneath the fire-girt crags of Brünnhilde's lair. Gandalf's staff is raised like Wotan's spear, both bar the way, and both fall, although not to their final ends. Gandalf returns, allegedly stronger than before, but his role becomes that of the diplomat and military adviser, with occasional sallies into heroic battle-action, as if to convince us he is not just a chief of staff. But he is surely being superseded by Aragorn before the end. His temporary absence after his fall in Moria opens the way for Aragorn to take the lead in the Fellowship of the Ring and after his return Gandalf rarely operates in the same spheres as Aragorn, who takes an increasingly active and decisive role in events. We should recall that Aragorn is the Siegfried-like inheritor of a broken sword remade. In keeping with Tolkien's revision of Siegfried, the immature wild-boy, into Aragorn, the king of men, he does not depict a crude direct conflict between Gandalf and Aragorn, or even suggest much rivalry, although there is the incident with the palantír, into which Aragorn chooses to look despite Gandalf's misgivings, and without telling him what he has done. Aragorn is always respectful to Gandalf and ready to defer to his wisdom, but in the end command passes to the new king, not the old wizard, and Gandalf, his work done, departs from the world.

Gandalf's work is also like Wotan's not just in the simple sense that both are shown trying to solve king-problems but also in the respect that both in effect exist to bring about order in their worlds. They are the embodiments of political and social visions of society that they try to realise in the worlds they inhabit. Both are beings of power and knowledge, their power derived from their knowledge. Both develop interrelations with other kinds of beings while remaining detached as individuals themselves. Both are portrayed as fatherly, as irascible, as wily and as capable of violent and decisive action. Both look forward and backwards in their time and see events in a large historical context, and see themselves and others in it, too. Superficially, Wotan the Wanderer, with his hat and cloak and staff-like spear, resembles Gandalf the Grey, so much so that Tolkien's claim that he based the visual appearance of his wizard on a German postcard seems like another of his attempts to disguise Wagner's influence on him, forgetting that in a letter to Stanley Unwin of 7 December 1946 he described Gandalf as an 'Odinic wanderer' (*Letters*, page 119). Finally, the outcome of both Wotan's and Gandalf's stories is their renunciation of the world as they become irrelevant to it and must leave the men in it to their own devices. This, as much as the destruction of a ring, is what makes the meanings of *Der Ring des Nibelungen* and *The Lord of the Rings* similar.

13. The Ring is returned to its origin, the River Rhine: The Ring is returned to its origin, Mount Doom.

Several Tolkien critics have claimed that *The Lord of the Rings* is original in being a quest not to find something but to lose it. The aim of the plot is the destruction of a valuable object, not its discovery or reclamation. *The Lord of the Rings* is like a quest story in reverse. But so too is *Der Ring des Nibelungen*, which begins at the bottom of the Rhine and ends with the river flooding the hall of the Gibichungs to allow the Rhinemaidens to swim up and take back their stolen gold. From Loge's first account of the theft of the Rhinegold there is the suggestion that true resolution can only be achieved by the return of the Ring to its origin. This point may be obscured in *Die Walküre*, where the Ring never actually appears, and *Siegfried*, where the hero who takes the Ring hardly knows what it is or what to do with it, but in *Götterdämmerung* the presence of the Rhine in the setting reminds us of the gold's origins and at the start of the third act the Rhinemaidens themselves re-appear to make their pleas for the return of the Ring. Wagner thus builds a grand and obvious ring-like circularity into his work.

Such a circularity is also present in the history of Tolkien's Ring but the outline is less clear because of the piece-meal development of his story. Historically and textually, the origin of his Ring is on the floor of a tunnel under the Misty Mountains in *The Hobbit*. Later Tolkien invented the back-story for the Ring, and placed its origins in Sauron's volcano in Mordor, where only it can be destroyed. One cannot categorically declare that Tolkien devised this circle of closure under the influence of Wagner, but equally one cannot deny the similarity. Both Rings come round to their origins, in which they dissolve and lose their shape and potency.

14. Hagen falls into the river: Gollum falls into the volcano.

It is perhaps misleading to say Hagen falls into the Rhine at the end of *Götterdämmerung*. Rather he dives into the rising waters, shouting 'Get back from the Ring!', in a desperate effort to seize it before the Rhinemaidens. Nevertheless, there is a similarity with Gollum's actions at the end of *The Lord of the Rings*, when he pounces on Frodo and struggles with him for the Ring, which he has to bite off, along with Frodo's finger. Too concerned with the prize, however, Gollum does not notice that he is dangerously close to the edge of the lava-pit, overbalances and falls to his destruction, and the Ring's. He takes the Ring with him to his death, unlike Hagen, and at first sight there seems only coincidence between the two characters here. But Hagen is the son of Alberich and becomes his representative, even substitute, and Alberich is easily seen as a parallel to Gollum. Both lose the Ring, both curse and both follow it about, trying to get it back. Thus the death of Hagen at the moment of the Ring's destruction can stand for the end of Alberich, too, and so continue the parallel with Gollum.

The other motif involved here is the ring-finger. Tolkien obviously wants to make Frodo's loss of a finger an echo of Sauron's, when Isildur hacked off his finger, with the Ring. Frodo ends up like Sauron, missing a digit. It is the mark of a secret connection between them. In *Der Ring des Nibelungen* finger-loss is not a feature but when Hagen, after Siegfried's body has been brought back to the hall of the Gibichungs, tries to remove the Ring from the ring-finger of the hero's corpse, the entire hand rises in ghastly resistance. The phallic implications of this are hard to deny, especially as a few moments later Brünnhilde will remove the Ring from her husband's finger with no trouble. This in turn points to the negative phallic implications of Tolkien's version of events.

There is one notable omission from Goldman's list of parallels between Wagner and Tolkien – the resemblances between Brünnhilde and Éowyn. Tolkien, I think, shared the late nineteenth-century fascination with warrior-women. It is another example of his links with essentially Victorian attitudes, like the interest in fairies mentioned already. In her book on *Tolkien, Race and Cultural History* (2010) Dimitra Fimi almost brings out Tolkien's interest in warrior women in her tenth chapter, 'Visualizing Middle-earth', printing two pictures of Norse warrior-women (pages 173f), but in fact her focus is only on their winged helmets, which she wants to connect with the winged crown of Gondor that Aragorn wears. Both Fimi's illustrations are of valkyries, the mythical daughters of Odin, chief of the Nordic gods, who sends them out to choose male warriors from the battlefield and bring them to his heavenly fortress Valhalla, there to enjoy long life as his elite bodyguard. The leader of the valkyries is Brynhild, or, in German, Brünnhilde, the heroine of *Der Ring des Nibelungen*, and in fact the character after whom the second of the operas, *Die Walküre*, is named. At least one of Fimi's illustration is of Brynhild (page 174). The image of a female warrior, in a chain-mail shirt and winged helmet, riding a horse and waving a spear, became common in the latter part of the nineteenth century, even in advertising, and lasted into the twentieth. It is now of course regarded as typical of Wagnerian opera. The nineteenth century was, I think, fascinated by this figure of the warrior-woman or shield-maiden, and she appears frequently in pictures and sculptures, such as images of Britannia, or the statue of Boadicea placed near the Houses of Parliament in London in 1905. I suggest it is not a coincidence that Éowyn, the most developed female character in *The Lord of the Rings*, becomes, for a time at least, a shield-maiden. While modern critics would like to think this is Tolkien trying to show a woman who is independent-minded and self-asserting, he was perhaps only indulging in the valkyrie-worship of his Victorian roots.

Éowyn brings in another connection between Tolkien and Wagner. When she disguises herself as a warrior in order to join the expedition to relieve Minas Tirith, she adopts the name Dernhelm, combining the archaic English word 'dern', meaning 'dark, secret or hidden', with an old form of the word 'helmet'. Etymologically, however, 'Dernhelm' is related to 'Tarnhelm', the name Wagner gives the magic helmet in *Der Ring des Nibelungen*, used by Alberich to make himself invisible and, more interestingly for the connection with Éowyn, by Siegfried when he disguises himself as Gunther to seduce Brünnhilde. The association of both Dernhelm and Tarnhelm with disguise and transformation adds to the close etymological connection of the two names to indicate that here is another detail that Tolkien must have known linked his work with Wagner's. As a student of Germanic languages he could not have been unaware of the fact that his invented name Dernhelm is cognate with the name of the magic helmet of disguise in Wagner.

The discussion of this list of resemblances and parallels between *Der Ring des Nibelungen* and *The Lord of the Rings* moves inevitably from the superficial to the fundamental. Though Goldman's list is, like all lists, essentially sporadic and at first sight offers no evidence for fundamental or sustained correspondences between the two works, only incidental ones, analysed in detail these have a cumulative effect, so that the shadow of a common narrative shape looms behind the string of details. Problems faced by main characters lead to solutions, questions have answers, actions have consequences and relationships develop along certain lines. Parallel effects in these terms connect the works in ways that go beneath the simple resemblances and suggest profounder similarities of meaning and purpose. Some may be sketched here. Both Wagner and Tolkien begin with a simpler world into which tension is inserted by greed and ambition. Both have major characters who attempt to deal with this disruption, and both these characters feel the need to work through others, rather than directly, to restore some sort of order. Both stories therefore involve those who one way or another have to learn what they have got themselves into, and a major issue is choice and freewill. The converse of this is the problem of leadership, or how a commanding figure can induce others to act according to his will without rendering them mere slaves to it. That this is a central danger is made evident by the main symbolic object in each work, the Rings that, whatever else one makes of them, stand for compulsion. But Wagner as much as Tolkien directs the narrative towards the destruction of the Ring and the power it represents, and both *Der Ring des Nibelungen* and *The Lord of the Rings*, for all the grandeur of their final scenes, tend to negative endings, to the passing away of an age of gods and heroes. Wagner came to see in the *Götterdämmerung* of his work an enactment of Schopenhauerian despair, but why should Tolkien follow a similar path in *The Lord of the Rings*? Answering that question not only takes us into the deep meaning his work shares with Wagner's, but also casts light on Tolkien's ideas about literature itself, and to that broad subject the next chapter turns.

CHAPTER THREE

What is *The Lord of the Rings* about?

The Lord of the Rings has been read by millions, in the original, somewhat difficult English and in translation, and taken seriously by most of them. It has not been taken seriously by mainstream critics, although it has by now generated a large amount of serious criticism, a great deal of which is directed at its general meaning, but much of this does not explain why the book is so popular and successful, or at least not in ways that would convince the mainstream critics. The weakness of Tolkien criticism is that it accepts the assumption of the mainstream that *The Lord of the Rings* must be about something other than what it says. Thus the dominant mode of exegesis has become allegorising, and the line of most confident writing about *The Lord of the Rings* is that of the Christian interpreters, who take Tolkien's own religion as fundamental and his own comments on the doctrinal Christian elements of his work at face value and apply them to *The Lord of the Rings* and his other works as thoroughly as they can. The result is largely paraphrase, retelling the stories in another form, and the Christian bias does not account for the response to Tolkien from non-Christians, and may indeed put them off. If the Christian commentators are right then most of the non-Christian readers of Tolkien should have been converted to Christianity by him, although actually, of course, it is already committed Christians who are most affected by this way of reading Tolkien, as they see in him the confirmation of what they already believe and are delighted to find at last a modern author they can agree with and who does not challenge, they think, their beliefs. As always with allegory, the application works in reverse from the theory: the prior beliefs are used to explicate the work, not the other way round.

The other main way of looking at Tolkien uses the other major aspect of his life, his profession as a linguistician or philologist, to explain his work in terms of language. The major exponent of this approach is Tom Shippey and he deploys it most convincingly. He shows the influence on Tolkien's fiction of his love of languages as such and of his experience of studying them, especially those of the Dark Ages. Shippey is persuasive in suggesting that there is a connection between Tolkien's professional activity, in trying to recapture the significances of ancient words and phrases, and his invention of a world to suit his own invented languages. Tolkien himself bestowed plausibility on this approach by several statements he made in interviews and letters. In a set of notes he sent to his American publisher in 1955, for instance, Tolkien wrote that '[t]he stories were made rather to provide a world for the languages than the reverse' (*Letters*, page 219). Middle-earth is therefore the cultural matrix both presupposed by Tolkien's elvish tongues and expressed by their nature (though Dimitra Fimi, in the introduction to the second part of her book *Tolkien, Race and Cultural History* (2010), has questioned easy acceptance of this idea). Again, however, this way of approaching Tolkien's fiction is mainly explanatory. Shippey describes with fine detail what Tolkien's fiction is like and makes us look at it more closely and admire its workmanship, but in the end he too is paraphrasing it, retelling it in different words. Like the Christians, he offers insights that are impressive and intellectually serious, but in his case they are often arcane, and hardly to be expected of ordinary readers. He makes Tolkien's fiction almost a part of his academic work and, while that may give it appeal to academic critics (though that has yet to happen in more than a minor way), it does not seem to explain what readers see. To be fair, Shippey has also tried to relate Tolkien's fiction to non-linguistic ideas and culture and history in the twentieth century, though again this is a kind of applied knowledge, in principle the same as the Christian readings, taking concepts from outside the books and applying them and saying the connection is the meaning. Even in Shippey's philological approach there is a large measure of biography.

There is also a strong sense that these critics want an interpretation that they think the author would agree with. Perhaps this is because of the powerful presence of the idea of Tolkien kept alive by his family, notably his son Christopher. The Tolkien publishing industry has its own weight and momentum and the operation of copyright laws and so on, along with the increasing merchandising of Tolkien, particularly after the success of the Peter Jackson films, generating more issues of rights and authorisations, pushes critics into aiming for orthodoxy. The Christian critics, naturally, are predisposed to the idea of an orthodox reading. Indeed, Tolkien, like C S Lewis, seems to have

Chapter Three: What is *The Lord of the Rings* about?   67

been taken over by the religious lobby in the USA and studies of his work are as likely to come out of departments of theology as from those of English or literature. This is partly by default, because the departments of English have ignored Tolkien as beneath serious notice. Yet approaches to texts that are the stock-in-trade of English departments ought to be applicable to Tolkien and they should provide a counterweight to the doctrinal studies that at their least subtle turn his works into the stuff of homilies.

What is needed is a step away from the biographical approaches that dominate so many studies of Tolkien's work. Almost every book about *The Hobbit* and *The Lord of the Rings* begins with a chapter on the author's life and the least subtle books simply take it as read that what they say about the life is the key to the work. Not that biography is completely irrelevant to criticism, but it ought to be treated sceptically, as a source of possibilities, of testable concepts, not of final truths. The best Tolkien criticism, such as Shippey's and Flieger's, is tentative in this way; much of the rest knows what it wants to find before it starts, and this certainty is projected on to Tolkien himself, so that, again like C S Lewis, he is becoming an image of the wise mentor, the prophetic sage. Tolkien is a wise and subtle writer all right, with a deep awareness of life and its problems and a considered attitude to dealing with them, but he perhaps needs to be rescued from the role of the Sage of Merton.

Actually, Tolkien's most trenchant statement about literature refers not to life but to death. In an interview he gave in 1968 he says this (as accurately as I can transcribe it: more refined versions have appeared in print elsewhere):

> If you really come down to any large story that interests people, holding their attention for a considerable time, or make the – the story is practically always a human story, it's practically always about one thing, aren't they? Death. The inevitability of death.

Tolkien says this about twenty-two minutes into a BBC television programme about him made by John Izzard, in a series called *Release*, first broadcast on 30 March 1968 and now available online at http://www.bbc.co.uk/archive/writers/12237.shtml. After making the statement quoted above, Tolkien is then shown taking out his wallet, from which he extracts a piece of paper that he unfolds, muttering as he does so that it is a quotation by 'Simone Beauvoir' he found the other day in a newspaper article about Carl Maria von Weber, a composer of whom he has always been 'extremely fond'. He then puts on his glasses and reads the following:

> There is no such thing as a natural death: nothing that happens to man is ever natural, since his presence calls the whole world into question. All men must die; but for every man his death is an accident. And even if he knows it and consents to it, an unjusti[fia]ble violation.

Then Tolkien takes off his glasses and says 'You may agree with the words or not, but those are the – are the keyspring of *The Lords of the Ring* [*sic*]'.

The quotation is from a book by Simone de Beauvoir, *Une mort très douce* (1964), a record of her experience of the death of her mother. Tolkien quotes, of course, not the original French but from a translation of the book into English as *A Very Easy Death* in 1965 by Patrick O'Brian (now better known as the author of novels of Napoleonic naval warfare). Tolkien quotes these, in effect the last, sentences from the book pretty accurately (more accurately than his reference to his own work's title, although he does insert the word 'whole' into the first sentence). Renée Vink, in her essay 'Immortality and the death of love: J R R Tolkien and Simone de Beauvoir', in the second volume of *The Ring Goes Ever On: Proceedings of the Tolkien 2005 Conference* (Tolkien Society, 2008, pages 117-127), suggests that he read the whole of de Beauvoir's book but that is unlikely. Tolkien's use of a newspaper cutting connected with Weber makes it probable that he found the quotation in a review of John Warrack's biography of the composer, first published in 1968 and reviewed in *The Times* by Michael Ratcliffe on Saturday, 3 February 1968 (page 20). Ratcliffe notes that Warrack 'prefaces his final chapter with Simone de Beauvoir' and then quotes what Tolkien reads out in the interview.

That quotation clearly made a strong impression on Tolkien, since he clipped it from his copy of *The Times* and put it into his wallet. From what he says, he saw in it a strong resemblance to the meaning of his own work. It seems surprising that he should suggest a link between *The Lord of the Rings* and a work by a French feminist philosopher notorious for her advanced views on marriage and sexuality, and for the way she lived by them. There is however nothing in the interview as broadcast to suggest Tolkien knew much about

Simone de Beauvoir beyond the sentences of hers quoted in Ratcliffe's review of Warrack's book on Weber.

Although the quotation from Simone de Beauvoir is surprising because of its source it is overshadowed by the statement that it is brought in to expand on, the statement that the subject of all great stories is death. Tolkien had by 1968 been interviewed several times. He never seems to have liked it and he appears to have developed a way of dealing with interviews by putting on an act, or rather, a protective display, half grumpiness, which comes out in his comments on interviews in his letters, and half shock tactics. Here he seems to be trying to frighten the interviewer and the audience by saying something he knows will upset them. He succeeded so well that very few commentators or critics have wanted to take his comment seriously and discuss it. Yet it is a significant key to his work. Death is indeed what much of Tolkien's writing is about.

In saying that stories are 'practically always about one thing [...] Death', Tolkien obviously does not mean that the most important works of literature are only those that describe death and dying. For one thing, that is not what he himself wrote about and we know that Tolkien's favourite reading from the Middle Ages, although it certainly contains death scenes, also contains much else, indeed everything else about characters and settings. When he said literature is about death he was being deliberately blunt and shocking, as academic tutors often are, throwing out outrageous-looking generalisations as the start of a discussion that will explore them further. The obvious next move is to expand the topic from just death to the meaning of death, its significance and consequences. This may be why Tolkien was interested in Simone de Beauvoir's book, not because he expected to agree with her but because he had a deep interest in attitudes to death and human reactions to it. The paradox is that the meaning of death is a matter for the living – it is about life. No doubt Tolkien was aware of the cliché that death is a part of life; we must all die and that knowledge must affect our thinking lives. One supposes that for a man in his seventies this was not simply an academic idea, but there is some reason to believe Tolkien had had a concern with the meaning of death from an early age, if not as a consequence of his parents' early deaths, then as a consequence of his experience of the First World War.

The implications of the idea that death is a part of life are not hard to work out, and indeed are the stuff of commonplaces about making good use of your time here, and so on. Since life is finite, and can be seen as short, because it will end in death, human beings must get on with it if they want to achieve something. If nothing is achieved, what have we lived for? Our cultural attitudes to death, and the place of death in our culture, have much to do with the summing up of the life that has ended and in every case, however grand or humble, the summation is in terms of what was achieved, what has been left behind for the rest of us, what the purpose of the deceased's life was and how far that has been fulfilled. We live in an obituary culture where everybody is expected to leave a monument, whether it is a statue in a public square or treasured memories in a family photograph album. These customs are for the living more than for the dead. The valuation of a life that is past is a promise to the living that they too will be valued and therefore that their lives are not pointless, and they will leave something behind. Hence the way, even after fatal accidents or avoidable deaths such as casual terrorism causes, surviving relatives or colleagues declare that the deceased did not die in vain, however difficult it may be to see what their deaths might have achieved. The pinnacle of this customary process is the ceremony of remembrance for the war dead, instituted in Britain in Tolkien's lifetime as a result of the war in which he served, and lost close friends, a ceremony maintained today in all seriousness and solemnity.

There are many references in Tolkien's letters to death as the theme of *The Lord of the Rings* – death and immortality. Most of these go back to a basic feature of his mythology, the comparison and contrast between men, who are mortal, and elves, who are in a particular sense immortal. Tolkien's elves do not die as men do. They can be killed and they can be worn out or so weakened that they fade away, but few do, and even those do not entirely end their existence. At first, Tolkien imagined that elves who lost their lives were simply reincarnated, but later the problems with this idea led him to a more elaborate scheme of a sort of elf limbo, in which the 'souls' of dead elves lingered until allowed to return to earth. Things got even more complex when he allowed elves and men to intermarry and he had to decide whether the half-elven were immortal or not. Fortunately, these beings were exceedingly rare and their fates could be treated as extremely special cases.

In many ways, however, the problems of an elven after-life are a distraction from Tolkien's main interest in elf immortals. Their real purpose is to allow him to analyse the mortality of men. His conceptualisation of undying elves is a means to exploring what it would be like to live for ever, and thus to explore what it means *not* to live for ever, that is, to face inevitable death, and why that is *not* the worst calamity in human nature. Tolkien's elves are thought-experiments in a debate about what endless life would be like. They are very like Swift's struldbruggs in Part III of *Gulliver's Travels*, except that Tolkien makes his elves articulate and thoughtful, usually physically healthy and aware of themselves, and in many ways attractive and interesting, where Swift's immortals are demonstrations that length of life in itself is not a boon. Tolkien's elves, of course, take on many of the attributes of the traditional elves of folklore (though it hardly affects the argument pursued here, it seems most probable that Tolkien came to contemplate the immortality of elves only after being drawn to them by their traditional qualities: see again Dimitra Fimi's book *Tolkien, Race and Cultural History*) and these they tend to retain in his system. They appear like beautiful people, they create beauty in their surroundings and their art, they are associated with the beauties of nature and they are both majestic and wise. In contrast with the struldbruggs they have all the best features of human beings and none of the obvious failings or weaknesses, and their freedom from death seems to be one of their advantages over us.

But this is in the end the opposite of what Tolkien wants to say. Despite all the seeming benefits of immortality that the elves have he, like Swift, wants their existence to seem a cruel burden, but where Swift makes his point directly and disgustingly by emphasising the physical deterioration of aging Tolkien wants to reach a similar conclusion without forcing the issue by referring to such material horrors. His approach is to allow for the ideal continuance of health, wealth and comfort and argue that *still* immortal life would be undesirable. His elves have nothing to live for because they have everything that makes life worth living except death.

Acutely, Tolkien describes what it would be like to live with unlimited time. While for short-lived mortals time is of the essence, always too short, always making us hurry on so as not to waste it, for immortal elves time is not pressing at all, and they are not pressed for it. Once they have, either individually or collectively, attained a certain level of amenity there is no reason to go further. Indeed, there is no reason to suppose that further progress is likely or possible, since after many centuries of experience it is improbable that the best ideas for improving the individual or society have not been thought of by somebody already. Where human society has a constant turnover of members generation by generation, and youth must quickly learn from age before it departs, and age must look to youth to complete or improve or maintain its achievements, long-lived beings like elves can have neither illusions nor aspirations of this sort. History and tradition are not repositories of knowledge and wisdom on which each generation must build but memories, usually personal, of past successes and failures. Immortal elves must live in a perpetual state of *déjà vu*.

Time will seem very different if you have a great deal of it. For humans the passing of the years and seasons is a measure of the shortness of existence and the need to take heed of the moment; for elves such changes are so frequent and so often experienced that they mark only the endless dull rotation of the world. For elves the alterations in their surroundings, the cycles of nature, the lives of mortal beings, are measures of the temporary and brief existences of things other than themselves, a mark of their impermanence and transitory nature. And because so much is transitory in contrast with themselves the elves cannot avoid treating the mortal as somehow less serious, less valuable, less momentous than they are. Yet on the other hand the elves lack goals and aspirations.

Life for immortal elves therefore becomes endless repetition for no clear purpose. Paradoxically, they are left longing for the one possible end (in both senses) of their existence, the final dissolution of their entire world and themselves with it, although they can do nothing to hasten this or anticipate it, other than to accept that some day it may happen. Meanwhile they go on doing what has to be done to maintain an agreeable existence and to fill time, or kill it. Tolkien accepts the traditional notion that the elves have perfected arts and crafts, and a knowledge of nature and much else, in a way that seems magical to humans because for us there is not time to do all that. On the other hand, much of what the elves do has the status of leisure activity in our world and is valued by us because we can only do it when we can, at times when we do not have more important things to do.

Chapter Three: What is *The Lord of the Rings* about?

It is true that the elves, like other beings on earth, have their politics and war. Tolkien's universe includes adversaries and antagonisms. The narratives of *The Silmarillion* are mostly about the wars of the elves against orcs and dwarves and among themselves, and the conflicts between elf-rulers and over-mighty subjects, and mortal men. In some ways this is inconsistent. What have immortal elves to fight for, having seen at first hand the collapse of empires and the futility of war? But Tolkien leaves the elves one thing they have in common with other beings, mortal or not, and that is the love of power. This is perhaps the only thing that can give their lives a sense of purpose. From it and the quest for it flow the heroic virtues of endurance, courage, steadfastness and honour that serve to animate the elves in their history, but also the concomitant vices of impatience, cowardice, weakness and treachery. Perhaps both virtues and vices seem the more irrational given that immortal beings such as elves should know what they really mean as lessons to be learnt from unreflective and ill-considered behaviour. Men may be excused by the brevity of their lives for not learning from their mistakes or not seeing the consequences of their actions, but immortal elves cannot make the same plea.

Despite, however, all the effort Tolkien put into imagining the lives of elves, they exist for him principally as grounds for the converse arguments about mortal men. When in his legends the elves, who are created first, encounter mankind the issue that dominates their intercourse is the brevity of human life, or the fact of death. Some men, of course, envy the elves' immortality. One human reaction Tolkien takes over from the traditions of faerie romance is the feeling of dismay of mortals when they encounter immortals. But more significant is his portrayal of the corresponding reactions of the elves to men, their envy of the drive and vitality of beings forced by the knowledge of the shortness of the time available to them to be up and doing. And of course where life is short and valuable the need on occasion to risk or sacrifice it is that much more heroic or tragic. The *ennui* of the elves in the face of the changeful repetition of mortal life is paralleled by a lack of moral intensity. What to some men seems an admirable calmness and deliberation about the elves can mask a sort of indifference that men cannot justify for themselves. In the end, men cannot wait for the ideal moment, they cannot hold themselves back in case it is too soon to be involved and they cannot refuse to take sides in a quarrel without at the same time taking a particular stand. There is too much at stake in a short life for men to be non-committal about it. In other words, Tolkien works towards the paradox that it is death, the end of life, that makes life worth living. Without a consciousness of an ending, of a foreclosure on existence, men's lives would be the drawn-out waiting for something to turn up that is the essential existence of immortal elves. Death is a part of life in that it determines that lives have a shape. For each man and woman that shape is different. Elvish lives lack this individuation. Without the prospect of death to concentrate their minds they must find something else around which to shape their existence. In Tolkien's works, as often in many traditional tales, that focus is provided by the lives of mortals.

In Tolkien's legendarium, then, men, the second race, created after the elves, are regarded not as cursed with but favoured by the Gift of Death, because it is the fact that mortal life is finite that gives it meaning. It is true, though, that Tolkien's Christian belief leads him to expand the meaning of the Gift of Death to include the gift of an after-life. Since life on earth is so short for men he thinks it follows that a benevolent creator must have intended mortals to have another existence elsewhere in compensation, a compensation denied the elves because they have the benefit of life on earth as long as it exists. One might see this as rather hard on the elves (where the dwarves fit into all this Tolkien was less than clear), but of course the meaning here is really that in actual fact men who long for immortality in this world should be aware that this means forfeiting whatever comes after death for the rest of us. The elves are images of a forlorn race of beings for whom heaven is forever barred, because they have accepted existence in this world for ever and will not go beyond it, or at least not as long as this world exists.

It is possible therefore to see Tolkien's writing about elves and men as a discussion of the meaning of death in human life and an attempt to justify human mortality. Biographical reasons for this are not hard to find. Tolkien's father died when he was three years old and his mother when he was twelve. Although he hardly knew his father he certainly felt the want of him, and it is possible to follow a strand of father-longing in his works. Both his leading hobbits, Bilbo and Frodo, are fatherless, both begin their adventures reliant on the paternalistic Gandalf, and both have to learn to do without him later in their stories. In addition to parental loss Tolkien also of course suffered the loss of close friends in World War I, into which he was plunged as soon as he had completed his Oxford degree in 1915. Before the Great War in which he and his friends served they founded a club, a literary, artistic and philosophical group that, with the earnestness of youth and their times, they intended should bring about great things. They had an English self-deprecation and humour about this, naming the club the TCBS, standing for Tea Club Barrovian Society, after the place in Birmingham where they met for tea after school, but they were quite serious, too. They went to war believing that this was a mere interruption in their real life's work, to which they would dedicate themselves as soon as the fighting was over. Even while it went on they tried to make plans and some beginnings. It is at this time that Tolkien begins writing poems and stories that he thinks of as expressing the ideas of Englishness that the TCBS stands for, but two of the leading members of the group were killed in the war and a third lost heart. Tolkien alone was left, feeling that the deaths of his friends had bequeathed to him the duty and the burden of carrying on and completing the task they had all set themselves before the war interrupted their lives. And so, as well as struggling to make a living from the academic abilities he had developed, Tolkien also embarked on the long sequence of mythological writings that constitute what has now come to be known as his legendarium.

As he said himself, in the 1951 letter to Milton Waldman (*Letters*, pages 143ff), he meant these to be the mythology he felt England, his country, had lost, or never had. He grew to despair of achieving this, and sometimes referred to it lightly, and in its later phases his writings gradually abandoned their more obvious connections (or pseudo-connections) with historical England and became more fiction than history. Yet embedded in much of his work is the idea of a survival of a lone witness to the past, keeping faith with ancient traditions that would be forever lost without his heroic persistence. The various frameworks for his legendary tales show these saviour figures and his time-travel fictions also depend on retrieval of the past for the present by special individuals. As Christopher Ricks said in *The New York Review of Books* in 1974, 'Tolkien is our Ossian'.

Another biographical manifestation of Tolkien's concern with life against death is his struggle with himself over the writing of *The Lord of the Rings*. This is at its height in the 1940s and out of it came two of his most autobiographical works, later collected under the title *Tree and Leaf* (1964), the essay 'On Fairy-stories' (1947, but based on a lecture given in 1939) and the story 'Leaf by Niggle' (1945). The latter presents in allegorical form Tolkien's worry that he has wasted his time 'niggling' at distractions from his serious work as an academic. By this time he must have been conscious of how his academic career was going, that is, not very well. He had a permanent post at one of the world's leading universities, from which he ought to have produced a stream of powerful and original research. As Tom Shippey however shows, in his essay 'Tolkien's Academic Reputation Now' in his collection *Roots and Branches* (2007), Tolkien's productivity was low and although some pieces are of great merit, others are of minor interest. What is most lacking is some great, definitive project that would be Tolkien's academic legacy, his monument. Instead, Tolkien was directing his energies into fiction, much of it, as had been recently confirmed to him, unpublishable at that time. His one notable success, *The Hobbit*, was in a genre that hardly counted in university terms (even now, but much less so seventy years ago). Yet he was engaged on a sequel to *The Hobbit* that threatened to become a monster. Tolkien clearly faced a choice, between committing himself to an attempt to retrieve and consolidate his academic reputation or abandoning that as far as was decent and turning instead to what he had always secretly preferred, and what showed one promising result.

At the same time, however, he was confronted by the precariousness of existence in the example of another war. This time he was not personally involved, although as a civilian in a Britain frequently bombed from the air and seriously threatened with foreign invasion, he could not easily assume that he would not be a victim of enemy action. Besides, the obvious seriousness of the war years must have made the writing of fantastic romance set in an imaginary world seem an indefensible indulgence, a waste of paper at a time when paper was in short supply. Yet before the war really started Tolkien tried to write a defence of fairy story in his lecture on that subject in St Andrews in 1939. Like 'Leaf by Niggle' this can be taken in an autobiographical sense. The defence of escapism as justifiable in a world of unpleasantness and modern technological horror applies directly to what Tolkien was doing into the small hours in his own study. So too the defence of fantasy as an exercise of a human creativity that is

God-given and God-like, along with the argument that such creativity is bound up with the defining human capacity for language, and language as the basis of culture itself. Finally, in fairy stories appears the desire to escape from death and to live happily ever after. In the 1939 version of the lecture Tolkien seems to have stopped there but later he would expand this point to make the Christian Gospel story the arch-fairy-tale, the ultimate and confirming example of the escape from death, for which he coined the term 'eucatastrophe'. As in 'Leaf by Niggle', in which the painter Niggle can only complete his over-ambitious project in a timeless after-life, perhaps Tolkien's eucatastrophic ending to 'On Fairy-stories' expresses a sense that he is doomed to leave his life's work incomplete, for it will take an eternity to complete it. What perhaps has not been sufficiently noticed, however, is how limited are the number of eucatastrophes in Tolkien's own work. Few if any of his legendary tales end happily and his whole cosmos is in a long decline (though no doubt his Christian apologists would argue that once the legendarium is tacked on to the history of the world as we know it the whole will head towards redemption at the Second Coming after all; the strange late dialogue between Finrod and Andreth, *Athrabeth Finrod ah Andreth*, Part Four of the tenth volume of *The History of Middle-earth*, certainly heads that way). One thing that makes *The Hobbit* and *The Lord of the Rings* exceptional in Tolkien's output is that they do end more or less happily, although dismay keeps breaking in, especially at the end of *The Lord of the Rings*. Tolkien's *Lost Tales*, on the other hand, are inexorably grim. For a writer who has become celebrated, at least in some quarters, for defending the idea of a happy ending Tolkien seems in practice to prefer the opposite.

'Leaf by Niggle' and 'On Fairy-stories' then are both concerned with Tolkien's personal worry about the purpose of his life and, if we set aside biography for a moment, the philosophical question of what life is for, particularly because of its shortness, because of death. It is clear that the issue resolves itself into a matter of the value of the life in question. What makes death more than just an ending is that the life that ceases has amounted to something, that it has not been wasted. There seems no doubt that the sort of values Tolkien has in mind by which to judge the success of a life were public rather than private ones. What we know of the ideals of the TCBS shows this, as does Tolkien's reported intention to devise a mythology for England. 'Leaf by Niggle' is partly about the artist's need for freedom to work but it is also about his public responsibilities, and one of the things 'On Fairy-stories' does not do is defend its subject in terms of art for art's sake. Tolkien is gracious in his references to Andrew Lang, in whose memory his lecture on fairy-stories was given, but he does not mention Lang's contemporary Oscar Wilde as a writer of fairy stories. Tolkien's personal dilemma was between his sense of public duty and responsibility, as a tenured professor, and his personal devotion, almost obsession, with imaginary worlds. One supposes he had religious doubts about this obsession, too, although his deft move to enlist the Gospels as the greatest fairy-story ever told has rather disarmed his Christian critics in this respect and they seem happy to accept the legitimacy of his concept of subcreation as justification for hours spent penning fantasy fiction. In the final analysis Tolkien's defence of himself, however, was in terms of the public, non-personal value of what he did, and this clearly connects with the effect of the Great War upon him. Tolkien felt very keenly the sense, common as a result of the war, that death had robbed the world, and England, of so many promising young men and what they would have achieved. He dedicated himself to trying to fulfil something of the dreams he and his friends had had as schoolboys before the war, and he frequently criticised himself for not applying himself enough to his life's work. It is a fierce irony of Tolkien's life that nevertheless he left so much unfinished and underachieved, both in his academic work and in his private writings. His painful awareness of his own failings adds tremendous point to his contemplation of the demands mortality imposes on human endeavour.

These biographical reflections allow us to move to a comparison with Simone de Beauvoir. Born in 1908, she was almost a generation younger than Tolkien and could not have experienced World War I as he did. She did have direct experience of World War II, living through the German occupation of France and involvement with the French Resistance. By that time she was the partner of Jean Paul Sartre, who was captured early in the war and held in a prison camp in Germany from which he escaped to join de Beauvoir in Paris. As well as the threat of death for herself, the war meant the deaths of people known to de Beauvoir, but before then she had developed a pre-occupation with the meaning of death, more or less directly because of her horrified recognition of her own mortality at the age of fifteen. This seems to have come to her as a violent shock, one that recurred several times more in her life, but she also set out to devise a philosophical reaction to death, if not a rational justification of it. By the time of her first dismay at her own mortality she had begun to abandon her Christian faith and so her ideas about death are not based around any idea of an after-life as compensation for the shortness of human life, but in significant other ways her approach is comparable with Tolkien's.

Like his, de Beauvoir's explanation of the value of mortality rests on a contrast with immortality. Endless life would lack purpose and intensity. It makes commitment impossible and valueless, since there would be no real personal risk involved. It would reduce human life to that of animals who, unaware of their mortality, are unable to give life meaning beyond the daily round. As Ray Davison says in his introduction to the Methuen edition of *Une mort très douce* (London, 1986), 'mortality is the plenitude of existence now in the present, and it is our freedom to define ourselves. Immortality would condemn us to the tedium of timelessness in a world devoid of preciousness and presence' (page 18). The second sentence here could easily be applied to Tolkien's elves, and the first by implication to his mortal characters, men and hobbits. But a further remarkable parallel between Tolkien and de Beauvoir is that she too turned to fantasy writing to make her point. During the war she worked on her novel *Tous les hommes sont mortels*, published in 1946.

The main character, Raymond Fosca, is a thirteenth-century nobleman in an Italian city state called Carmona that is riven by factional strife. He becomes city-ruler, struggling against local rivals and internal plots while trying to improve his domains, aware that this means curbing the self-indulgent excesses of the aristocracy and fostering basic industries. In a moment of crisis, realising that he is likely to suffer an early death (probably, like most of his predecessors as ruler, at the hands of an assassin), he drinks what a strange old man claims is a potion of immortality and indeed becomes unable to die. Still struggling against his self-centred relatives and other people, he at last contrives to give Carmona a period of peace and prosperity. His only son, however, impatient to take responsibility, demands the right to run city affairs. He embarks on a pointless war with a neighbouring city, wins a victory, during which he is fatally wounded, and, to Fosca's dismay, dies happy in the knowledge that he is a hero, despite the fact that Carmona will now become embroiled in the warfare between the Italian city-states. Fosca is forced to become a participant in these wars, continually frustrated by the short-sightedness and selfishly limited aims of the mortal men he must rely on, especially the mercenaries he has to lure into fighting for him.

By the fifteenth century, with the intervention of France and the German Empire in Italy, Fosca realises that he cannot bring peace and progress to Carmona alone and must contend with the politics of the whole of Italy, and indeed of the whole of western Europe. He leaves Carmona and attaches himself to the new emperor, Charles V, to whom he reveals the secret of his immortality. Charles responds to Fosca's advice and aims to create a stable, progressive empire in Europe, but these plans are repeatedly postponed in the face of outbreaks of violence within the empire and between it and other states, particularly France, many as a result of the Reformation. Religious fanaticism ruins Fosca's expectations that he can use reason to persuade people to work for their own best interests. In despair, he leaves for America, where he believes that a new empire is possible, according to the reports of Charles's governors of the Spanish colonies there. But he soon finds that in Mexico and Peru the Spanish conquistadors have brutally destroyed states that were closer to his ideal than any in Europe (the novel is somewhat idealistic about the Aztec and the Incas) and they have committed barbarities as bad as anything in Italy or Germany. Whole populations have been exterminated.

Losing all hope, Fosca wanders into North America, spending years in the wilderness of the mid-western prairie, until, late in the seventeenth century, he comes across a lost French explorer, Pierre Carlier, who is seeking a river route from Montreal to the Pacific. Fosca, somewhat half-heartedly, becomes Carlier's companion on several expeditions, often saving the Frenchman by his ability to travel indefinitely without food or water. They make significant geographical discoveries but Carlier comes to regard them as hollow triumphs, recognising that for the immortal Fosca exploration is risk-free and lacking in reward. Eventually Carlier kills himself. Fosca's immortality has made his life and ambition pointless. Fosca himself, however, finds his life pointless, too. He no longer believes he can improve the lives of mortals, or share them, and begins to think he is of another species.

Chapter Three: What is *The Lord of the Rings* about? 81

He returns to Europe and becomes a misanthropic hanger-on in fashionable circles in eighteenth-century Paris. He torments a man who offends him, partly ruining him by divulging his secret to him, knowing now that most mortals cannot come to terms with the thought that he will outlive them. Fosca attends intellectual salons, ridiculing the optimistic Enlightenment talk and betraying other people's confidences. He fights a number of duels, winning them all because he can always recover from even the most serious wounds. But he meets an idealistic young woman, Marianne de Sinclair, who insists that he ought to dedicate his intellectual abilities to human progress. Fosca falls in love with her, and she with him. He marries Marianne and joins in her projects but does not tell her his secret. It is however revealed to her by the man that Fosca humiliated. Marianne feels cheated and betrayed and her love for Fosca expires, despite his pleas, since he continues to love her. In time she dies, embittered, and Fosca is left in despair again, vainly trying to preserve her memory although he knows from experience that she will soon become just another vague episode of his long past.

He plays no part in public affairs for about fifty years, including the period of the French Revolution. The next episode in his life begins in the 1820s. He takes up with the son of his daughter by Marianne. Armand guesses that Fosca is the immortal that family tradition speaks of and, undismayed, tries to enlist Fosca and his experience for the sake of his revolutionary politics. Reluctantly, and half-heartedly again, and while refusing to take full responsibility, Fosca allows himself to be used by Armand and his revolutionary group in promoting republican and socialist rebellion against the French state. He takes part in political journalism, meetings and riots, even serving ten years in prison as a political prisoner, although privately he regards human progress as impossible. His mind is filled with the parallels between current events and his early experiences of human failure and disaster, in Italy and the Americas, and with the deaths of all the people he has known. He becomes obsessed with the fact that mortals keep on living and planning and acting as though they did not know that soon they will be dead and they can make no real difference in the world. He meets another young woman, Laura, a socialist, who, like Marianne, appeals to him to exert himself for her cause, but this time, having experienced the anguish of losing Marianne, Fosca refuses to become involved.

He goes off alone and falls asleep in a wood for sixty years. When discovered, he is regarded as a madman and put in an asylum. Eventually he leaves it and takes up residence in a small provincial hotel in France. There he is found by a young actress, Regina, ambitious and arrogant, who decides that she will rouse Fosca from his lethargy and make him live a real life. She takes him to Paris, not knowing his secret. These modern scenes are the framing narrative of the novel, told in the third person around Fosca's first-person account of his life from Carmona to nineteenth-century Paris. In the Paris of the following century, Regina tries to convert Fosca while pursuing her own narcissistic career. Soon enough Fosca tells her his secret. At first she is attracted to the idea that through his memories of her she can achieve a kind of immortality herself but Fosca's repeated insistence that to him she is just another woman, no different essentially from all the others he has known and will know, saps Regina's confidence in her own individuality. She begins to find her own existence as empty and pointless as Fosca says his is. She announces that she is abandoning her acting career just as she is about to sign a contract for a starring role. Fosca, to save her from herself, tries to run away but she follows him and insists she will never leave him. They wander aimlessly into the countryside, resting now and then. Regina insists on Fosca's telling her his full life-story (this forms the bulk of the book). At its end Fosca walks away from her again, and she is left abandoned, her mind weakening in despair.

The novel has two contrasting themes. The first is that mortal human beings never live long enough to identify what is good for them and waste their lives on self-regarding, limited aims. Even those who try to live by higher ideals, of service and care for others, cannot see clearly beyond the limits of their own short existences and so pursue the wrong aims and are doomed to fail. On the other hand, an immortal being like Fosca is eventually unable to take life seriously enough to want to do anything with it. Fosca takes the immortality potion because he thinks that it will give him the power to overcome the difficulties he faces as an enlightened political reformer but relatively soon after he realises that he cannot persuade other people to share his long-term perspective and in turn he becomes contemptuous of the short-term views of the mortal beings whose lot he set out to improve. Eventually the thought of having to spend eternity struggling to make progress knowing that even if some improvement is made it is likely to be only temporary, and in any case small in relation to all that remains to be done, drives Fosca to misanthropy and apathy.

Connected with Fosca's despair at the possibility of progress is the cost of it. At first Fosca sternly accepts that, to change things, he will have to sacrifice other people. He is prepared to believe that the price of progress has to be the deaths of many people and the destruction of whole cities. Only when he sees what has been done by the Spanish in America does he realise that this is a false idea but he then takes to believing that, since all progress involves violence and death, no change is worth the attempt. The last episode of his history, the period of socialist agitation in nineteenth-century France, is full of his reflections on how those preaching revolution and the cause of working-class rebellion are blind to the death and misery they are bound to cause if their dreams come true. He has a kind of admiration for those so committed to their cause that they risk their lives for it but he also sees such commitment as futile, since he does not believe any real result is achievable. From his long-term perspective, no mortal human being can make any real difference, even by dying for a cause, and for the most part the causes themselves are wrong and misguided. The novel therefore seems to end in utter despair and nihilism. Fosca goes off alone, presumably to sleep out the rest of his existence; Regina, her life in ruins, stands in the street, unable to come or go, about to scream in despair.

Fosca is very like one of Tolkien's elves, an imaginary being whose only significant difference from humans is his immortality, and de Beauvoir uses him much as Tolkien uses his elves to make arguments about the Gift of Death. To be sure, her arguments have a more pessimistic tendency than his. She shows that, from the perspective of a being with endless life, the short-lived expectations and endeavours of men are often futile, irrational and doomed to failure. Tolkien, on the surface level at least, wants to argue for a more positive view of what men can do, although it is arguable that he cannot quite convince himself or the reader about this. *The Hobbit* and *The Lord of the Rings* may, unlike most of his other stories of Middle-earth, end with triumph of a kind, but victory is not unmixed and as pointed out above all his Middle-earth writings are characterised by a sense of loss and decay. De Beauvoir's philosophising in the face of death is said by Davison (page 16) to be an attempt to combat the attitude 'à quoi bon', or 'what's the use' of life, since we are all going to die anyway. Arguably both Bilbo and Frodo end up feeling just this attitude and that is why they join the elves who are giving up on life in this world in favour of passing over the seas to the elven limbo, the Isle of the West, the Undying Lands, there to await the end of all things.

Tolkien was not an existentialist any more than Simone de Beauvoir was a hobbit-lover. It is almost as impossible to believe that she read *The Lord of the Rings*, or *The Hobbit*, as to think Tolkien read *All Men Are Mortal* or *A Very Easy Death*. *Almost* impossible, for Tolkien *did* read and remember at least two sentences of one of these books. Yet, if the direct literary connection between them is so slight, a deeper connection of ideas and attitudes surely exists. In the middle of the twentieth century these two writers, so different in so many respects, nevertheless shared an over-riding concern, and one that has a special urgency in a century of massive human mortality, in two instances of which they were involved. There is, indeed, a cluster of works, not only literary, in the first half of the twentieth century that deal with the idea of immortality or extended longevity. One example is *Věc Makropulos* (*The Makropulos Affair*), a play by Karel Čapek (1890-1938) first performed in 1922 and a few years later made into an opera by Leoš Janáček (1854-1928), in which the heroine proves to be over three hundred years old thanks to an elixir. Like de Beauvoir's Raymond Fosca, Emilia, as the heroine has become known, has turned into a cold and unfeeling person because of her long experience of life, and is glad to die. Conversely, in Bernard Shaw's cycle of plays *Back to Methuselah* (1921), it is argued that the normal life span of human beings is too short for them to achieve their true potential. Coincidentally, Shaw asserts that humans must learn to live for three hundred years. Though it is unlikely that Tolkien had heard of *The Makropulos Affair* until late in his life (the opera was not performed in England until 1964), he may well have known about *Back to Methuselah*, which became something of a feature at the annual Malvern drama festival, begun by Sir Barry Jackson, a Shaw enthusiast, in 1929, almost like the Wagner festivals at Bayreuth, where a performance of *Der Ring des Nibelungen* is a yearly fixture. Another work dealing with longevity is *Lost Horizon* (1933), a novel by James Hilton, more famous as a 1937 film directed by Frank Capra that won two Academy Awards. Both novel and film tell of the discovery of the Tibetan monastery of Shangri-La, whose inhabitants live for hundreds of years. It is not hard to see all these works as responses to the loss of life of the First World War, coupled with a decline in belief in an after-life as compensation for the brevity of life in this world, but also at stake is the question of how much more might be achieved if time were not so short.

Tolkien's response to the consideration of the meaning of mortality was, then, in accord with a large area of modern sentiment. Our monumental culture demands justification by works and few indeed are those who practice a solipsistic denial of public accountability. Tolkien surely was not one of those, in either his life or his works. In all his stories men (or elves) and women must achieve. Those who deny the imperative are condemned if not to oblivion then certainly to neglect, and very often inaction or lack of commitment is the cause of downfall. For one aspect of the need to offer public service is the consequent self-exposure to public appraisal and judgement. The problem is not just about finding purpose in life beyond private satisfaction. It is also about engaging public attention. More, it is also about how others are affected by your intentions. You cannot have a life of public service without impinging on the lives of others and so you have to confront the problem of how others see you and how they are affected by you. If it is not enough to save just yourself and avoid danger, but you must try to help others to a better life, you face the problem that they may not want this, or not want your version of it. As Bernard Shaw said, 'Do not do unto others as you would that they should do unto you. Their tastes may not be the same' (*Man and Superman*, 1903). But if you wish to change people's lives how then do you do it? You cannot order them to be better or tell them what to do, nor can you guide them or teach them without their knowing, although if you are open about your intentions you may only start a debate and get nothing done. This is the age-old problem of political leadership, the tension between the will of the ruler and the consent of the people. It has its artistic and literary counterpart in the tension between the inspiration of the artist and the preferences of his or her audience. But it is not just a political problem. It is more fundamental than that. If, in the face of death, life must be lived with purpose, and that purpose must be for the benefit of others, we are all faced with the problem of how to translate good intentions into successful outcomes that do not infringe the rights of those we seek to help.

These are fundamental questions. They are also ones susceptible to narrative, but narrative of a desperately modern kind. It is the modern novel that has refined the presentation of the moral dilemmas of leadership. The classical epic can deal with the burden of the leader, the need for courage and steadfastness. The mediæval romance can deal with the soul of the hero, his purity of intentions, his conflicts between personal desires and the perceived responsibilities of a man living in God's universe. The renaissance tragedy sharpens these problems by its stronger awareness of the depravity of man and the inscrutability of the deity. But it is in the secularising modern period of the novel that the individual, cut off from divine assurances and closed within his own empirical sensations, has to confront the problems of how his desires manifest themselves to others and how he can encompass them in combination with, and sometimes in competition with, what he must assume are other self-defining individuals with similar desires to his own. It is in this Humean world of sceptics that the novel places its characters and enacts its narratives and however much Tolkien thought his quasi-mediæval settings and archaic language made his fiction different from the standard novel these core aspects of the form remained. He could almost avoid them in the cosmological myth of the early parts of *The Silmarillion* but as the legends moved through time into a world of narrative action so his fiction converged on modern narrative, on the novel. *The Hobbit*, as a children's story, could pretend not to be fiercely governed by the rules, but even *The Hobbit* loses its playfulness as it goes on and becomes a different, more serious thing by its end. *The Lord of the Rings* mimics the starting-point of *The Hobbit*, and much of its structure, but in a tone that leaves the children's story behind.

In modern narrative the plot is contrived to be driven by crucial negotiations and conflicts between the wills of individual characters. The outline of the story is the accumulated outcome of the negotiations between characters, against a background of plausible other events. The meaning of a novel usually lies in the perceived moral sum of these events, the ethical direction they seem to take. If the non-character driven events are over-strong, or over-determined, the whole meaning will appear forced and unconvincing. Readers will call it unrealistic. A book can get away with many and far-reaching marvels, provided some consistency is maintained, but too many and it becomes about them, not about the moral lives of its characters. At that point it ceases to be a novel and will be treated as essentially a lesser form, an allegory or a homily or a simplified story.

There are different kinds of characters in a novel. There are not just the flat and round ones of E M Forster (see chapter 4 of his *Aspects of the Novel*), or the primary and secondary characters of simple criticism, but a range of types as defined by their roles in the plot, depending on how strong they are in driving the story, or in effect other characters, or how far they are themselves driven, by events or, more significantly, by other characters. It is possible for a major character, in terms of prominence to the reader measured in, say, amount of space devoted to him or her in the text, to be in fact a lesser character in terms of influence or significance to the plot. Many narrators in novels, especially from the novels of Sir Walter Scott onwards, have this ambiguous status. Conversely, there are novels in which the driving force is a character who rarely appears, or who takes up less word-space than others. Such characters may be absent from large sections of the text, or present only by hearsay or reminiscence. Analysis of a novel in these terms often alters its apparent significance from what might be expected, forcing the recognition that what seem to be leading characters are actually lower in the plot structure than some they seem to over-shadow. The question to ask is which character has authority in any given context, that is to say, which is not only able to give direction to others but also able to take an initiative and pursue it. The character with authority may be the hero but equally may not and of course some characters of authority may lose it as the plot unfolds. The dynamics of character relationships are crucial to an understanding of what the story is telling us, how the narration shapes towards its conclusion. By applying these dynamics to Tolkien's fictions what results is an emphasis on the character of Gandalf and his role as the driving force of the action in both *The Hobbit* and *The Lord of the Rings* and how they both attend to the imperative of achievement in this world, and the constraints of leadership in attempting such achievement.

It is worth mentioning *The Hobbit* in this context because its similarities to *The Lord of the Rings* make it a useful test-bed for interpretation of the later work. As has been argued above, Tolkien had a general theory of literature that, while it applies strongly to *The Lord of the Rings*, is equally relevant to its predecessor, *The Hobbit*, and by discussing it first we can clear some ground before looking at the longer work. In fact, it is quite possible to look at the two works together, as the next chapter will try to show.

CHAPTER FOUR

The Hobbit as paradigm

The Hobbit is more than just a prequel to *The Lord of the Rings* in terms of plot and characters. The shape of the earlier novel and its plot and the articulation of that plot are such clear anticipations of the later work that Tolkien is liable to the accusation, levelled at many writers, that in effect he wrote the same book more than once. The similarities between his two novels are on the whole clear enough to be tabulated:

	The Hobbit	The Lord of the Rings	Notes and Exceptions
1.	Summoning of Bilbo by Gandalf.	Summoning of Bilbo/Frodo by Gandalf.	
2.	Gathering of (dwarf) companions.	Gathering of (hobbit) companions.	
3.	'An Unexpected Party'.	Bilbo's Birthday Party.	Bilbo's Birthday Party precedes the gathering of companions in *LotR*.
(3a)		Dark Riders, Tom Bombadil, Bree, Strider.	Not in *H*.
4.	Wilderness Encounter: Trolls.	Wilderness Encounter: Weathertop.	Temporary absence of leader (Gandalf, Strider) followed by his rescue of the party.
5.	Rivendell, and the counsel of Elrond.	Rivendell, and the council of Elrond and others.	

	The Hobbit	*The Lord of the Rings*	Notes and Exceptions
6.	Journey continues into mountains.	Journey continues into mountains.	
7.	Journey continues underground, leading to flight from goblins/orcs and encounter with Gollum.	Journey continues underground, leading to flight from goblins/orcs and encounter with Gollum.	In *LotR* the encounter with Gollum is slight and precedes the flight.
8.	Fight with the wolves and goblins and rescue by the eagles.	Indirect parallels in *LotR*: the fight with the goblins and the fire element (balrog) occurs before emergence from underground. Party escapes rather than is rescued.	
9.	Encounter with Beorn.	The equivalent is the encounter of Merry and Pippin with Treebeard later in the plot.	The separation of Gandalf from the others in *H* is the rough equivalent of his 'death' after 7 in *LotR*.
10.	Journey into an enchanted wood and encounter with elves.	Journey into an enchanted wood and encounter with elves.	Mirkwood and Lothlórien have on the whole opposite values, as do their elvish rulers, although neither is simply bad or good.

Chapter Four: *The Hobbit* as paradigm

	The Hobbit	*The Lord of the Rings*	Notes and Exceptions
11.	River journey.	River journey.	At the end of this journey the plot of *LotR* divides and follows two independent groups of characters, but parallels with *H* continue. There are however a number of events that intrude into *LotR* at around this point: Fangorn, Edoras, Helm's Deep, Isengard, and so on. Some of these, however, have parallels with *H* (see below).
12.	Lake Town and the return of the king.	Minas Tirith and the return (eventually) of the king.	In neither case is the king's return straightforward, although in both there is an unreliable steward or regent to be dealt with.
13.	Journey across wasteland to the Lonely Mountain.	Journey across wasteland to Cirith Ungol/ Barad-dûr.	The journey in *LotR* has more stages (including the encounter with Faramir) than that in *H* but has the same ultimate effect.
14.	Finding the back door to the mountain.	Finding the way through Cirith Ungol.	

	The Hobbit	The Lord of the Rings	Notes and Exceptions
15.	Inside the mountain and encounter with the monster (Smaug).	Inside the mountain and encounter with the monster (Shelob).	The encounter with Shelob also of course parallels the fight with the spiders in Mirkwood in *H*.
16.	Smaug flies to the attack, and is killed.	Nazgûl flies to the attack and is killed.	The attack and killing of Shelob is another parallel with *H* in *LotR*.
17.	Debate and diplomacy, followed by battle between the forces of good and evil.	Debate and diplomacy, followed by battle between the forces of good and evil.	In effect, this happens twice in LotR, in both Rohan and Gondor.
18.	Bilbo's sacrifice of the Arkenstone.	Frodo's sacrifice of the Ring.	This parallel is exact neither in the action nor its timing.
19.	Battle won by intervention of reinforcements (Beorn and eagles).	Battle won by intervention of reinforcements (Riders of Rohan and Aragorn).	This also happens at Helm's Deep, with the intervention of Gandalf and the Ents and Huorns.
20.	Death in victory of Thorin.	Death in victory of Théoden.	
21.	Acknowledgement of true king and restoration of peace.	Acknowledgement of true king and restoration of peace.	
22.	Bilbo returns to find disorder in the Shire.	Frodo returns to find disorder in the Shire.	
23.	Order restored in the Shire.	Order restored in the Shire.	

Chapter Four: *The Hobbit* as paradigm 93

The chief formal difference between the two books is the division in *The Lord of the Rings* at the point where Frodo and Sam separate from the rest of the Fellowship of the Ring to make their own way to Mordor, while Aragorn, Legolas and Gimli pursue Merry and Pippin across the plains of Rohan. It is difficult to tabulate the parallels between the novels from this point onwards because what is one line of narrative in *The Hobbit* has to be compared with two separate lines in *The Lord of the Rings*. The events at the end of the earlier novel are more clearly paralleled by the Aragorn strand of narrative in the later one rather than the Frodo strand, although there are key incidents, especially those involving Bilbo in the Lonely Mountain, that relate to aspects of the story of Frodo (and Sam) in or around Mordor. But a further complication is that the story of the defence of Rohan against Saruman is obviously itself a parallel or anticipation of the defence of Gondor against Sauron, so that there are two sets of incidents and situations in the later books of *The Lord of the Rings* that parallel developments in the last third or so of *The Hobbit*.

Yet it is not impossible to read the split narrative of *The Lord of the Rings* back into *The Hobbit*. By the time Bilbo reaches Lake Town with the dwarves he is beginning to develop some distance between himself and them. His magic ring is not the only thing that has given him a sense of superiority and self-esteem. He takes little part in Thorin's assertion of his rights as the returned King under the Mountain and, although he fulfils his duty by accompanying the dwarves on the last stage of their expedition, when he reaches the Lonely Mountain there are signs that he is at last confronting the question of what the goal of the quest really is. Smaug's cynical attempt to put a wedge between Bilbo and the dwarves by insinuating that they will only use the hobbit for their own greedy ends are on the face of it unsuccessful but they do raise Bilbo's (and the reader's) awareness of the material desires of the dwarves, especially Thorin, and make him ask how far he shares his companions' love of treasure (not to mention practical questions about how he can carry a share of it home). When Bilbo finds, and realises that he has found, the Arkenstone, the jewel almost without price that is the treasure most coveted by Thorin and the dwarves, Bilbo faces a dilemma not unlike Frodo's with the Ring. Fortunately for Bilbo, the Arkenstone has none of the mind-bending fascination of the Ring apart from its value and he is able to rise above that temptation, see the object for what it is and trade it for what he hopes will be a peaceful and bloodless outcome. There is then, in Bilbo's part of the story at the end of *The Hobbit*, a parallel to the story of Frodo in the second half of *The Lord of the Rings*. They both make dark, lonely journeys to encounter monsters and the fears and temptations they represent, and they both face a crisis of renunciation; and conversely, Bilbo plays as little part in the fighting at the climax of his book as Frodo does in his. The grand political events surrounding Bilbo at the end are literally above his head. He is largely out of the story of the restoration of the dwarf Kingdom under the mountain and the city-state of Dale.

This makes for a certain oddity about the ending of *The Hobbit* in so far as the reader, in response to the book's title, regards Bilbo as the central character, the hero. When the story reaches its climax both reader and character begin to wonder what the hero will find to do, and it seems from the early drafts that the author too had a problem with this. Much of the business in Laketown and after was unforeseen by Tolkien when he began the book. He had the map and the general aim of defeating the dragon to recover the treasure but the exact means to do this, and the role of the hobbit in it, was not clear to him. *The Hobbit*, like *The Lord of the Rings*, is essentially about the education of the hobbit-hero, his transformation into a real hero. Both Bilbo and Frodo begin as anti-heroes. Bilbo is more obviously a comic reversal of heroic characteristics. Tolkien plays this aspect of Frodo down at the start of *The Lord of the Rings*, partly no doubt because he has done it already in *The Hobbit* and partly because the later work is aiming for a more serious impression on the reader. Nevertheless the hobbits, their world and their ethos as humorous undercutting of epic seriousness are still apparent in *The Lord of the Rings*, but Tolkien displaces all this from the main hobbit character. He can continue to use Bilbo as an anti-hero at the beginning of the work, and at his reappearances later, maintaining the character from the earlier novel and adding to the sense that we have moved on from him by superseding Bilbo by Frodo. But if Frodo is more serious, and ultimately tragic where Bilbo is comic, comedy is retained in Frodo's hobbit companions, Merry, Pippin and Sam. All of these will follow Frodo on a journey of self-discovery, by the end of which they will become more serious, less anti-heroic, than when they started, but Merry and Pippin and Sam are always several stages of seriousness behind Frodo and they never quite attain the gravity, and depression, that he represents well before the ending. The lesser hobbits, then, are usually available to play the undercutting role that Bilbo plays for himself throughout *The Hobbit*.

That aside, Bilbo and Frodo follow a similar path. Both become leaders and must learn to take decisions and responsibility. Both go from an initial apathy, indifference and a desire to stay out of the world to commitment, action and a purpose to improve the world. They both begin in an essentially pastoral retreat, where nothing happens or has happened. The Shire is a place of historical stasis. We are told of past events there, battles and political developments, but these are long-gone and appear to have no contemporary implications or effects. There are no tensions within the Shire and none with anything outside it. Indeed, connections with the outside world are remarkably slight. The Shire, at the beginning of both books, is bucolic, innocent, child-like and isolated. To make this possible at the start of the second book, of course, Tolkien has had first to make the ending of *The Hobbit* as much of a closure as possible, bringing Bilbo back alone and with very little to show for his adventures – so little, indeed, that at first Tolkien could not conceive of a way to extend them into a sequel until he transformed the one specific thing Bilbo brought back, the ring he got from Gollum, into the One Ring of Power. Bilbo's ignorance of what the Ring is at the very start of *The Lord of the Rings* preserves the early innocence of the Shire at the beginning of that work.

It cannot last, of course, because the Shire must fall to the traditional fate of all pastoral realms, fulfilling the prophecy *Et in Arcadia Ego*. Into Arcadia must intrude the outside world, the forces of history and time and death. For one thing, these lead on to narrative, rather than the pictorialism of pure pastoral. The intrusion of history, time and death is more obvious in *The Lord of the Rings* than in *The Hobbit*. The Black Riders are surely some of the most direct examples in literature of the deadly serious breaking into a pastoral world and forcing the hero to turn from the timeless and innocent to confront the choices of moral and political action. This effect is far more muted in *The Hobbit*. Bilbo's complacency and peace are disrupted by much less obviously death-like intruders, Gandalf and the dwarves. The humour of the opening of *The Hobbit*, and the ironic tone of its narrator, distract the reader from the significance of what is enacted. Bilbo's bourgeois existence may not be recognised as a form of pastoral, his comic confusion at the series of incursions on his hospitality may seem the main point, a mild satire on conventionality, and the high-handed actions of Gandalf in choosing him may seem adequately explained as just what grumpy wizards do, especially at the beginning of a fairy story. Looking back from *The Lord of the Rings* it is easier to see the associations between Gandalf, and the dwarves, and death. There the wizard will appear as a bringer of war. He will be greeted with fear and accusations of bringing death and destruction with him. He will assail a fiery monster in what seems like a suicidal combat, from which he will return like a ghost, like the undead. When Tolkien wrote *The Hobbit* he had of course no knowledge of what Gandalf would become in its sequel, but these things are inherent in the character.

As for the dwarves, they too appear at first as humorous characters in *The Hobbit* and yet may be associated with dark forces. By focusing on Bilbo's comic reactions to their grim acceptance of the risks involved in the quest they intend to undertake, Tolkien distracts attention from that grimness. Their love of jewels and precious metals mined out of the earth connects them with ideas of burial and the underworld. They are the opponents but not wholly the opposites of the dragon who sits on their treasure in the bowels of the Lonely Mountain. He displaced them (or their ancestors) and they now wish to displace him in their turn. Such displacing means the spilling of blood, something the dwarves are more than prepared to accept. Tolkien makes light of death as an occupational hazard by the parody of business language in the letter of appointment Thorin gives Bilbo when he is hired as the party's burglar, but the point of the joke about funeral expenses is that we have moved from a world in which such things are not discussed into one in which it is reasonable to anticipate them, and all their implications. The dwarves are emissaries from a world where death is an obvious eventuality.

Bilbo, then, like Frodo, must leave the pastoral simplicity of the Shire for the great world outside, with all its dangers. He then becomes subject to forces beyond his control. Another way of expressing the nature of the pastoral retreat is to say that within it the individual has power over his own existence. To get this he has to lead an existence of such simplicity and regularity that it is hardly a life at all, and certainly not one the reader can really think of sharing. Bilbo's life before *The Hobbit* opens gives him a kind of existence that while common in books is wishfulness out of them. Once he is driven out of his hole, however, his life is no longer his to direct as he will and he becomes as much (if not more) the servant of the forces of existence than their master. This is most plainly seen in the fact that, although Bilbo is the main character of *The Hobbit*, virtually its eponymous hero, he is not the driving force of the story. He is not a character with authority, one who not merely carries out the action of the plot but directs it and the actions of lesser characters. The character with authority in *The Hobbit* is Gandalf. He it is who moves the action on at critical points and his motivation is crucial to the meaning of the book. Tolkien reveals as much in his later efforts to relate *The Hobbit* to *The Lord of the Rings* and his legendarium as a whole. The chief of these is a first-person account of Thorin's expedition by Gandalf from his point of view, giving his reasons for instigating the quest and for including Bilbo in it, and his justification of the outcome in terms of the struggle against Sauron for the safety of Middle-earth. This appears as 'The Quest of Erebor' in Appendix A of *The Annotated Hobbit* and in *Unfinished Tales* (1980).

These writings are of course from outside *The Hobbit* itself, and much later than it. They follow after the writing of *The Lord of the Rings* and are partly motivated by Tolkien's desire to integrate his fictional writings, a desire that at one time induced him to begin a revision of *The Hobbit* that would have diminished Bilbo's role while aligning the text more closely with *The Lord of the Rings* (see 'The 1960 Hobbit' in John D Rateliff, *The History of the Hobbit* (2007), Volume 2, pages 765-838). Such a re-reading of his own work by the author is no more critically sound than that of anyone else but it does show how precarious Bilbo's position is in the narrative structure. It reflects the way that Tolkien in *The Hobbit* tries to disguise Gandalf's fundamental part in the plot and mystify his motives. Tolkien does not want the reader to know too much about Gandalf and tries to prevent the reader from probing into the wizard's actions. No matter what he thought of Bilbo's importance twenty-five years later, when he wrote *The Hobbit* Bilbo was the main character and the narrative had to give him full prominence. This could be done ironically, with the constant suggestion that Bilbo is partly an anti-hero, but the book avoids fully inverting the adventure format and satirising the hobbit as the antithesis to the conventional hero. He is not to be a complete coward, or immoral, or indeed a real thief or burglar, and he must not seem a mere pawn in a game played beyond his knowledge. There is an element of subterfuge in this, as Tolkien distracts the reader by confining the point of view to Bilbo and neglecting other viewpoints, and there are places where the text's silence is significant. This is particularly true of its silence on some of Gandalf's actions, actions of underlying importance crucial to the real meaning of *The Hobbit*. The first of these has already been noticed, Gandalf's choosing of Bilbo.

In plot terms the choice of Bilbo is a given: Bilbo must be chosen and Gandalf must choose Bilbo for the story to be *The Hobbit* and for it to begin. A plot must have a beginning and by definition that will appear at least arbitrary and fortuitous. The famous opening of *The Hobbit* – 'In a hole in the ground there lived a hobbit' – fits the definition of a beginning excellently, and the story of the origin of this opening sentence marks its originary nature. Tolkien's well-known account of how he found a blank page while marking exam papers and spontaneously wrote on it the first sentence of what became *The Hobbit* reinforces the point that this was a fresh beginning so well that the cynic might suspect the account had been invented. Tolkien's comment that having written the word 'hobbit' he did not know what it meant and so would have to find out builds up the impression of an unpremeditated, unforeseen and, at the time, inexplicable event that could only be a beginning, not a link in a continuing series of events. All this serves to draw attention away from the question of what happened before the story began. In fact Tolkien knew very well that much had happened. Even if he did not immediately or consciously connect the sentence about the hole-dwelling hobbit with his other writings such a connection was so inevitable that it would be true to say it always existed. Tolkien was bound to look for the meaning of 'In a hole in the ground there lived a hobbit' in terms of his own, long-standing interests in mediæval literature, especially that of England and Northern Europe, in mediæval languages and in the mass of fiction he had already written, both stories for his children and the secret store of myth and legend he had been accumulating since his early adulthood. In that sense, 'In a hole in the ground there lived a hobbit' comes out of Tolkien's earlier writing, even if at first he did not recognise it.

But let us postpone discussion of fitting *The Hobbit* into Tolkien's legendarium and ask straightforward questions about the first events of the story, in particular

Chapter Four: *The Hobbit* as paradigm

why Gandalf chooses Bilbo. Some of the analysis comes from considering who the two are. First, it is evident that Gandalf is a being of some power. He is a wise and powerful wizard, able to achieve things ordinary mortals, including hobbits, cannot. He has, we assume, great skills, a wealth of knowledge, experience of the world and the combination of self-command and authority needed to get things done. So why does he need Bilbo at all? Why does he himself not go with the dwarves to the Lonely Mountain, kill Smaug and restore Thorin to his throne and treasure, if that is what he wants? What is stopping Gandalf from setting the world to rights with his superhuman magic powers?

Perhaps these powers are not strong enough. There are indications in *The Lord of the Rings* that Gandalf's magic cannot be used indefinitely at high output. He can sustain a low level of magic use, like producing light in the mines of Moria, for long periods but can only perform grand actions, such as driving back a monster, once or twice before he must rest and recuperate. Although Tolkien never quite explicates the process, it seems to be not dissimilar to what his games-playing fans have devised. In the Tolkienesque fantasy games spawned by his work it is usually the case that magic-users have a limited amount of spell-power which, once expended, needs to be replaced, either by acquiring suitable potions or other reserves of magic energy or by a period of inactivity during which the character's reservoir of magic gradually refills by a kind of natural process analogous to recovery after physical exertion. In game terms this mechanism functions to limit the use of magic and prevent its becoming a kind of superweapon, an endless stream of spells that will get the user out of any situation. Tolkien, of course, faces in Gandalf the paradox posed by all superhumanly powerful characters, that it is not the extent but the limit of their powers that is critical. In the simpler world of comic-book characters like Superman the revelation of the hero's strength has almost immediately to be matched by the discovery of his weakness for any sort of narrative, other than the monotonous repetition of the hero's inevitable triumphs, to proceed. Tolkien's Gandalf is not so simple a superman that Tolkien has to resort to such a crude device as kryptonite to curb his powers but he does have to mark some sort of limit to the wizard's abilities.

But if Gandalf cannot do everything for himself because he is not strong enough he surely does little to add to his strength by enlisting the help of a hobbit.

Bilbo has no magic powers (at least, not until he finds the Ring) and he has little physical strength either. We can only deduce from Gandalf's choosing of Bilbo that he must have some other thing, not to do with magic power or physical strength, that Gandalf needs, something Gandalf needs for getting the result he wants. From the start Gandalf insists that he sees something like this in Bilbo. He repeatedly claims there is more to Bilbo than meets the eye, more than Thorin and the dwarves can see in him, and indeed more than Bilbo sees in himself. In one sense the whole of *The Hobbit* is the explanation of what this thing about Bilbo is; or, in other words, *The Hobbit* is about why Gandalf chose Bilbo. The obvious place to look for the answer is at the conclusion of the story and what Bilbo does, and what he has become, by the end.

Earlier it was said that unlike Gandalf Bilbo is not a character with authority, one that directs and controls the action, but that is not wholly true. By the end of the plot Bilbo does take on responsibility for doing things, for directing events and for inducing other characters to take certain actions leading to outcomes he favours. He acts on his own initiative, without prompting from Gandalf or anyone else, when he uses the Arkenstone to force Thorin to negotiate with Bard and the Elvenking. He does this by considering how all those involved will act and react and making them do so in ways that will suit his purpose. What is more, the end Bilbo aims at is related not to his own benefit, or not solely, but for the good of others. He wants to avoid a battle between the dwarves and the elves and men and to bring about a just settlement between Thorin and Bard, a settlement reached by negotiation for mutual benefit, with the prospect of continuing co-operation and harmony between the restored King under the Mountain and the new King of Dale and the Lake. There is little in this for Bilbo himself, except the short-term relief of escape from the besieged mountain, and he risks, not only although most obviously in the short term, the enmity of Thorin and the dwarves, a setback both personal as well as a professional (given his contract with the dwarves). Bilbo's main reward would seem to be the setting up of peace and order in a part of the world recently subject to disorder, even devastation. He does not even seem to expect public acclaim for his actions, as he works secretly and, beyond suggesting what to do, leaves others to carry out the diplomacy required.

In this, of course, he acts much as Gandalf does, but that is not the most important point. What is really significant is that Bilbo acts like Gandalf spontaneously, without prompting by the wizard. A key aspect of the concluding events in *The Hobbit* is that Gandalf is absent from them. Bilbo, shut up inside the mountain with the dwarves, cannot ask Gandalf's advice and indeed does not know where Gandalf is. Bilbo must take charge for himself. This marks the difference between the hobbit as agent at either end of the story. At the beginning Gandalf makes Bilbo into the dwarves' companion, and he is dragged along with them, hardly knowing what he is doing; at the end, Bilbo achieves a victory for common sense and the commonweal such as Gandalf can applaud, but without anyone else's instructions, not even Gandalf's. And this too Gandalf can applaud.

This takes us to an understanding of the consequences for Bilbo of his choosing by Gandalf but what about Gandalf himself? We can now see that he chose Bilbo partly because he saw in the hobbit the potential for growth into spontaneous responsibility for action for the benefit of others, but why does Gandalf need such a development in one small hobbit? If the end is the restoration of order in (a part of) the world, why does Gandalf take such a roundabout route to this end? He could easily manœuvre Bilbo (or anyone else) into doing what he wants or what is needed, and so for what reason does he prefer to see Bilbo find his own way, and without prompting or assistance? It would seem easier to direct Bilbo in an unmistakable way, and less risky, just as it was easier to choose Bilbo rather than let him emerge.

There is perhaps a clue in the manner in which the choice of Bilbo is made. Gandalf's actions here seem to have self-imposed limits. These actions consist mainly of marking Bilbo's door with the sign that leads the dwarves to suppose that within lives the burglar they seek for their mission. There is a little more to this, it is true, in so far as Gandalf has had to persuade the dwarves that they need a burglar and that the hobbit he knows will suit their purpose. But as far as Bilbo is concerned all Gandalf does is mark his door. He does little or nothing to induct the hobbit into his role as burglar or to school him in it. He does not even tell Bilbo in advance that the dwarves are coming or say that he has told them Bilbo is a professional burglar ready for hire. Gandalf leaves the purpose of the choosing to emerge, mainly from the assumptions of the dwarves. This hands-off approach is an important indicator that what Gandalf wants is not just someone to bring about his intentions but someone who will do so not as a tool but as a free agent – or as free as possible. In other words, it is as important to Gandalf how his ends are achieved as whether they are achieved, and he wants them achieved freely, not under his control, direction or compulsion. He can only bring this about by choosing an agent who is ignorant of the purpose for which he is being chosen to the point of being virtually unprepared for it. Bilbo is so unprepared that until the last moment he does not realise he is actually going on the expedition and runs out to join the dwarves without even a handkerchief.

There is then a practical risk for Gandalf that Bilbo, his chosen agent, will turn out to be inadequate and so jeopardise the success of the mission. In the matter of the handkerchief Gandalf avoids failure by making up for Bilbo's omission himself, and at the same time bringing to Bilbo from his house some of the things he should have prepared for the journey. But this leads to a philosophical problem about the situation: how independent can Bilbo be as long as Gandalf is there to help? Arguably any help from Gandalf, even finding him a handkerchief, or any influence, even the bare choosing of Bilbo, infringes the hobbit's independence of action and makes him Gandalf's instrument, carrying out the wizard's quest by proxy, and yet it seems that this is what Gandalf wants to avoid. He chooses Bilbo because the task he wants completed he wants done, truly done, by somebody other than himself.

What is this wonderful task, and why does Gandalf think it must be done by some independent agent? The answer to this question is another version, perhaps the most fundamental one, of the action of the narrative defined in its essence; that is to say, not simply the revenge of the dwarves on Smaug but in a general sense the improvement of the world, by the restitution of order and peace to the region of the Lonely Mountain through the elimination of Smaug and the redistribution of his ill-gotten wealth. Such an improvement is not just for itself, charity for the sake of it, order imposed by whoever has the power. Benevolence must not be imposed from above but must be won by those who are to benefit, so that they benefit in spirit as well as in material terms, just as Bilbo grows and is not just transformed into a hero by a wave of Gandalf's magic staff.

Chapter Four: *The Hobbit* as paradigm   103

Here at last we see Gandalf's dilemma. He wishes to improve the lives of dwarves and hobbits, and of men and elves, and to do so conceives the intention of disposing of Smaug and repossessing the treasure, but he cannot truly and lastingly improve the lives of the peoples of Middle-earth if he carries out this task entirely himself. Then he would make men, elves, dwarves and hobbits his dependents, his puppets, his slaves. If however he totally respects their freedom they may never take the steps necessary to achieve the goal. Gandalf has to discover how far he can compromise between respecting the freedom and directing the actions of those whose well-being he wishes to foster. This is of course the eternal dilemma of the benevolent leader, the benevolent ruler, the benevolent god. The dilemma lies at the heart of *The Hobbit* (and *The Lord of the Rings*, and indeed *The Silmarillion*). Much of the narrative structure and plot of Tolkien's work can be explained as his fictional reaction to the dilemma. Like Gandalf, Tolkien chooses in *The Hobbit* (and later in *The Lord of the Rings*) as main actor the most unlikely person he can find who may yet have it in him to carry the project of improvement through, to make it look as if the choice has the minimum of direction in it. Then Gandalf has to hope for the best and try not to interfere too much himself.

Of course, he *has* interfered by the choosing. Tolkien disguises this as he may by trying to make the choosing seem arbitrary, almost whimsical, and in addition by avoiding explanation of the reasons there may be for the choice. After all, if it is Gandalf's whim to choose Bilbo, there is no point in seeking profound reasons for his choice. But the *absence* of profound reasons is meant to be part of the paradox of Gandalf's relation to the action of the book. Not only does Tolkien want the reader not to form a clear idea of Gandalf's motives, but Gandalf wants Bilbo, and indeed the dwarves, not to form a clear idea of them, either, for otherwise they and their actions become merely manifestations of his will.

The same kind of argument surrounds another aspect of the story's beginning in which Gandalf has a key role that neither he nor Tolkien wish to have debated. This is the matter of Thror's map. Why is it that Gandalf has this and not Thorin? It would seem more natural that this map drawn by a dwarf to lead to a dwarf treasure should be in the hands of a dwarf, not a wizard, and indeed Thorin says so when Gandalf first produces the map. The wizard pushes aside Thorin's complaint by telling the story of how Thror himself gave the map to Gandalf. Tolkien's technique of distraction here is different from the case of the choosing of Bilbo. There he closes off reader speculation by presenting the choice as above discussion, a sudden and undisputed act; here, he avoids a real discussion of Gandalf's motives by substituting a piece of narrative. To Thorin's implicit question *why* Gandalf has the map the wizard replies with an explanation of *how* he obtained it. Gandalf's reasons are really non-reasons that serve only to distract Thorin and the reader from questions about the map: why does Gandalf have it, why does he value it and why has he decided at this time to use it to begin the quest?

One thing the map does is lead us to a consideration of events before *The Hobbit*. It is a piece of back-story, but it is also a bridge back to the world of Gandalf before he appears in *The Hobbit*. As such, it is a reflection of that world, but Tolkien keeps the details hazy. No doubt at first this was because he himself only dimly saw the connections between *The Hobbit* and the rest of Gandalf's world, and in fact he hardly knew what connected Gandalf, or anything else in *The Hobbit*, with the rest of his stories until he got down to writing *The Lord of the Rings*. There are however some things that can be deduced from Gandalf's possession of Thror's map. One is that there is indeed a back-story, there is a world before *The Hobbit*, a wider world, and that *The Hobbit* is connected back to that wider world. Further, Gandalf's possession of the map shows that he is an active participant in that world. It also implies that the project represented by the map is not Gandalf's only concern in the world. We can hardly believe it is the first scheme of improvement he has undertaken, or that it is different from his other concerns. Indeed, the story of how he acquired the map shows that it is not unusual for him to go out of his way to find such things, and his long delay in doing anything about it indicates that he has had other, more pressing matters to attend to, probably of a like nature. There is no reason to suppose that Gandalf wastes his time on trivialities or takes extended holidays. His initial encounter with Bilbo gives a strong impression of someone businesslike and well-organised, faintly displeased by Bilbo's leisurely attitudes.

We can deduce then that Thror's map, and the expedition against Smaug, constitute only one of Gandalf's projects, one example of the things he wants to do to improve the world; and therefore we can conclude that Gandalf's general role in the world is to try to improve it, to right wrongs, bring about beneficial changes, organise projects to make things better and drive back chaos, darkness and evil. These profound implications tell us more about Gandalf than the explicit comments on his possession of Thror's map and they add to what has already been said about his purposes, and the dilemma he faces in trying to realise them. In a sense Gandalf's possession of the map is more fundamental than his choosing of Bilbo; it comes before it not only chronologically but also logically. Both actions help to characterise Gandalf for us and help to show what the underlying meaning of *The Hobbit* is.

Knowing what Gandalf is about also helps to make sense of some of his more puzzling actions in *The Hobbit*, especially his habit of absenting himself from the expedition. The most noticeable example of this is when Gandalf insists on leaving the dwarves and Bilbo at the entrance to Mirkwood, just as they are about to enter an obviously dangerous place where they will need all the help they can get. Gandalf's refusal to accompany the others beyond this point is surely one of the most unsettling and intractable incidents in the book and the justification for it that he gives is never convincing to readers. He flatly insists that he has other business elsewhere that he must attend to and cannot stay. Of course, on a simple level Tolkien removes the wizard from the action at this point just because he is sorely needed. If Bilbo and the dwarves are to get into trouble in Mirkwood they must be deprived of the means to avoid this. Here is another reflection of the Superman problem: the powerful superhero has to be got out of the way if the other characters are to confront real hardship and danger. Presumably if Gandalf had stayed with the party he would have been able to conjure up food and drink for them, prevent them from straying from the path and alert them to the threats from the inhabitants of the forest. Without him, the dwarves and Bilbo must rely on their own resources, and of course one result of that is that Bilbo becomes indeed resourceful and seriously embarks on the process of maturing into a hero in his own right. The larger aspect of Tolkien's removal of Gandalf from the story is that his place as leader of the mission is left open and Bilbo must rise to the opportunity to fill it (it is noticeable that Tolkien goes some way to restrict the powers of action of the nominal leader of the band, Thorin, to enable Bilbo to rise and he even develops an open rivalry between them before the end).

This is clearly part of the underlying scheme of setting the conditions for Bilbo's spontaneous development of the skills and courage needed to become a hero and bring about the change in the world Gandalf is aiming at. But by definition this motive cannot be revealed to Bilbo or the dwarves, so that Gandalf's excuses for his departure have to be half-truths and prevarication. Tolkien cannot avoid this and really fails to disguise it, partly no doubt because he in fact did not have, when he wrote *The Hobbit*, a genuine answer to the question why Gandalf had to leave the story before its end. Only later did he try to work out what the pressing business was that took the wizard away at this critical moment. His answer, however, reinforces some of the points already made about Gandalf's purposes since it relates to his larger role as inspirer of the struggle to save the world from chaos. Clearly the only kind of business more requiring Gandalf's presence than helping the expedition to defeat Smaug he himself has set going would be some project even more directly concerned with safeguarding Middle-earth. Tolkien therefore picked up on the idea that a powerful evil figure, named in *The Hobbit* as the Necromancer, lived not far from where the party had reached and decided that Gandalf was needed to conduct operations against him. Later Tolkien would try to identify this Necromancer with Sauron himself, thus trying to connect the plots of *The Hobbit* and *The Lord of the Rings*, although in fact problems of chronology would in the end defeat him. The point to note, however, is that Gandalf's period of absence from *The Hobbit* is related to his overall mission of combating the forces of evil in Middle-earth. In *The Lord of the Rings* Gandalf will also be forced to leave the main party, though in more drastic circumstances than in *The Hobbit*, when he falls over the cliff in Moria in combat with the balrog and is presumed dead by the rest of the Fellowship of the Ring, who must carry on without him. Again, this leads to a crisis of leadership in the group, resulting in its division into those led by Aragorn, the returning king and so the equivalent of Thorin, and those (only one, as a matter of fact) led by a hobbit, Frodo. As in *The Hobbit*, the absence of Gandalf forces the others to take decisions for themselves, notably Frodo's decision to leave the others and strike out for Mordor on his own (although Sam insists on joining him). This ensures that at the climax of his story Frodo acts without Gandalf's influence, just as Bilbo does at the climax of *his* story.

Chapter Four: *The Hobbit* as paradigm

The exploration of Gandalf's role in *The Hobbit* leads on to exposition of his similar role in *The Lord of the Rings*. That this is so is due to the strong parallels between the two books. The extensive similarities between *The Hobbit* and *The Lord of the Rings* in structure, characters, plot and themes mean the earlier book can direct us to an understanding of the later one. *The Hobbit* is somewhat simpler and easier to deal with. Although its ending has the beginnings of the duality of the latter two-thirds of *The Lord of the Rings*, this is not so thoroughly developed. Indeed, the simpler structure of *The Hobbit* in this respect makes it easier to see the reduplication of plot in *The Lord of the Rings*, and what it means. *The Hobbit* also helps us to see Tolkien's tactics of distraction, the techniques he uses to disguise from the reader the exact roles of his main characters, that is, Bilbo in the first book, Frodo in the second, and Gandalf in both. It is embedded in Tolkien's strategy in both books that the fundamental significance of Gandalf's purposes should be placed in the background and the foreground occupied by the hobbits. This of course was demanded in *The Hobbit* by the generic requirements of a children's story, with a prominent role for a small, humorous character, and in so far as *The Lord of the Rings* began as a sequel it started with the same generic rules. But Tolkien seems happy with this. He does not want the reader to see the fundamental significance of what Gandalf stands for. But the connection between both books, and the way the simpler, earlier one yields to analysis of the basic importance of what Gandalf's business is, leads to a closer analysis of *The Lord of the Rings* that gets around the obstacles Tolkien places in the reader's way. The critical question about both books then becomes who or what Gandalf is.

CHAPTER FIVE

Who is Gandalf?

There are two ways of answering this question: one, by examining the texts and, two, by referring to what Tolkien said about them. The first has the greater critical respectability since the second uses material from outside the texts to try to explain them. The fact that this material comes from the author may seem to give it special authority compared to the theories of other readers or the opinions of academic (or non-academic) critics but once the writing stops the writer himself is no longer inside his work but outside it like the rest of us. His comments on what he has done, although perhaps based on a greater familiarity with the text than that of other readers, at least for a time after publication, are not in some mysterious way to be privileged over other readers' responses or understandings or interpretations. In the end, the author's attempts to explain his own work are to be judged only as are the explanations of other readers, that is, on the basis of whether they do indeed explain the work or not. It has to remain conceivable that the author may not be the best or even the most interesting interpreter of his own work. This may be because he is not, as a matter of fact, as good a critic or reader as he is a writer, or it may be because the closeness to his work that seems to give him the right to explain it is actually the reason he cannot be relied upon to see it clearly. And in the end, as the years pass, the author's special position of being the earliest reader of his text declines in significance. Nor can he simply maintain it by constant rereading, since the man who reads his own novel ten years after it was written is not the same man as wrote it. He may claim to have more intimate knowledge of his earlier self, just as he may claim to have more intimate knowledge of his work, than anyone else, but again it must be conceivable that he may not be the best or the most interesting interpreter of his earlier self, and that there may be somebody else who can do it better.

Let us start, then, by looking at what we can make of Gandalf in *The Hobbit* and *The Lord of the Rings* without the aid of Tolkien's own commentaries on them. In the case of the former, however, there is an immediate problem: if our study is to be text-based on which text of *The Hobbit* should it be based, the early editions written before *The Lord of the Rings* was conceived or executed or the later ones in which Tolkien revised the text to bring it more into line with *The Lord of the Rings*? Between them, these versions are perfect examples of the problem of authorial authority discussed above, since it is clear that Tolkien uses his privileged position as author to try to impose on his earlier work a reading consistent with his later one. But fortunately the alterations to *The Hobbit* very largely affect characters, notably Bilbo and Gollum, other than Gandalf. Indeed one could argue that Gandalf remains much the same in both early and late versions of *The Hobbit*, and that in turn makes him much the same as he is in *The Lord of the Rings*, and the reason for this is that a fundamental feature of the development of *The Lord of the Rings* out of *The Hobbit* is Tolkien's effort to find out who exactly Gandalf is. The later book can be seen as in part (but a large part) the exploration of the Gandalf character as he appeared in *The Hobbit*. The continuity of the character between the books is therefore no accident since Gandalf in *The Lord of the Rings* is intended to be a consistent development of the Gandalf in *The Hobbit*.

What is Gandalf like in *The Hobbit*? His character is straightforward enough, as we saw in the last chapter. He is an elderly but vigorous man of superior skills and wide experience, a natural leader who assumes that others will accept him as such and that his advice will usually be taken. He is capable of expressing doubt in his plans or conclusions and he is careful not to fall into the trap of presenting himself as, or believing himself to be, infallible, and yet he has greater confidence in his own abilities and his own decisions than he has in anyone else's, and he can be brusque with those who contradict him, although he will listen to objections, and knows that those who follow must on occasion be allowed their say, and sometimes even the opportunity to go their own way.

Gandalf is capable of direct and energetic action. He is a doer as well as an instructor. He will take physical risks, endure hardships and go out into the world beyond comforts and conveniences. In principle he does not ask others to do what he would not do himself. Conversely, he will share the dangers and discomforts into which he leads others. He has physical strength to match his intellectual ability and his age does not seem to have brought him any infirmities. In fact, he has all the advantages of looking old and wise with none of the disadvantages of physical weakness, except perhaps a suggestion of less-than-perfect eyesight. But his hearing is good, as is his digestion, he can walk or ride for days without tiring, he can sleep rough, climb trees and mountains, ford rivers and withstand rain and cold weather. He can also play a leading part in skirmishes with a range of enemies.

His fighting prowess, along with his intellectual ability, is partly explained by his magical power. It is not in fact clear how much his capacity for physical endurance, his general good health and his mental sharpness are simple, though outstanding, human virtues and how much they owe to superhuman or supernatural powers. In moments of extreme crisis, physical or intellectual, Gandalf will resort to magic as an aid to his extraordinary normal abilities. It is arguable that for him magic is a matter of specifically-cast spells for specific occasions, not long-term, sustained supernatural support, but there is not enough information about his magic or his use of it to be sure that he does not use it to give himself his physical resilience and sharp wits. The converse of this, however, is that, if magic is not responsible for Gandalf's remarkable physical and intellectual abilities, then these must be taken as natural and normal in him and therefore in so far as he exceeds human expectation and standards he is not simply human but of some higher order of being.

This question might be settled if we were given fuller information about Gandalf's origins, such as his parentage, his education and early life, his place of origin and the race or species to which he belongs. *The Hobbit* gives no information on these. As suggested above, *The Lord of the Rings* can be seen as a working-out of some answers to these questions, answers that in turn generate the actions of Gandalf in *The Lord of the Rings* and so the shape of the plot that surrounds him. In *The Hobbit* the absence of explanation of Gandalf's origins is passed off as a given of the story, along with much else about him. This is not the only aspect of *The Hobbit* where Tolkien relies on the narrative conventions of the adventure romance, especially one written for children, to truncate formal expectations. Cleverly, he uses the narrator's voice (often criticised, even by Tolkien himself) to give the reader the impression that more need not be said to introduce Gandalf or explain him, partly because the narrator treats the character as too well-known to need explanation. At first Tolkien did not in fact have a full explanation for Gandalf and so devices of avoidance were inevitable, and of course he was right not to clog the narrative with elaborate back-stories for his main characters. Nevertheless, the absence of information about Gandalf is a serious matter for understanding the character and the book, because of his significant role in it.

Gandalf, after all, is the main reason for the action of *The Hobbit*. It is Gandalf who produces the map the expedition follows, it is he who persuades Thorin to form a party of dwarves to undertake the quest, he it is who deliberately involves Bilbo in the venture and he who leads them for half the way, in the process forming them into a group and showing how to deal with what they encounter on the way. Why he does all this is not clear. His acquisition of Thror's map is, as he describes it, an accident. His meeting with Thorin at which he arranges to see him to discuss his plans is another accident. There is no particular reason given to explain Gandalf's interest in the Shire that leads to his hearing about Bilbo and choosing him as a key member of the expedition. Tolkien leaves it vague what motivates all this. The suggestion hangs in the air that this is only the sort of thing wizards like Gandalf do, but this of course begs the questions of what kind of wizard Gandalf is.

We can however draw some conclusions from these essentially descriptive comments on Gandalf in *The Hobbit*. If we assume that Gandalf really is a good example of the kind of wizard he is, we can try to say what that sort of wizard is like. Setting aside what may be classed as Gandalf's personal traits, his mild irascibility, his orotundity, his no doubt forgivable impulses to patronise those less quick to understand than him, first we can note that tendency to the superhuman. Notable about that is the slightly more than human longevity of Gandalf. Although we have little or nothing to go on to determine his exact age we can get the impression that he is both older than he looks and not as old, in ideas or capacities, as he should be in human terms. And so, although he looks like a man, in some ways he is more than an ordinary one and perhaps not really a man at all. When we consider what he does a similar conclusion emerges. His instigation of the expedition to the Lonely Mountain is in some ways human but in the end not quite that, chiefly because it is hard to see what he himself gets out of it. Why should he care if Thorin becomes King under the Mountain or not? He might of course care to see the end of Smaug, the dragon who has driven the dwarves out of the mountain and devastated the surrounding area,

Chapter Five: Who is Gandalf?

which he keeps in thrall, but even this goal seems an altruistic one, a desire for the welfare of others that is unusual among humanity in so pure a form. Yet it is hard to resist the conclusion that it is just this sort of thing that wizards do. To do it Gandalf can afford to spend his own time and energy organising and leading. It is true that before the task is completed he announces that he has other business to attend to and leaves the party to continue without him, but we conclude that this other business must be more of the same. We do not come to believe that Gandalf has a job to go to, that he is retained by some master or that he holds a permanent post at some court or other institution.

No doubt because of his story of how he met Thror and received the map from him, and because of Gandalf's ability to travel through rough country with the dwarves and Bilbo, we readily view him as a sort of roving trouble-shooter, a kind of freelance upholder of order and justice, a 'have-wand-will-travel' maverick Lone Ranger without a Tonto, the Middle-earth equivalent of the US marshal in Wild West stories, or the knight errant in tales of the Round Table. As such, he has no real home, no family ties or permanent connections. He moves through the land, known to everybody at least by sight, and to many by name, or a name they know him by, ready to strike up conversations with anybody, conversations that will lead to plans and schemes all tending towards the benefit of those ill-done-by or misled. Each scheme, small or large, will add to an overall trend towards the general good, which rather than any particular advantage to him seems to be the wizard's aim. He is not even especially anxious to be seen as the leader or chief agent in what comes out of his plans. Although he unquestionably takes the lead when he is present, he is content to leave the operation to others if he has to, or can, and they can have the credit for success. Despite a certain exterior gruffness and air of not suffering fools gladly, he is basically not egotistic and places the needs of others above his own. Paradoxically, he is a leader and initiator who shapes his powers into service of the general good. Like some latter-day Enlightened Despot, he is the first servant of the people, or at any rate of those who represent honesty, decency and ordinary human values. He maintains his link with these in his pleasure in simple things – simple food, drink and tobacco, and conviviality. Like most Western (and Wild Western) heroes, he embodies heroic values for the sake of non-heroic ones, and lives a life of epic adventure to safeguard the right of the majority to live humdrum, quiet lives of domestic peace and social harmony.

The Lord of the Rings amplifies these impressions of Gandalf without adding a great deal to them. In that work he begins, as he did in *The Hobbit*, as a visitor to the Shire who instigates action largely by passing on information. In the process we learn some more of his background and way of life. He is now no longer a unique individual but a member of an order of wizards and he tells us of two of them, Saruman and Radagast. The latter seems to be a wanderer like Gandalf, although his purposes are obscure. Saruman, on the other hand, occupies a permanent base and acts as leader of the order of wizards. At first Gandalf refers to him as his superior in respectful terms, and tells of going to him for advice and support. Saruman, we conclude, is engaged in much the same tasks as Gandalf, although perhaps with a more political bent, as the ruler of a domain of some sort. As such he must, we suppose, have diplomatic relations with other rulers in the vicinity and as a respectable wizard, full of wisdom and learning, must surely offer an example of good political practice and stewardship to his neighbours. There is something papal about our early idea of Saruman, not least because of the description of him as Saruman the White. Gandalf, by comparison, is a sort of wandering friar, grey like the Franciscans, not exactly a mendicant but certainly one who eschews wealth, comfort and possessions so that he can go about the land watching for danger and organising the defences against the enemy.

A major change between *The Hobbit*, especially in its original form, and *The Lord of the Rings* is of course the nature of the enemy Gandalf faces. The rather vague sense of injustice and disorder he appears to be trying to combat in setting up the expedition against Smaug, and even in his fostering the coming together of dwarves, elves and men against the goblins at the end of the story, is made more specific in *The Lord of the Rings* by the focus on an actual villain, Sauron the Dark Lord. A simple and obvious colour-symbolism becomes fundamental to *The Lord of the Rings*, the clash between the blackness of Sauron and the whiteness of his opponents. Tolkien attempts to avoid the crudest form of black and white contrast by such compromises as making Gandalf grey at first and giving Aragorn's heraldic blazon a sable field (although the principal charge upon it is argent), but the simple contrast nevertheless obtains in many instances, great and small, from the white light of Galadriel's phial in the blackness of Shelob's lair to the star that shines through the clouds in Mordor, the flowers on the tombs at Edoras, and Gandalf's horse and the Black Riders'. These devices convert Gandalf from the generalised do-gooder of *The Hobbit* into a champion of the light in *The Lord of the Rings*. He is not alone in this. Other characters also take on a crusading role. The Fellowship of the Ring is unlike the band of dwarves, with hobbit and, sometimes, wizard in tow in *The Hobbit*. The Fellowship has an almost sacral quality, blest and twice blest by elves in Rivendell and Lothlórien, as they set out, like knights on a quest, or a party of missionary explorers, into the wilds bearing the hope of civilisation. But of all the Fellowship it is surely Gandalf who most clearly represents dedication to a higher purpose, not only because he is the obvious leader but also because the object of the expedition is so much in accord with his own objects, his life's work, his *raison d'être*. The explicitness of *The Lord of the Rings*, in contrast with *The Hobbit*, about the epic and ethical nature of its action, which defines its antagonist in clear and stark terms as a metaphysical evil, also defines Gandalf in terms of a metaphysical goodness. In the face of this Tolkien has a hard time retaining from *The Hobbit* the superficies of Gandalf's character, his grumpiness, his sense of humour, his occasional condescension and not infrequent acceptance that he makes mistakes. When Tolkien remembers to put references to these into *The Lord of the Rings* they often appear somewhat jarring to the reader, used by then to Gandalf's otherwise commanding authority.

He has command in *The Hobbit*, too, but in *The Lord of the Rings* Gandalf becomes literally a commander, and in a military way, after his return in *The Two Towers*. By the siege of Minas Tirith in *The Return of the King* the wizard has become both a field marshal and an Achilles or Arthur, leading men in battle and also organising armies, tactics and strategy. In the build-up to the final battles he also shows the flowering of his diplomatic skills, evident at the end of *The Hobbit* but now in full operation, both in Rohan and Gondor. Where earlier he had seemed to operate behind the scenes, now he appears on an international stage, arguing with statesmen and influencing the politics of rulers. Before, he had, as he says when he describes his research into the Ring to Frodo at the start of *The Fellowship of the Ring*, worked in archives and libraries, digging out information to be used to persuade and inform individuals to whom he delegates much of the task of applying new information to events. When he arrives in Rohan, however, we see him accepted as a kind of ambassador, an emissary from a recognised power, to whom attention must be paid, and he is treated in the same way in Gondor. This is made the more striking by the fact that in both cases he is regarded as the purveyor of unwelcome news and advice. The respect he is given is often grudging and querulous, and he himself recognises that he has a need to win people over. He cannot simply hector them into compliance with his will.

This is a significant point. Although Gandalf becomes such a commanding figure, or at least a commander-in-chief, in *The Lord of the Rings*, he remains as in *The Hobbit* unable or unwilling simply to direct others to do what he wants. We suppose he has magic powers to control and compel people, as indeed his opponents, Saruman and Sauron, do, but he never uses them as such. The whole point of his conflict with Grima over Théoden is that Gandalf breaks Wormtongue's spell over the king in order to leave him free to judge and act for himself. Gandalf does not just replace Grima as Théoden's *eminence grise*. Sauron uses his rings to turn their wearers into his tools, and he wants the One Ring as a means to total domination of the minds of others, but Gandalf refuses the Ring when Frodo offers it to him. The meaning of this refusal is made unmistakable for the reader when Galadriel also refuses to accept the Ring from Frodo, explaining that if she took it she would become a terrible force, a queen who could compel obedience, and even love and admiration, from her subjects. She declines this fate, acknowledging that to terrify people into a show of affection is to drain their actions and feelings of all significance. Only the spontaneous and free can feel and display true love and duty. Galadriel's vision of what she might become with the Ring is only the starkest and clearest demonstration of a truth that flows through *The Lord of the Rings*, and *The Hobbit*: that goodness, virtue, positive action and positive feeling, cannot be compelled or bought but must be freely given. It therefore follows that whoever desires or needs love, friendship or support from his or her fellow-beings will have to earn it, not take it, and whoever has a grand design for the world will

Chapter Five: Who is Gandalf?

need to avoid dictating or driving and aim at persuasion and diplomacy instead. Out of Tolkien's work therefore emerges the paradox of power: that to wield it successfully it must not be seen to be applied, or even applied at all.

Let us now turn to what Tolkien himself says about Gandalf in his comments made outside *The Lord of the Rings*, and in most cases after it was written, to see how they relate to what we have said above about the character as he appears in the texts themselves. A clear place to start is with some of Tolkien's letters, notably that of 4 November 1954 to Robert Murray SJ, number 156 in Carpenter's *The Letters of J R R Tolkien*, and the end of the draft of a letter to Michael Straight, number 181 in Carpenter and dated by him 'probably January or February 1956' (*The Fellowship of the Ring* was published on 29 July 1954, *The Two Towers* on 11 November 1954 and *The Return of the King* on 20 October 1955). In the first of these Tolkien begins by discussing Gandalf's return from the dead in *The Two Towers*. He confesses that the way this is presented is a defect partly because it was driven by the needs of the plot, which required Gandalf to return at this point in the narrative, although there is no space for a full explanation of his return. Tolkien admits that he has tried to keep references to his mythology down to hints only and thinks that therefore the death and return of Gandalf are left mysterious. He goes on to make some amends by trying to say in the letter who Gandalf is and how he could have survived the fall with the balrog in Moria.

The first point is that Gandalf is not human. Tolkien says he is neither a man nor a hobbit and immediately offers a term to define him. He calls Gandalf an angel (he immediately puts in the Ancient Greek for this), thus introducing an obvious religious overtone. Literally, as Tolkien would know, an angel is a messenger. Tolkien goes on to translate the word as 'emissary'. Gandalf is one of the Istari, which Tolkien translates as 'wizards', because of the etymological connection of 'wizard' with the English 'wit', meaning 'knowing' or 'knowledge', a parallel to the etymological connections in his Elvish of the word 'istari'. The Istari were sent to Middle-earth to oppose the rising threat of Sauron. Although superhuman they were physically embodied in human-like form and flesh. Tolkien describes them as incarnate, that is, to take the word literally, enclosed in flesh, which means that although capable of great feats of endurance and slow to weary they nevertheless do feel pain and other afflictions and can be killed, in a sense. Tolkien goes on, however, to make an interesting comment on the *limitations* of the Istari or wizards:

> At this point in the fabulous history the purpose was precisely to limit and hinder their exhibition of 'power' on the physical plane, and so that they should do what they were primarily sent for: train, advise, instruct, arouse the hearts and minds of those threatened by Sauron to a resistance with their own strengths; and not just do the job for them. (*Letters*, page 202)

Tolkien then brings out a surprising but logical implication of these limitations: that the wizards, like most of the quasi-divine beings in his mythology, are fallible and make mistakes, and because of their fleshliness the wizards are that much more likely to fail. Indeed, he says that as a group the wizards *did* fail. Obviously he is referring here to Saruman, and perhaps also to the inefficacy of Radagast, the third wizard in *The Lord of the Rings* (of the other two Istari Tolkien says existed nothing is known; they make no appearance in his tales). Gandalf also fails in so far as he has to sacrifice himself in Moria to enable the rest of the Fellowship to escape, with the consequence that they lose his leadership and fragment (although it is of course arguable that this might have happened anyway and after all it turns out to be all to the good, and a prime example of how what seems to be disastrous is in the event a paradoxical virtue). Tolkien claims that Gandalf's self-sacrifice shows that he is not powerful enough to do the job he was sent to do and, to succeed, he needs to be given enhanced powers, hence his transformation, by the beings that sent him, from Gandalf the Grey to Gandalf the White. Who these beings are Tolkien leaves not fully stated. He says they are not the gods of this world, and therefore hints at a power beyond them. This is consistent with his mythology, in which the Valar, or lesser gods, who roughly correspond to the gods of a classical or Nordic pantheon, are placed as underlings of the one true God. Tolkien's system is therefore intended to be strictly speaking monotheistic although for practical purposes polytheistic, with a range of demigods and their supernatural servants, such as the Istari, running the day-to-day operations of the world in time and space, under the supreme if withdrawn supervision of an ultimate divinity. All except him are fallible, to a greater degree the further from him they operate, and all but he are vulnerable to the machinations and temptations of the Satanic rebel in Tolkien's cosmos, the fallen demigod Melkor or Morgoth (he has several names), whose chief servant Sauron becomes.

Chapter Five: Who is Gandalf?

The powers of Gandalf the White are still, according to Tolkien, limited, although greater than those of Gandalf the Grey:

> He is still under the obligation of concealing his power and of teaching rather than forcing or dominating wills, but where the physical powers of the Enemy are too great for the good will of the opposers to be effective he can act in emergency as an 'angel' [...] He seldom does so, operating rather through others [...]. (*Letters*, pages 202f)

Tolkien refers to occasions in *The Lord of the Rings* when Gandalf the White uses his full powers, but he continues to stress that Gandalf is still a physical being and as such he still feels care and anxiety and worry about the future, which he cannot foresee much more than other people. In fact, the temptation for beings like Gandalf is to believe that they can know the future and to try to force it into existence by controlling and directing other people: 'their constant temptation [is] to do, or try to do, what is for them *wrong* (and disastrous): to force lesser wills by power; by awe if not by actual fear, or physical constraint' (*Letters*, page 203). Tolkien restates this more succinctly in the second letter, the draft of 1956 for Michael Straight (Letter 181), where he writes of how the incarnated wizards because of their incarnation are liable to 'fall' into sin:

> The chief form this would take with them would be impatience, leading to the desire to force others to their own good ends, and so inevitably at last to mere desire to make their own wills effective by any means. To this evil Saruman succumbed. Gandalf did not. (*Letters*, page 237)

Behind these letters, it seems likely, lies the short essay on 'The Istari' published in *Unfinished Tales* (pages 388ff) and dated by Christopher Tolkien to 1954. This explains who the Istari are and where they come from, and the tensions among the three, Gandalf, Saruman and Radagast, who appear in *The Lord of the Rings*. There is also a character-sketch of Gandalf. It is noteworthy that, although the essay states that the Istari 'were forbidden to reveal themselves in forms of majesty, or to seek to rule the wills of Men and Elves by open display of power, but [...] were bidden to advise and persuade Man and Elves to good' (page 389), this point is far less stressed than it is in the letters. The brief note on the Istari or Wizards in the section on the Third Age in Appendix B of *The Lord of the Rings* is similar. It says the wizards 'were forbidden to match [Sauron's] power with power, or to seek to dominate Elves or Men by force or fear' (page 1084). The passage in the section of *The Silmarillion* called 'Of the

Rings of Power and the Third Age' that conveys the same information about the Istari, and is verbally close to the appendix in *The Lord of the Rings*, does not say as much about the exercise of power by the Istari. Christopher Tolkien, in volume 5 of *The History of Middle-earth* (page 199), dates this section of *The Silmarillion* to the period between the publication of *The Fellowship of the Ring* and *The Two Towers*. It is here that Tolkien tries to connect *The Hobbit* with *The Lord of the Rings*. He answers the question of Gandalf's absence from the adventure as Bilbo and the dwarves enter Mirkwood by equating the necromancer with Sauron, who has taken up residence there to be near enough the river where Isildur, last known bearer of the Ring, was killed by orcs. Not knowing that Gollum has the Ring after his friend retrieved it from the river, Sauron is searching there for it, but when Gandalf learns this he persuades Saruman and others to drive Sauron from Mirkwood. This is a temporary victory, however, as Sauron then flees to a prepared stronghold in Mordor, from which he will soon threaten Gondor and the rest of Middle-earth. Coincidentally, of course, Bilbo has already found the Ring and carries it with him through Mirkwood and on to the Lonely Mountain, and then back to the Shire. Rather surprisingly (from the point of view of this later linking of *The Hobbit* and *The Lord of the Rings*), Gandalf does not realise what Bilbo has found and it takes some time, and research by the wizard, before he knows exactly what it is – so long, in fact, that he gives a full explanation of it not to Bilbo the finder but to Frodo his nephew, some years after the Ring has been passed to him. However satisfying this process is in the narrative structure of *The Fellowship of the Ring*, it poses an awkward set of questions for the history of Middle-earth as outlined in 'Of the Rings of Power and the Third Age' in *The Silmarillion* and for Gandalf's part in it. But this is just one of many problems Tolkien faced in trying, retrospectively for the most part, to fit *The Hobbit* into his legendarium, a task he worked at several times but in the end had to concede was impossible (largely for geographical reasons, he could not fit Bilbo's journey into the same map as Frodo's, even although they both travel from Hobbiton to Rivendell: see 'Timelines and Itinerary', in Rateliff, *The History of the Hobbit* (2007), Volume 2, pages 813-838). In the end the reader is left with the strong impression that *The Lord of the Rings* is a sequel to *The Hobbit* although in fact the links are not complete and in some cases, especially in matters of time-scale and geography,

Chapter Five: Who is Gandalf?

incoherent, a result of the fact that *The Hobbit* began as an independent tale only casually related to Tolkien's mythology by passing uses of names and references.

Tolkien's various writings about Gandalf and the Istari, then, are partly generated by his need to build *The Hobbit* and *The Lord of the Rings* into his mythological history, a task made difficult by the intractable independence of *The Hobbit* from his legendarium, despite the fact that it was the reason for his writing *The Lord of the Rings*. In the process he also articulated his idea of Gandalf in his own mythological terms. In so far as this explanation is meant to apply to the Gandalf of *The Hobbit* there is surely no clearer example, as noted earlier, of an author using his privilege as author to impose on a text meanings it did not originally possess, an imposition that goes as far as rewriting the text to suit the new interpretation. In the case of *The Lord of the Rings* the process is more complicated, since that work is written with more conscious awareness of the legendary background into which it is set, but that knowledge was not itself fixed, or even complete, when Tolkien wrote the story. The appendices offer the impression that *The Lord of the Rings* is based on a fully-detailed and extensive pre-existing quasi-historical foundation but in fact much of this was constructed, as had to be the case, after the main text was written. One might argue that the appendices are actually part of the text and so not to be set against it (the same might be said of the prologue to *The Fellowship of the Ring*), but this would be an awkward position to maintain, since we know that the appendices were written afterwards and they present themselves as commentary on the main text. Again Tolkien exploits his position as author to try to direct the reader's understanding of the text. This is not to say that this is unwelcome or altogether unhelpful. Tolkien's commentary enriches the reading of *The Lord of the Rings* for us and adds to our understanding of it, but the status of this commentary remains outside the work itself and therefore open to judgment as to its relevance or accuracy to the work, no matter how well it fits in with the rest of Tolkien's ideas. And in fact, as part of a work in progress, it does not necessarily fit the outside legendarium that perfectly, either. We can justifiably suspect an element of special pleading and adjustment on both sides, with *The Lord of the Rings* being interpreted to fit the mythology and the mythology being adapted to fit *The Lord of the Rings*. It would be naive to treat the appendices as statements of unalterable facts against which to compare the text of *The Lord of the Rings* for some sort of veracity. Here Tolkien falls foul of the weakness of his privileged position as author: his exegesis of his own work is suspect because he is his own advocate, and his invention of material outside the text to explain it is open to the charge of circular argument.

Nevertheless, when all is said and done, Tolkien's attempts to explain who Gandalf is outside *The Hobbit* and *The Lord of the Rings* are not so distant from our understanding of the texts as to lack value. On the contrary, in many ways they confirm the basic insights derived from the texts alone. Whatever we think of the labels Tolkien puts on the character, Istari and angel, Gandalf does appear to be more than human though less than godly. He is a character between the human and the divine, gifted with supernatural powers but subject to almost normal human physical weaknesses. His power is partly magical, that is, beyond the ordinary abilities of normal humans, but it is also a matter of wisdom and knowledge, partly drawn from experience, partly from access to sources of information and insight, and partly from his contact with others of his kind, and perhaps with even higher beings. A central issue, however, is his use of this power, and the limitations on that use. In the stories we can see him delegating and deferring, using persuasion and diplomacy, and refraining from imposing his will or applying supernatural force. In Tolkien's external accounts of Gandalf's role we correspondingly find a strong emphasis on the constraints under which Gandalf must operate, the need for him to teach and instruct others in their actions and duties rather than force them to act, or, what seems as bad, himself act for them. Thus, there is a paradox in as much as a being with superior abilities, but not overwhelming ones, who therefore needs the co-operation if not the assistance of other beings, including those lesser than him in many ways, must learn *not* to use his powers to the full and restrict himself essentially to means and methods that are open to ordinary human beings. The final end, represented in *The Lord of the Rings* by the destruction of the Ring, does not justify the use of any means that overbear the minds, the free will, of others. As we shall see, this makes for a significant parallel between Tolkien's wizard and Wotan, Wagner's chief god.

CHAPTER SIX

Gandalf and Wotan

We have already explored the question of Tolkien's knowledge of Wagner's *Der Ring des Nibelungen*. Assuming from that that his knowledge extended beyond a general acquaintance we discussed a set of superficial resemblances between Wagner's *Ring* and *The Lord of the Rings*, a discussion that at times led into deeper levels of meaning and suggestions of much more profound correspondences of structure and theme than Tolkien and his admirers have been prepared to admit. What these point towards is an interpretation of *The Lord of the Rings* (and its prequel *The Hobbit*) that is less exclusively concerned with Frodo and the destruction of the Ring than the now standard critical accounts. Instead, our attention shifts towards the other half of *The Lord of the Rings*, that concerning Gandalf and Aragorn. The comparison with Wagner's *Ring* makes these characters more prominent in interpreting *The Lord of the Rings* because they are clear parallels with two of the leading characters in Wagner, Wotan and Siegfried. Paying attention to this side of *The Lord of the Rings* not only restores significance to parts of the book that have often been regarded as secondary to the main plot of Frodo and the Ring but also reveals connections between *The Lord of the Rings* and Tolkien's other Middle-earth writings, represented by *The Silmarillion*. The standard account of the origin of *The Lord of the Rings*, given authority by Tolkien himself, out of *The Hobbit*, whose own origins are presented as spontaneous and unconnected with anything that went before, tends to obscure continuities between *The Lord of the Rings*, especially the stories of Gandalf and Aragorn, and the rest of Tolkien's legendarium. These would arguably have been more obvious if the comparison between Wagner's Ring and Tolkien's had been acknowledged. *Der Ring des Nibelungen* is almost a hidden key to the *whole* of *The Lord of the Rings*, and without it only a partial reading has prevailed.

To equate Gandalf with Wotan seems at first sight tendentious. The one is a wizard, the other a god. But Wagner's god is very far from the idea of an omniscient, omnipotent being and we must get away from the definitions of a god that are familiar from the monotheistic religions that dominate modern Western thinking. Wotan in *Der Ring des Nibelungen* is never a god in the Christian sense of the word. For one thing, he is not alone as a divinity, however minor his fellow-gods are. For another, although wise and powerful, he is not all-knowing and all-powerful. He is subject to a range of other forces, in time and space, and must pay a price for what he knows, and often for what he does. He is not even, in the end, immortal. On the other hand, he is a dominant force in the first half of *Der Ring des Nibelungen* and not insignificant in the second half, although with diminishing power. He embodies not just wisdom and power but also will and purpose, so that he is the mainspring of the plot of the work. But not only does he set things going and try to press to conclusions, he also defines the terms under which action is undertaken. He chooses the modes of action and the constraints to be observed. It is a part of his nature, and function, that rules are set and obeyed. He is an embodiment, and creator, of principle, not chaos and whimsy, and he not only recognises boundaries to his actions and desires but also expects others to do so too. Yet he is human enough (there is no other way of putting this) sometimes to resent the difficulties his own principles put in the way of his intentions, and the frustrations caused by the limits set on his actions. Nevertheless, he is not egotistical. He accepts the existence of others, relies on them and indeed readily sees the need to operate with and through them. He is a leader, not a solipsist, and as a leader he needs followers. He cannot do everything on his own.

All of this brings Wotan very close to Gandalf. The wizard too is wise and powerful, but there are limits to both of these qualities, and therefore to achieve his aims Gandalf must work with what he has and use the assistance of others. Like Wotan, Gandalf is an instigator, planner and director of events, more particularly so at the beginning of the story (this is true of both *The Hobbit* and *The Lord of the Rings*). Tolkien often tries to disguise Gandalf's role as the central force in the plot, frequently removing him from the centre of the action, most drastically by apparently killing him off in Moria, but Gandalf's influence is still there when he is not, and repeatedly those left by him try to imagine what he would do, or wish that he was there to tell them. Like Wotan, Gandalf has to hope that in his absence his followers will have understood enough of what he thinks is needful to be able to take decisions and make progress towards the goals he has set. Almost all the good characters in *The Lord of the Rings*, including Frodo, are carrying out Gandalf's orders. The equivocal characters, like Boromir and Denethor, are those who resist Gandalf. There are others who, like Théoden, are undecided at first and have to be persuaded by Gandalf to do what he thinks is right. Like Wotan, however, Gandalf does not act out of his own desires alone. He represents higher values. Wagner is far less explicit than Tolkien about what these are, and what Wotan's relationship with them is. Largely he confines himself to reminders that Wotan is bound by the laws inscribed upon his spear to regulate his actions by promises and contracts, and we are left to extrapolate these to an idea of law and order that transcends Wotan himself and his personal wishes and preferences. Tolkien, working in a more spacious form, is more articulate about Gandalf as a servant of higher powers, and in his writings around *The Lord of the Rings* can define him as an *angelos* or messenger, placing him in a hierarchy of powers that reaches above and below him. Wagner can indicate something the same about Wotan by the appearances of Erda in *Der Ring des Nibelungen*, but inevitably this can only be a token representation of Wotan's position. Yet it is enough to confirm the parallel with Gandalf's.

In what they are and what they do, then, Gandalf and Wotan are similar. There are also similarities in their parts in the narrative. Both begin as central figures, directing the action and organising other characters. Then both overreach themselves, almost as though for both Wagner and Tolkien these characters have become too dominant and for the story to continue they must face a setback. Wagner makes the removal of Wotan from centre stage a humiliation for the god. Not only does his scheme to recover the Ring through Siegmund go wrong but it is shown to be a misconceived plan in the first place. The profound implications of using somebody as a tool to gain your ends are made central to the narrative necessity of displacing Wotan to make room for other figures. Tolkien's displacement of Gandalf is less well developed. The wizard's supposed death in Moria operates quite obviously as a device for opening up the narrative and diverting it from an orderly procession towards its conclusion. Up to the point where Gandalf falls with the balrog it has seemed that the story will consist of a series of encounters between the Fellowship of the Ring, ably led by Gandalf, and supported by his magic abilities, and sundry threats as they travel to Mount Doom and a final climactic encounter that ends the quest and the book. After the success of *The Lord of the Rings* simple narratives of this shape abounded. Tolkien, to his credit, avoided this foregone pattern (as he had tried to do in *The Hobbit*), although he did not altogether succeed in explaining what the death of Gandalf meant. Here the comparison with Wagner helps, because it is clear that in *Der Ring des Nibelungen* the issue has to do with human freedom and responsibility. Tolkien was less daring than Wagner in suggesting that, to develop true freedom, humans had to break with supernatural guidance and so he muffles the crisis and even brings Gandalf back from the dead as if little has changed.

Nevertheless, both *Der Ring des Nibelungen* and *The Lord of the Rings* show in their second halves a waning of the power of the figure so central to their earlier parts and the initiation of their action. Wotan as the Wanderer in *Siegfried* becomes more observer than agent and lingers on only as an off-stage presence in *Götterdämmerung*. Gandalf seems more prominent in the latter parts of *The Lord of the Rings* but the fragmentation of the Fellowship turns him into one of several elements and his actions embroil him in human affairs in ways that, while they confirm his importance, also reduce its scope relative to that of others. We are conscious in *The Return of the King* of a comparison between Gandalf and Aragorn as centres of narrative interest, and of narrative power. By the end Gandalf, like Wotan, has become a bystander, politely honoured by others and included in the final celebrations but not the centre of attention, in the present or for the future. Wagner, of course, dismisses Wotan in a blaze of glory. Tolkien is less histrionic with the twilight of Gandalf but the outcome is similar. Once again the comparison between the two works draws attention to an aspect of *The Lord of the Rings* that is usually overlooked. Gandalf, his mission done, fades from the scene, leaving humanity to get on with their lives.

Comparing Gandalf and Wotan leads to other parallels between characters in the two works. The next obvious one is between Aragorn and Siegfried. Perhaps one of Tolkien's motives for resisting the comparison between *The Lord of the Rings* and *Der Ring des Nibelungen* was that he did not want anyone to see likenesses between his ideal king and Wagner's tainted hero, but they surely play the same role in each work. They are the human heroes who take over and fulfil the aims of the supernatural semi-divine beings who govern the action.

In both cases there is a significant ancestry, symbolised by a broken sword. Siegfried is the son of Wotan's first attempt at a delegated saviour, Siegmund. Wotan's miscalculation, by which he reckons he can gain his end but leave the responsibility to the means, leads however to Siegmund's refusal to abandon his own prime interest, his sister-bride Sieglinde, for Wotan's, a refusal backed up by Brünnhilde. Siegmund, then, is a nay-sayer, an obstinate human resistant to doing what higher powers require, and it is out of this recalcitrance that Siegfried is born. Aragorn, too, has a background of recalcitrance. He is the heir of Isildur, the man who defeated Sauron by chopping off his Ring-finger and seized the Ring itself, but instead of destroying it he retained it. His refusal to give up the Ring led to his death, just as Siegmund's refusal to give up Sieglinde led to his. The refusals are different in value, perhaps. Siegmund's sacrifice is noble, even honourable; Isildur's seems neither. Tolkien surely plays down this dark aspect of Aragorn's ancestry, no doubt to protect him from readers' suspicion, even although at his first appearance in *The Fellowship of the Ring* Aragorn seems suspicious enough. By the time he arrives in Rivendell, however, Aragorn is losing his Strider persona and leaving that rather fugitive existence behind. Aragorn's Strider existence actually makes him seem like Siegmund, another fugitive with good intentions, but it also has parallels with Siegfried's early life in the forest, a wild man of the woods and as such not welcome among decent folk. Wagner dramatised that wildness with gusto; Tolkien tamed it into a kind of Robin Hoodery. This makes acceptable Aragorn's equivocal status as Strider and assimilates it to a heroic and virtuous myth. Aragorn is justified by his intentions, despite his initial appearance and some of his actions. He is originally a social outcast, if not an actual outlaw like Robin Hood. Although he proves himself to the hobbits, even Sam, and confirms the truth of Gandalf's repeated expressions of faith in him, it is notable that he has to go through a similar process of winning acceptance in each phase of his story, in Rohan and Gondor.

The shape of that story is much like Siegfried's. Aragorn comes in from the wilderness, with something of a reputation for heroic deeds, and enters the world of human affairs, of politics, where simple valour is not enough. Tolkien of course directs his narrative to a happy outcome: Aragorn proves himself, is accepted as a superior individual and takes the throne. Wagner's version has an unhappy outcome: Siegfried is tricked and played upon and taken for the fool at court that he is, and eventually murdered by his rivals there. The difference is partly to do with character, partly with upbringing. Siegfried, an orphan brought up in the forest by a dwarf, would have had to be extraordinarily intelligent to be anything but ignorant and socially inept after such an upbringing. Wagner may have believed that such things as bravery and openness of heart were innate qualities (this is the message of the later opera *Parsifal*) but, to judge by Siegfried, he does not seem to have thought the same about manners or political finesse. Tolkien, on the other hand, was surely determined that his wild man would have the grace and perceptiveness of a natural aristocrat. Aragorn is both a more traditional and a more conventional version of the outcast hero than Siegfried and his eventual triumphant return as a king fulfils a narrative pattern that Wagner could be said to be subjecting to deconstruction.

Tolkien confuses the parallel between Aragorn and Siegfried by the doubling of part of the narrative, showing the return of the leader not once but twice, in first the story of Rohan and second that of Gondor. Siegfried comes to one court and his downfall is enacted there only. Aragorn comes first to Edoras and then to Minas Tirith. There are awkwardnesses about this. Aragorn's status among the Rohirrim hovers between his rangership and his kingship. Tolkien gets away with this by including Gandalf in the early part of the Rohan episode. He literally brings the wizard back from the dead so that he, not Aragorn, can struggle for Théoden's soul against Grima Wormtongue. The latter is essentially the equivalent of Hagen at the court of the Gibichungs in *Götterdämmerung*, an evil counsellor out for his own ends who disguises himself as a friend of the prince and secures mastery over his will. Neither Gunther nor Siegfried is a match for Hagen and one wonders whether Aragorn alone could have disposed of Grima. That is however a hypothetical question since Tolkien makes sure Gandalf is there to do the job for him. Théoden, the Gunther figure in Rohan, is turned to the good side and Aragorn enlists as a champion in his army of resistance to Saruman.

The other Gibichung, Gunter's wife Gutrune, is paralleled by Théoden's niece Éowyn. Like Gutrune, Éowyn is a figure of female temptation for the hero. Again Wagner and Tolkien take different paths. Siegfried succumbs to Gutrune's charms, with the help of a love potion from Hagen, whereas Aragorn gently resists Éowyn. The sense that Tolkien is rewriting *Der Ring des Nibelungen* with a morally more robust hero than Siegfried seems strong here, especially when we consider the reason for Aragorn's resistance to Éowyn, his prior commitment to Arwen, the equivalent to Siegfried's prior relationship with Brünnhilde. More of the comparison between Arwen and Brünnhilde will be said later. The odd thing here is how little Tolkien says about Arwen. Indeed, our current understanding of Aragorn and his love surely owes more to Peter Jackson's films of *The Lord of the Rings* than the book itself. Jackson builds on hints and the brief note on Aragorn and Arwen in the appendix to the book to make a love-story for his version, not unsympathetically, but with remarkably more explicitness than the original. One is struck on the one hand by how this shows how much Tolkien was reluctant to express his hero's sexual and emotional life and on the other by the suspicion that Jackson fleshed out Tolkien's bare account by paralleling Wagner here. The scenes in which Aragorn catches sight of Éowyn in Théoden's hall, and she finds meek but artful ways to keep herself in his eye and mind, seem modelled on equivalent passages in *Götterdämmerung*.

Aragorn's heroism at the defence of Helm's Deep, however, does not bring him nearer to Tolkien's goal for him. Faced with the danger of repetition in a second episode of arrival at an established court, Tolkien, before moving the story on from Rohan to Minas Tirith and another weak monarch who needs to be saved from his weakness, splits Aragorn from Gandalf and sends him on a long detour, to emerge in the nick of time to save the city from its besiegers. Gandalf it is who must travel into another Gibichung-like court, but here the Gunther-figure, Denethor, has no Hagen to subvert him. Denethor is his own bad counsellor and his despair is not projected on to a separate figure. There is no Grima whose banishment will automatically lead to the monarch's recovery of true vision. The agent of Denethor's sickness of mind is not a person (or personification) but a thing, the telepathic palantír that Sauron himself uses to control Denethor's mind. This is like an internal disease, a mental infirmity, and as such much less easy to combat without killing the patient. In the end Gandalf may be said to fail in treating Denethor because he does not diagnose the cause of his mental weakness. Aragorn avoids any blame for this failure and his triumphant return is untainted by it, and his supremacy over Gandalf enhanced.

Yet Aragorn's adventures between Helm's Deep and Minas Tirith, when he is separated by Tolkien from Gandalf, actually extend the parallel between the characters. Here is yet another instance of the doubling of characters and situations that Tolkien does so often that it is almost a hallmark of his narrative style. Just as earlier Gandalf in Moria undergoes a near-death underground trial from which he emerges changed, so Aragorn, in leading his followers through the Paths of the Dead, travels underground and confronts death in a trial that establishes his final authority. Though the processes are the same the outcomes are subtly different. Gandalf, as already suggested, emerges from Moria apparently stronger and grander than before and throws himself energetically into saving Middle-earth from Sauron, but try as he might Tolkien cannot recapture the aura of mystery surrounding the earlier Gandalf. He becomes a busy diplomat and soldier, but in the process comes down to the level of mortal men and is judged by their standards. The story gradually moves away from him until by the end, the episode of the Scouring of the Shire, he has faded from sight. Aragorn, on the other hand moves decisively to the centre, filling the gap left by Denethor, and by Théoden, and even that left by Gandalf himself. It is Aragorn who takes on magic powers, in healing the sick, and it is he who distributes rewards and favours. He accepts the crown of Gondor from Gandalf, but it is Aragorn himself who chooses the style of his coronation.

Aragorn's journey through the dark underworld as a preparation for his emergence as a great hero has a parallel in the career of Wagner's Siegfried. Though a major difference between Aragorn and Siegfried is that the former is not a dragon-slayer, after Siegfried has killed Fafner he goes down into the dragon's cave to find his treasure, notably the Ring. When he emerges he is a different man. Siegfried's descent into the dragon's den is of course paralleled by that of Bilbo in *The Hobbit*. Tolkien does not repeat this in *The Lord of the Rings* but, in another instance of the doubling of Gandalf and Aragorn, he has the wizard, not the hero, fight a fire-monster, the balrog, in Moria. Conflating Gandalf in Moria and Aragorn on the Paths of the Dead creates a composite parallel to Siegfried's slaying of Fafner and his raid on the dragon's hoard, but again the significance of this is not just that there is a parallel but how it makes clear Tolkien's intention to keep Aragorn away from the more obvious violence and physical activity of Siegfried. His hero is too refined, too much of an aristocrat, to get involved in slaying dragons and robbing their lairs. He is also to be shown as resisting the lure of the Ring. He has more sense than to take it like Siegfried, and so he avoids the rash dragon-slayer's fate. While this may make Aragorn a more fortunate figure, and a wiser and more reliable one, it also makes him seem more reserved and calculating. Perhaps Aragorn never quite shakes off the association with dissimulation that his initial appearance at Bree in the guise of Strider creates. Here his association with the Gandalf of the early parts of the story, Gandalf the Grey, who moves about on his own errands, rarely confiding in others, and never quite fully, works to suggest a secretive side to the hero.

Aragorn's reserve and reticence is nowhere more apparent than in his dealings with women, particularly the two most significant in his life, Arwen and Éowyn. The reticence here is mainly Tolkien's, though, especially in the case of Arwen, a shadowy figure in *The Lord of the Rings*. This is quite odd, as noted in Chapter 2, given that her relationship with Aragorn, that of an immortal elf with a mortal man, is the same as that of Beren and Lúthien, whose story Tolkien identified with so strongly and personally. The tale of Beren and Lúthien was one of Tolkien's major concerns and the whole idea of an elf woman sacrificing her immortality to bond with a human hero seems to have moved and obsessed him. Was it because he had tried to deal with this theme so fully elsewhere that he did not do so in *The Lord of the Rings*? Versions of the story of Beren and Lúthien already existed when Tolkien wrote *The Lord of the Rings* and perhaps he felt that they had precedence. If they were ever to be published perhaps it was his preference that these original legends of Middle-earth should speak for him, not the later and less authentic sequel to *The Hobbit*. Or perhaps Tolkien believed the theme was too great to be contained by *The Lord of the Rings* and so was best left almost unsaid. It is hard to argue that Tolkien kept the story of Aragorn and Arwen out of *The Lord of the Rings* because it is a tale of action and adventure, since he does include the romantic entanglement of Éowyn with Aragorn.

However neglected the part of Arwen, Aragorn's true sweetheart, in this threesome, it corresponds, as suggested earlier, with that of Siegfried, Brünnhilde and Gutrune in Wagner. Perhaps the greater prominence of the Aragorn-Éowyn side of this triangle relates to something Tolkien said in the introduction to his lectures on the Eddaic poems (see *The Legend of Sigurd and Gúdrun*, page 55), that 'curiously enough' he was more interested in Gudrún than Brynhild (to give the characters the Icelandic versions of their names). It is a measure of how far Aragorn is meant to be different from Siegfried, and Tolkien's story from Wagner's, that, where Gutrune succeeds in seducing Siegfried (with, to be sure, the assistance of Hagen), Éowyn hardly diverts Aragorn from Arwen. Brünnhilde is originally a non-human, a semi-divine valkyrie and as such probably immortal, like Arwen. To marry Siegfried Brünnhilde must turn her back on her valkyrie past, just as Arwen must renounce her elfhood to marry Aragorn. Éowyn, like Gutrune, presents a more normal, human match. From Brünnhilde Siegfried receives superhuman protection and advice, and one supposes that Arwen also offers Aragorn special assistance, if only in the form of elvish wisdom, and the friendship of her kin. Éowyn, like Gutrune, really offers little more than love and human pleasure, at the price of involvement in the politics of her world. As if warned by the disaster that overtakes Siegfried when he blindly accepts the offer of Gutrune, Aragorn declines that of Éowyn and survives to live happily with Arwen. Aragorn's caution saves him, but so does the absence from the scene of a Hagen to plot the hero's downfall.

This absence makes things easier for Aragorn but harder for Éowyn. Unlike Gutrune, she is left to fend for herself, hardly daring to reveal her love for Aragorn to anyone. She too becomes a figure of reticence and restraint. The contrast between the operatic intensity of Wagner's version of this love triangle and Tolkien's muted treatment is very striking. Was this deliberate? It is harder to deny this now that we have Tolkien's own version of the story of Siegfried, Brünnhilde and Gutrune in his adaptation of the Icelandic originals in *The Legend of Sigurd and Gudrún* (see Appendix B). In writing that he must have known he was challenging comparison with *Der Ring des Nibelungen* and when the same theme emerged in *The Lord of the Rings* he was surely not unaware of it. Perhaps another reason for not elaborating on the relationship of Aragorn and Arwen was that, as well as the tales of Beren and Lúthien, Tolkien had already covered similar ground in *The Legend of Sigurd and Gudrún*, even if that work was unpublished (and, if the letter to W H Auden of 29 March 1967 is any guide, the manuscript had been mislaid). That Tolkien worked a variation on the story of Siegfried, Brünnhilde and Gutrune in *The Lord of the Rings* is apparent in his development of Éowyn virtually from a Gutrune-figure into a Brünnhilde-like shield-maiden, if not a valkyrie. Éowyn's disappointment in her love for Aragorn leads to her disguising herself as a warrior and joining the expedition to relieve Minas Tirith, an operation in which she plays a leading part by killing a Nazgûl, almost as though she moves backwards through a Brünnhilde existence to a Siegfried-like monster slaying. Tolkien then revises the awakening of Brünnhilde by Siegfried in the scene of Aragon's rousing of the wounded Éowyn from unconsciousness after the battle. The transposition of this from a mountain-top to a hospital corresponds with the other ways Tolkien presents a tamer version than Wagner's. He then brings forward Faramir as a replacement for Aragorn in Éowyn's affections and thus again avoids tragic consequences.

Clustered around Aragorn, then, are a set of echoes and parallels that link him to Wagner's Siegfried, often as a contrast or correction as he avoids the mistakes of Wagner's hero and heads towards success and fulfilment. Aragorn also brings in comparisons between other figures in *The Lord of the Rings* and *Der Ring des Nibelungen*, notably Éowyn as a kind of Gutrune and, with less detail, Arwen as Brünnhilde. The location of the Wagnerian love triangle at the court of the Gibichungs suggests an analogy with the courts of Rohan and Gondor, taken together as a complex duplication of effect characteristic of *The Lord of the Rings*. Théoden then appears to be a Gunther redeemed, freed from the Hagen-like Grima to achieve true alliance with the visiting hero Aragorn. Denethor, on the contrary, is a Gunther with an internalised corruption that nobody can save him from, not even Gandalf or the healing king Aragorn, but his self-destruction leaves the way open for Aragorn's accession to the throne. In all this Aragorn is assisted by Gandalf rather directly, unlike the way in which Wotan is left to struggle between his wish to see Siegfried succeed and his need not to interfere. Tolkien suppresses the problem of responsibility and influence that Wagner confronts, leaving the cause of Aragorn's success to a vague sense of destiny derived from his family history and various legends, including the contrived business of the stewardship of Gondor, with its vacant throne awaiting the return of the true heir. All this points to a happy ending, an easily foreseen closure, where Wagner's Wotan instead foresees catastrophe and the passing of him and his kind. Tolkien displaces the vision of destruction out of the political world of Aragorn and Gandalf, Rohan and Gondor, and into the other half of his story, the journey of the Ringbearer Frodo to Mount Doom. In another act of doubling Tolkien takes the Ring out of the human story and sets it in a parallel narrative.

There are however also submerged connections between these two streams of narrative and the parallels visible between characters from *The Lord of the Rings* and those in *Der Ring des Nibelungen*. Aligning Gandalf with Wotan leads on to aligning Aragorn with Siegfried but it also leads to an alignment of Gollum with Alberich, and that in turn suggests a connection between Gandalf and Gollum, like that between Wotan and Alberich. Alberich is explicitly called 'Schwarz-Alberich', or 'Black Alberich', in *Der Ring des Nibelungen*, in contrast to Wotan as 'Licht-Alberich', or 'Light Alberich'. Wotan does this when he talks about the Nibelungs and the gods to Mime in the first act of *Siegfried*. Wagner thus hints that Alberich is Wotan's *alter ego*, the dark Hyde to his Jekyll. What links them, of course, is the Ring, to which both are drawn. After he has lost it Alberich leaves his subterranean realm, where his treasure was accumulated, and takes to lurking around Fafner's cave, waiting for a chance to retrieve the Ring, and is assuaged by proximity to it. When Siegfried kills Fafner and descends into his cave, Alberich comes out of hiding to quarrel with his brother Mime over who shall take the ring – prematurely, of course, as neither has any more chance of getting it off Siegfried than off Fafner. Later, at the beginning of Act 2 of *Götterdämmerung*, Alberich will turn up, following Siegfried, at the Gibichung court by the river Rhine, where his son Hagen is, he hopes, his means to recover the Ring. In one of the most eerie scenes in *Der Ring des Nibelungen* Alberich appears at the ear of the sleeping Hagen to urge him on to take the Ring. The dwarf has become a creature of the shadows, hardly detected, who creeps closer in times of darkness to mutter about his only obsession, the Ring. The parallels with Gollum are obvious but the Wagnerian linkage between Alberich and Wotan brings out a surprising possibility in *The Lord of the Rings*: that the Wotan-like Gandalf is secretly linked to the Alberich-like Gollum.

At first this looks absurd. It is usual to think of Gandalf and Gollum as having next to nothing in common and as polar opposites, if not actually enemies. One might, however, have said the same about Wotan and Alberich had Wagner not built a connection into his text by calling Wotan 'Licht-Alberich'. Tolkien

Chapter Six: Gandalf and Wotan   135

does not of course use such a play on names to connect Gandalf and Gollum (although turning the wizard into Gandalf the White might be seen as a parallel to Wagner's use of light to symbolise Wotan), but there are features of Gandalf that can be paralleled with Gollum. They are both, for instance, searchers for the Ring, Gollum for the actual Ring, Gandalf more for its significance, in his research of its history and its meaning. Gandalf famously rejects the Ring when Frodo offers it to him but that does not mean he turns away from it entirely, or indeed very much. Though we might not call him obsessed by it, he is nevertheless always concerned by it, frequently thinks about it and shapes his life, and that of others, around it, to the extent that it is surely true to say his life becomes dominated by it, like Gollum's (and, by a different Ring, Wotan's and Alberich's). To that extent, then, Gandalf too is transformed by the Ring.

Gandalf's most obvious transformation, however, is that from grey to white after his fight with the balrog in Moria. This is only indirectly a consequence of the Ring but it nevertheless shows a strong parallel with Gollum's experience. He too undergoes a transformation at the roots of a mountain, deep underground away from the light, as a result of which he becomes a pale, death-like thing. Gollum's transformation takes longer and so is not so easy to see as a death-and-rebirth like Gandalf's, but in fact it is more like a death, not less. The old Smeagol expires and Gollum takes his place. But Gollum also takes Gandalf's place after he falls in Moria. Gollum reappears in the story as the Fellowship begin their journey through the dwarf mines, though at first only Frodo notices this. He disappears from sight at the climax of the episode but somehow escapes from the orcs in Moria and begins stalking the rest of the party. When they leave Lothlórien by boat to travel down the river Gollum follows, clinging to a drifting log. He has become the unacknowledged replacement for Gandalf and inevitably when the Fellowship breaks up and Frodo and Sam, with the Ring, set off in a different direction from the others, Gollum follows them. Soon he becomes part of this group, distrusted but essential as a guide on the journey to Mordor, in effect the role that Gandalf had played in the first stage of the journey of the Fellowship from Rivendell to Moria. In another example of doubling in *The Lord of the Rings*, Gandalf's role as guide from one elf-haven, Rivendell, to a passage underground, in Moria, and an encounter with a monster, the balrog, is reflected by Gollum as guide on a journey from another elf-haven, Lothlórien, to another underground passage and a meeting with a monster, Shelob the spider, at which point Gollum, like Gandalf in Moria, disappears, although he, again like Gandalf, will return. Gollum as guide is of course much riskier than Gandalf, but then it would hardly suit the story if he was reassuringly competent. From a literary point of view Gollum acts as a device to keep everybody, hobbit and reader alike, nervous and gloomily aware that things are likely to go wrong, and even if they go right that only means something terrible when the Ring meets its destruction. Gandalf himself could not have protected us from the horror of the marshes, Shelob, the orcs and the plains of Mordor, and certainly not those of Mount Doom. Indeed, Gandalf is responsible for these, since he is the one who sends Frodo with the Ring to destroy it. Gollum the accursed guide takes on the burden of the cursed journey Gandalf ordained, and should have led himself. Gollum as Gandalf's substitute leads us back to Alberich and Wotan and the thought that the former is the latter's substitute not at the end so much as at the beginning of *Der Ring des Nibelungen*.

Alberich steals the gold to make the Ring and to do that he has to curse himself by forswearing love, but to possess the Ring after him such a self-abnegation is not needed. The price has been paid by Alberich once for all. He tries to exact his own price on those who exploit his sacrifice by cursing the Ring himself and vowing that none who own it will come to any good, but this is clearly spite for his loss, like Gollum's curses on Bilbo and Frodo for taking his 'precious'. Both Alberich's and Gollum's curses take their power from our sense that they have paid a terrible price for owning the Rings, a price that others seek to avoid. The Rings, then, represent a sort of moral and emotional calculus. To own them must cost something. You can have nothing for nothing. Alberich knew this when he chose the gold before personal happiness. Gollum knows it because he preferred the Ring to his friend Deagol, and then to his whole way of life, and having lost the Ring he knows he has lost the only thing he valued instead of his normal world before he found it (or rather Deagol did, from whom he took it). Wotan nearly makes the same mistake, refusing to give up the Ring to rescue Freia from the giants until Erda makes him see sense. Even so, he then tries to find a way to get the Ring after all, until he comes to realise that the desire for the Ring is alone enough to end the world he knows. Gandalf is wiser and avoids the Ring's temptation, unlike Saruman, who takes to its damned conclusion the path Wotan so nearly trod. But avoiding the curse of the Ring does not end it and someone has to take it to its destruction. That someone in *The Lord of the Rings* is Gandalf's substitute Gollum.

These developed parallels between pairs of key characters in *Der Ring des Nibelungen* and *The Lord of the Rings* justify an attempt to explain the meaning of the latter in parallel with that of the former. That is the subject of the next chapter.

CHAPTER SEVEN

The Ring and *Der Ring*

A consideration of Wagner's influence on Tolkien should not stop at listing similarities and exploring patterns of resemblance. It should also extend to using the explanations of *Der Ring des Nibelungen* as starting-points for trying to interpret *The Lord of the Rings* and explain its success and appeal to readers. This will have the advantage of allowing the reading of *The Lord of the Rings* to break out of the rather confined areas it has largely occupied hitherto, areas defined by Tolkien himself and his biographers and their implicit judgement that Tolkien's fiction is unique and so unattached to other literature. That *The Lord of the Rings* is not divorced from other literary and artistic works should not seem unusual, nor should it be seen as an adverse criticism of it or an attempt to show that it is derivative, or second rate, or unoriginal.

The thoughts about the meaning of *The Lord of the Rings* that this book will attempt to explain have been heavily influenced by one book on Wagner in particular, *Finding an Ending: Reflections on Wagner's 'Ring'*, by Philip Kitcher and Richard Schacht, published by Oxford University Press in 2004. Indeed, it was reading this book that first crystallised my conviction that Tolkien's *The Lord of the Rings* shares much of the meaning of *Der Ring des Nibelungen* and must have been influenced by it, despite what Tolkien said to deny this, and that began the process of investigating Tolkien's knowledge of Wagner and of comparing *Der Ring des Nibelungen* and *The Lord of the Rings*. Anyone who has read this far in the present work and who knows Kitcher and Schacht's book *Finding an Ending* may already have guessed that their work is an influence on this, if only because of the references to Wotan and Gandalf as characters of authority, ones who take decisions and direct the action of the plot. The concept of character authority and how it shapes narrative and its effect on the reader or spectator is a prominent part of Kitcher and Schacht's discussion of *Der Ring des Nibelungen*. It is not however the real point of their interpretation but only a technical device used in constructing it.

Kitcher and Schacht are professors of philosophy and, although they do not regard Wagner himself as a philosopher, they do think *Der Ring des Nibelungen* has a serious philosophical subject. Their book tries to defend this position by explaining what that philosophical subject is. My contention is that this subject has a great deal in common with what *The Lord of the Rings* is about. It is perhaps worth mentioning that, although Kitcher and Schacht do refer to Tolkien in their book, not without approval, they do not discuss *The Lord of the Rings* as such. In the course of their brief remarks on it imply that they do not find it of as much interest to them as *Der Ring des Nibelungen*, which they describe as a different kind of work, one with which it is misleading to compare *The Lord of the Rings*. Before attempting to explain how the two works are in fact more closely related in their fundamental significance, however, it is first necessary to try to outline what Kitcher and Schacht have to say about Wagner's *Der Ring des Nibelungen*.

They begin with this question, which, with the substitution of Tolkien's name for Wagner's, and one or two other slight adjustments, might be asked of *The Lord of the Rings* as well as *Der Ring des Nibelungen*:

> Why should people, many of whom profess a thoroughly demystified view of the world, ruminate – and even argue passionately – about the exploits of gods, dwarves, giants, and dragons, or about the magic powers of gold, potions, and headgear? What justifies the claim that Wagner was a great dramatist, and that his elaborate myth, concocted from a variety of sources, deserves the serious attention of mature and thoughtful adults? (page 2)

Their answer begins with the bigger questions, that they regard as philosophical, of the meaning of human life. This is an issue going all the way back to Socrates but it becomes more acute, perhaps, after the Enlightenment in the eighteenth century when the range of answers to it becomes freer. Kitcher and Schacht suggest there are three sorts of answers to this philosophical question: 'one that sees a source of meaning in an order that is independent of human beings; another that rejects the question entirely, and seeks to deflate it and rid us of the desire to ask it and the craving for an answer to it; and a third that takes the question seriously, but contends that any answer to it must recognise the source of meaning to be in ourselves' (page 50). The first of these is of course the approach of major religions like Christianity, but Kitcher and Schacht take that approach 'to be unpromising at best' (page 54). They think 'the adult Wagner had many reasons for rejecting the idea that lives obtain their meaning through their relation to the divine will' (page 53). For them, the problem with that approach is that humans cannot discover 'how the route to bliss is blocked or delayed, how the ultimate bliss compensates for the tribulation along the way, how denying that bliss to some (if indeed some are denied) accords with the demands of justice (and love)', and they add that '[i]f what we do makes no difference, then our earthly life becomes pointless, an irrelevant prelude to something more glorious which is, inexplicably, postponed for us' (pages 52f). Such a philosophical dismissal of religion flies in the face of the assumption that because Tolkien was himself what is called a devout Christian *The Lord of the Rings* must be a fundamentally religious work, upholding the concept of a divine justification for human lives, and so it might be said straight away that Kitcher and Schacht and their ideas about Wagner cannot apply to *The Lord of the Rings*. But, to make a simple point at this stage, that work is notable for the virtual absence of the divine or of formal awareness amongst its characters of 'a source of meaning in an order that is independent of human beings' (whether we confine 'human' here to a strict meaning or include various of Tolkien's other fictional races, such as hobbits or elves, as well as men). Whatever Tolkien said about it afterwards, *The Lord of the Rings* as published reads well enough without the need for attaching to it 'a source of meaning in an order that is independent of human beings', and many readers accept it as such. In fact, Kitcher and Schacht, in their description of the problem of believing in a justification of life in terms of a non-human, other-worldly purpose, actually point to a fundamental issue in *The Lord of the Rings* for the characters if not for the author, and his Christian apologists, in that the question of the meaning of life in Middle-earth is presented without reference to anything beyond Middle-earth.

The second approach Kitcher and Schacht mention is presented by them as a kind of reaction to the acceptance of the impossibility of resolving the questions, such as 'how the route to bliss is blocked or delayed, how the ultimate bliss compensates for the tribulation along the way', that the first approach raises, to its detriment. 'The idea that such questions are not worth asking and that they are wrongly posed or pompously empty,' they write, 'is often accompanied by a celebration of the ordinary' (page 53). They cite two literary examples,

Shakespeare's Falstaff and James Joyce's last two novels, *Ulysses* and *Finnegans Wake*, where '[a]ll of the sides of life, grand or respectable, mundane or shameless, are to be accepted for what they are' (page 54). Kitcher and Schacht say that 'as far as we know [... Wagner] never seriously entertained our second way of dealing with questions about the meaningfulness of human life' (page 53) and one might be tempted to say the same of Tolkien, were it not for his hobbits. One would have to admit, though, that in *The Lord of the Rings*, as well as in *The Hobbit*, the unreflecting, cosy world of the Shire is shown to be limited and inadequate, as those hobbits who leave it discover. The episode of the Scouring of the Shire at the end of *The Lord of the Rings* functions surely as a rebuke to the hobbits' refusal to see the meaning of life in anything more than food, drink and family parties. Again, as with their formulation of their first approach to the meaning of life, Kitcher and Schacht, in what little they say about their second approach, offer an insight into Tolkien's work.

Their third approach, however, is the most important because it leads into their deeper discussion of the meaning of *Der Ring des Nibelungen*. 'Wagner', they write, '*starts* from the view that there are more and less significant ways of living a human life, taking seriously the question of what grounds or engenders significance' (page 56), and the same must surely be said of Tolkien. In very general terms this is why *Der Ring des Nibelungen* and *The Lord of the Rings* deserve 'the serious attention of mature and thoughtful adults', to echo Kitcher and Schacht (page 2). There is however a formidable obstacle to the notion that a human life dedicated to seriousness and significance can be worthwhile and that is that all life is finite and the achievements of any one person can only be transitory, and may well be incomplete. In other words, Kitcher and Schacht confront the problem of death. Their answer is of considerable interest, in relation to Tolkien and his works as well as to Wagner and his. They admit that the brief and temporary nature of human achievements *sub specie aeternitatis* (and they refer explicitly to 'a time when humanity is no more' on page 58) may induce despair and 'a passionate resolve to abnegate all willing (Schopenhauer's recommendation) or a bitter nihilism' (pages 58f), but they respond with a challenging question: 'Why should we suppose that the appropriate perspective from which to render judgment [on human achievement] is that of the timeless

Chapter Seven: The Ring and *Der Ring*　　　　　　　　　　　　　　　　　　143

observer of the whole universe?' (page 59). Nevertheless, they have to concede that the achievements of mortal beings will usually be partial or incomplete:

> Human attempts at knowledge [...] are inevitably limited, partial, and distorted. Justice is ever only imperfect. Comfort and aid can only be given in inadequate measures. And human love is flawed and vulnerable to corruption and erosion. Thus, one might suppose, genuine values though these may be, human efforts to realize them are doomed to fail, falling so far short as to be exercises in futility. (page 59)

They respond to this by pointing out that '[i]mplicit in the considerations about the partial character of our efforts is the idea that we achieve nothing if we are not completely successful', and they add that 'there is no good reason to think in such "all or nothing" terms' (page 60). They conclude that 'we can regard exemplary lives as meaningful in terms of their imperfect realization of the values of knowledge, compassion, justice, and love' (page 60). Failure is not the last word, which is just as well, since it is far more likely than success in human endeavour.

Kitcher and Schacht of course are arguing towards an evaluation of the actions of the main characters in Wagner's *Der Ring des Nibelungen*, among them Wotan, Brünnhilde and Siegfried, all of whom in an obvious sense fail. *Der Ring des Nibelungen* notoriously ends with what its last opera calls 'Götterdämmerung', which however it is translated into English is taken to mean the defeat of the gods and their passing into nothingness, and Siegfried and Brünnhilde both suffer death at the same time. Kitcher and Schacht are dealing with the philosophical problem of tragedy: why are audiences more concerned and even uplifted by tales of defeat and death than those of easy success? *The Lord of the Rings* is not a tragedy in the accepted sense of that term, although it might be said to have tragic elements. It does not however avoid the issue of human failure (using 'human' here again in a broad sense). Although it reaches a climax with the destruction of the Ring and the return of the king of Gondor, these are not unalloyed triumphs. Frodo, for example, fails in the quest to destroy the Ring, for at the last moment he changes his mind. The Ring is destroyed because Gollum seizes it from Frodo and in so doing overbalances and falls with it into the volcanic fire. What Kitcher and Schacht say about the partial nature of achievement and how that relates to the judgment of whether a life was meaningful or not has, then, a bearing on *The Lord of the Rings* as much as on *Der Ring des Nibelungen*.

Kitcher and Schacht sum up their discussion of how life can be meaningful by setting out the steps of their argument in this way:

- The question of whether and how human life may be endowed with significance is of the utmost importance and deserves to be taken seriously.
- That question need not – and perhaps cannot plausibly – be answered by reference to the purposes of some external agency (e.g., a divine creator).
- The answer is also not dictated by the plausibility of the idea of the perfect attainment and unending perpetuation of the realization of values transcending those of merely natural existence, either in this life and world or beyond them.
- If there is a positive answer, it may – and perhaps even must – be given instead in terms of the possibility of the realization of such values in more limited, imperfect, and transient ways, in this life and world.
- Exceptional significance attaches to efforts that not only realize such values in finitely attainable ways in one's own life but moreover contribute to the possibility of their realization in the lives of others as well.
- What matters most, however, is contributing to and participating in the transfiguration of merely natural and commonplace existence, in ways revealing and expressing its capacity to be endowed with and enriched by such values.
- This conceivably might be done by instituting and maintaining conditions conducive to their concrete realization and perpetuation on a broad scale; but that is difficult at best in the short term, and impossible in the long run.
- This also – and ultimately more importantly – can be done even in failure and defeat, if a transient and imperfect realization of important values finds an ending that preserves and even enhances its significance, and so is vindicating despite all. (pages 61f)

This, they claim, is the philosophical position of *Der Ring des Nibelungen*. They can then explain what they think the main characters in the work are trying to do and why their actions are meaningful even although they do not succeed. 'Striving to achieve something ultimately unattainable,' they write, ' can make sense only if it does not issue in *blank defeat* – in a state of affairs essentially no different from the starting point, or in a conclusion that negates the value that was sought' (page 63). As with much else they say, this statement, I want to maintain, also applies to *The Lord of the Rings* and in its implications lies the deeper meaning of that work, and of its wide appeal to readers.

It is not just Kitcher and Schacht's theory of what *Der Ring des Nibelungen* means that is useful in understanding *The Lord of the Rings*, however. Because of the parallels between situations and characters in the works that we have already

Chapter Seven: The Ring and *Der Ring*

observed, the interpretation of Wagner's *Der Ring des Nibelungen* by Kitcher and Schacht throws much light on *The Lord of the Rings*, and so it is worth outlining their reading of Wagner to see how it relates to a similar reading of Tolkien. Although they do not set it out in any sort of table or list, Kitcher and Schacht essentially reconstruct the events of *Der Ring des Nibelungen* in a full chronological and causal order, from the beginning of the world to its end, or the end of the world of the gods. The scope of Wagner's mythology therefore bears comparison with that of Tolkien's and for much the same reasons and philosophical purpose.

Der Ring des Nibelungen begins with a single low note, from which other harmonising notes arise until one by one the elements of the orchestra are drawn into a swelling, swirling outpouring of sound that becomes the image of the river Rhine in which the Rhinemaidens swim, guarding their gold. The sense is of a simple, primitive world coming into being out of nothing, represented in the opera house by the silence and darkness from where the music emerges, to be followed by (in most productions) some onstage light effects and then the physical appearance and (if Wagner's stage directions are at all observed) movement of the Rhinemaidens, who at first sing meaningless echoes of the orchestral music before enunciating some simple and self-regarding verses. The beginning of *Das Rheingold* is therefore very much like the beginning of the world, but actually this is only a representation. In fact much must have happened in this world already before the music starts, as we shall gather when the story gets under way. Still, the impression that the story starts at the very beginning of things is appropriate and significant, and Wagner's way of making us know this, and feel this, without confusing us with too many thoughts and words about it, is also appropriate. Later in *Der Ring des Nibelungen* he will provide us with hints and ideas about the world's beginning that are the basis for the action of the drama.

The chief sources of information about the beginnings of the world in *Der Ring des Nibelungen* are the Norns in the prelude to its last section, *Götterdämmerung*, though there are fragments of information earlier. In the beginning the world was a simpler and more primitive place, both elemental and organic. The Rhine is a good representation of the first, and the second is symbolised by the World Ash Tree, Yggdrasil, with its roots in the earth and its boughs in the heavens, and potent waters flowing from beneath it. The Rhinemaidens, with their insouciance and grace, belong to this virgin world, but they are not alone in it. There are two opposed but subtly linked forces that will change this world and in the end between them drive it to destruction. The one we meet first in the opera is Alberich the dwarf. He it is who, on seeing the Rhinegold and learning from the unsuspicious and careless Rhinemaidens that it can only be taken and forged into a Ring of Power by somebody who renounces love, promptly renounces love, steals the gold and makes the Ring. It is not hard, then, to see Alberich as an intrusion into this world of selfishness, self-regard and difference from others and their needs, together with a desire for power of a self-centred kind. This is not to say that the Rhinemaidens are not also in their own way self-centred and unwilling to see anything but their own point of view, as their taunting of the ugly Alberich and their failure to anticipate what he might do to their gold suggests, but in the end the Rhinemaidens' self-absorption is limited and static whereas Alberich's is not. Unlike them, he is out to change the world, for his own ends.

There is however another force for change – Wotan. Throughout *Der Ring des Nibelungen* Alberich is linked with Wotan as both his main rival and as a dark opposite, most notably in the first act of *Siegfried*, in Wotan's riddle contest with Alberich's brother Mime. There Wotan actually calls himself 'Licht-Alberich', or 'light-Alberich', having already referred to the dwarf himself as 'Schwarz-Alberich', or 'black-Alberich'. The connection between them is not just a matter of name-calling. Like Alberich, Wotan also introduced change into the primal world. His early story is told in a fragmentary way in *Der Ring des Nibelungen*, by himself and by the Norns, and by implication elsewhere, but he like Alberich turned away from love (although not entirely) in search of power and came to the World Ash Tree Yggdrasil where, in return for the sacrifice of one of his eyes, he was allowed to drink from the magic waters under the tree and so gain wisdom about the world. This knowledge gives him the power to change the world. As a symbol of this he tore a stem from the tree and made it into a spear. Like Alberich, with the theft of the Rheingold, Wotan gains power by violation, and according to the Norns the injury he does to the Ash Tree eventually leads to its death and the end of its world, and along with it the gods themselves.

Chapter Seven: The Ring and *Der Ring* 147

Wotan's violation of Yggdrasil differs from Alberich's theft of the gold in its motive. Alberich wants power for himself, whereas Wotan wants it to bring about improvement in life. His spear becomes more than just a symbol of a new order in the world because on its shaft will be carved runes recording treaties and contracts, the promises made by Wotan and extracted by him from others that he intends shall settle disputes and bring harmony and peace. Wotan, in other words, is attempting to answer the challenge Kitcher and Schacht see as the fundamental philosophical question in *Der Ring des Nibelungen*, the question of 'whether and how human life may be endowed with significance' (page 61). For himself, Wotan's answer is that he will strive to bring order and government to the world, and within that intention is his answer for others, that they too should set aside differences and forego opportunistic gain for the sake of a higher level of order out of which a better life for everyone can emerge. To realise this ideal Wotan is prepared to do two rather unattractive things. First, he is prepared to see the end of the seemingly innocent, unprogressive kind of existence that is represented by the Rhinemaidens, swimming and singing all day long in the Rhine. Perhaps he sees in them a lack of purpose that provides no answer to the question of how life can be made significant. Secondly, Wotan is prepared, as his violation of the World Ash Tree shows, to take dangerous steps to achieve his aims, steps that include violence, double-dealing and anything he can get away with. This is not very uplifting, however necessary it may be to get things done, and it leaves Wotan open to the accusation, from Alberich himself, that the god is no better than the dwarf. That Wotan *is* better, however, is shown by his motives, his basic concern to take others into account and his capacity for reconsidering his actions and revising his plans. Wotan may be flawed but Alberich indicates that there is no better alternative, and now that there is an Alberich with a Ring in existence Wotan's rule of law, however rough his justice, looks necessary.

There are problems with his justice, though, as the contract with the Giants to build Valhalla shows. Valhalla itself is a questionable project. Wotan has decided he needs a citadel from which to exercise his power and a place to defend himself and the other gods. The implication is that the law-and-order project is not without some resistance (Alberich represents this, too) and Wotan is having to escalate the level of force he requires for it. This, however, is beyond his own resources and he has had to engage the services of those emblems of raw physical power, the giants Fasolt and Fafner, but to achieve this he has had to offer them a reward that he cannot afford to give them, the goddess of youth and beauty Freia. To renounce her would in effect be to join Alberich in foreswearing love. Wotan has in fact no intention of honouring this bargain with the giants and, though he knows he cannot break it, since to do so would negate his whole project, he means to get out of the contract by persuading the giants to accept a substitute for Freia. What that substitute might be Wotan cannot say, but he hopes the clever god of fire Loge will discover something in time.

Loge does find a substitute – Alberich's gold. Wotan persuades himself that, since Alberich stole the gold, it is all right for him to take it from the dwarf. Loge persists in reminding Wotan that the gold ought to be returned to the Rhinemaidens but Wotan's need for it as a substitute for Freia as payment to the giants is too great. Fasolt and Fafner are convinced and accept Alberich's gold, but insist on all of it, including the Nibelung's Ring, which Wotan is forced to give up. At first, he is most reluctant to do so, realising that to let such a powerful object out of his hands risks disaster for all he has been trying to do. On the other side, though, is the inevitable decline and disappearance of the gods without the presence of Freia among them, since it is her magic apples that keep them young and vigorous. The other gods clamour for Wotan to yield the Ring, but he only does so after the intrusion of Erda, a strange elemental being who rises up out of the ground to warn Wotan that he must give up the Ring.

Kitcher and Schacht pay a great deal of attention to Erda and what she says to persuade Wotan to yield the Ring. She seems to represent some sort of primordial force that antecedes Wotan, Alberich and the others, although probably not the Rhinemaidens, but unlike the latter she has some instinct for how the world changes and where those changes might lead. Her presence in *Der Ring des Nibelungen* is the most obvious sign that Wotan himself is not an ultimate force and that there are powers beyond or even above him to which he must respond. Conversely, the vagueness and the static quality of Erda contrast with the activity and decisiveness of Wotan. This is strongly conveyed in the dreamy, shifting music associated with Erda, in contrast with the vigorous and often clear-cut music associated with Wotan, notably the *leitmotif* usually identified with his spear, a stentorian descending scale often blared out by the trombones in the orchestra. Erda seems sleepy and passive where Wotan is wide-awake and active. If he is in some sense contained within her overall view of things, he is like the energetic articulation of her half-formed ideas. To call Erda's ideas half-formed is however to misunderstand them. The fulcrum of Kitcher and Schacht's interpretation of *Der Ring des Nibelungen* is provided by taking Erda's warning to Wotan in *Das Rheingold* quite literally. She seems to speak so generally, and her music so creates a feeling of mistiness and mystery, that it is tempting to see her as that conventional dramatic device, the fortune-teller who gives the audience enough suggestions in a general way of what is going to happen without ever being specific enough either to be wrong or to give the details of the plot away (Tolkien flirts with this device in the Mirror of Galadriel episode in *The Lord of the Rings* but, like Erda, the Mirror is not quite as cloudy as it may seem). In most accounts of the plot of *Das Rheingold* synopsis writers are content to describe Erda's effect on the immediate situation, the question of whether Wotan should give up the Ring to the giants, and the impression is left that her warning to Wotan is that if he does not give up the Ring the end will come of both himself and the other gods. The point Kitcher and Schacht make is that she means much more than this:

> She is not saying that the ending of the gods will come if Wotan keeps the Ring (and thereby hinting that the ending could be averted if he gives it up). She leaves no doubt about it: 'All that is, ends' – and the gods are no exception [...] the point is not that he [Wotan] has a way out if he is clever or resourceful enough to take it. Rather, it is that there are *endings and endings*. Erda is reminding Wotan of something he knows, if not fully explicitly: he, too, must pass. The task for him, in view of the inescapability of his approaching ending, is to find *the right kind* of ending – and retaining the Ring would preclude that. (page 46)

'Alles was ist, endet,' says Erda, and Wotan, like everyone, must consider how he will meet his end. This, say Kitcher and Schacht, is why Wotan is so struck by Erda's words that he immediately decides he must seek her out to discover more from her, why he so soon after her intervention begins working on new plans and why, in their view, the grandiose 'Entry of the Gods into Valhalla', the scene that follows Erda's appearance and concludes the opera, is undercut by Loge, so that, though it may provide a very loud ending to *Das Rheingold*, it is far from the end of *Der Ring des Nibelungen*.

Erda's intervention, in other words, lifts Wotan's project up to another level. No longer can it be just a matter of his imposing his notion of law and order on the world, for it must now also take account of the fact that whatever he achieves he himself will not exist long enough to sustain it for ever, and indeed he may not exist for long enough to put it in place in any really finished state. If what he makes will not outlast him, it is difficult to see anything meaningful in it at all. On the other hand, if, to be meaningful, what he has to make has to be complete, he is likely to be facing the impossible, and his difficulties with the giants, and Alberich, and the Ring, suggest that he will never complete the system he has been so long working for. But some sort of system is better than none, and so some sort of meaningful contribution is possible, but what that may be needs consideration, and that consideration has to take account of how things will be left at Wotan's ending, so that he, or those who come after, can look back and see some significance in what he has done, even if it is incomplete, or in some respects a failure. The rest of *Der Ring des Nibelungen*, say Kitcher and Schacht, consists of Wotan's efforts to find a new way of shaping events that will lead to a meaningful ending, an ending that will leave the world better than it was before and will not introduce new calamities to it.

After this long account of the fundamental meaning of the first part of Wagner's *Der Ring des Nibelungen*, let us now go back to Tolkien's *The Lord of the Rings* to see how it follows a similar path. To do so requires moving back before the beginning of that work, and even before *The Hobbit*, to the outline of Tolkien's legendarium of which *The Silmarillion* contains a representative sample. As with *Der Ring des Nibelungen*, we must begin at the beginning, with the creation of the world. It is perhaps only coincidence that Tolkien's world begins, like Wagner's, with music. *The Silmarillion* contains the most accessible version of Tolkien's musical creation myth in its first section *Ainulindalë*, subtitled 'The Music of the Ainur'. The one god Eru, known in Middle-earth as Ilúvatar, having created a set of demi-gods, the Ainur, communicates with them in music, suggesting themes for them to sing, at first solo, then together in harmony, until they produce what Ilúvatar calls the Great Music together. But one of the Ainur, Melkor, insists on introducing into the music themes of his own that clash with the music generated by the others from the basic themes of Ilúvatar's creating. After two attempts by Ilúvatar to overcome the discord introduced by

Melkor, he brings the music to an end 'in one chord, deeper than the Abyss, higher than the Firmament, piercing as the light of the eye of Ilúvatar' (page 17). Then Ilúvatar takes the Ainur and shows them that on the pattern of their music, including the discords of Melkor, he has created in the Void a new world that is an embodiment in time and space of their singing.

Christopher Tolkien dates the earliest versions of this creation myth to a period shortly after the First World War, long before Tolkien met C S Lewis. There is no evidence that Tolkien had heard, or heard of, the opening of *Das Rheingold* before this time, although it is not inconceivable. There are however no compelling similarities between Wagner's music and the music Tolkien describes in *Ainulindalë*. He likens the voices of the Ainur not to a nineteenth-century orchestra but to 'harps and lutes, and pipes and trumpets, and viols and organs, and [...] countless choirs singing with words' (page 15), a list that owes more to the Bible than to any concert platform of his time. The language Tolkien uses of the music seems equally detached from musical practice, lacking technical terms and consisting mainly of conventional epithets such as 'power', 'beauty', 'rippling' and 'loud'. When the discords of Melkor are introduced they turn the music into 'a raging storm' (page 16), and Melkor's theme at its height is described as having 'little harmony, but rather a clamorous unison as of many trumpets braying upon a few notes' (page 17). The words 'harmony', 'unison' and 'notes' are almost the most technical Tolkien uses in the passage. It does not seem that he is much interested in the music of the Ainur as music but more in an idea of music as a representation of creation. Comment on the *Ainulindalë* tends to refer to such traditional ideas as the music of the spheres rather than to any interest of Tolkien's in music or its performance. Tolkien liked music and attending concerts but he did not play an instrument and, although he enjoyed making up songs, he never seems to have sung in a choir. His wife was a pianist, and his father's father had run a music publishing company in the mid-nineteenth century, tantalising information for anyone seeking a connection between Tolkien and Wagner, but Tolkien's father died when he was very young and his mother became estranged from her husband's family so that her son never knew a connection with what one guesses must have been a musical circle.

Nevertheless, the significant point is not Tolkien's musicality but that his creation myth, like the opening of *Das Rheingold*, involves a process of evolving harmony into which discord is introduced. The beginning of Tolkien's world, like Wagner's, is melodious and beautiful but into it there intrudes a different, harsher set of sounds, just like those of Alberich when he breaks in on the Rhinemaidens, and out of this discord the history of Middle-earth develops. For both Wagner and Tolkien, one assumes, the pattern of harmony disrupted by discord derives from the Old Testament creation stories and the corruption of the Garden of Eden by Satan. Tolkien probably cast his creation myth in musical terms both to differentiate it from the Biblical version and to avoid the accusation that he was trivialising Holy Scripture (whether the disguise is adequate for this purpose, or whether a believer in Holy Scripture should be involved in writing a rival version at all, is another matter).

Tolkien's use of a musical metaphor for his creation myth, if we take into consideration Wagner's embodiment of the same, endows that myth with certain qualities. The most significant is its concept of the relation of creation to time. Ilúvatar begins the music and it is taken up by the Ainur who, in musical parlance, develop it so that it grows more complex and varied. All this takes time. This is not creation as fiat, with worlds and beings and all coming into existence when called upon. The idea of a musical creation puts emphasis on the creation of processes, not entities. When he gets into his narration of the mythological history of Middle-earth Tolkien will recount the stories of the making of the sun, the moon and the stars, of the various intelligent races and of their homelands, but he does not describe these being called into existence in the way that Genesis does. However unmodern he may think of himself as a writer, Tolkien is sufficiently of his time as a twentieth-century narrative artist to adopt the conventional modern prose narrative pattern of an account of events that succeed each other in time in a reasoned order and for the most part as a chain of cause and effect. The musical metaphor, with its implications of a structure of melody and harmony in which one note leads to another, and chords progress and link together, usually heading towards closure, contributes fundamentally to the sense that Tolkien's is a universe ordered in time, just as Wagner's compositional technique in *Der Ring des Nibelungen* always implies movement in time towards an ending or endings that fulfil harmonic patterns

Chapter Seven: The Ring and *Der Ring* 153

and expectations. Music as a metaphor for creation contains not only an image of development through time but also the presentiment of an ending.

Finding an ending, to echo the title of the book on *Der Ring des Nibelungen* by Kitcher and Schacht, is as important an issue for Tolkien as it is for Wagner. It applies to the author but also to the characters within his legendarium, since they are all imagined as existing within the music-like movement of history that follows the score of the Ainur's singing. Basically, Kitcher and Schacht's question 'whether or how human life may be endowed with significance' is answerable in Tolkien's Middle-earth in terms of how far that life contributes to the onward movement of the divine music. In Middle-earth, then, the answer to the question is set as of the first type that Kitcher and Schacht consider, the one that 'sees a source of meaning in an order that is independent of human beings' (page 50), but unless you can convince yourself that Ilúvatar and his Ainur actually exist, or you insist on equating them with some other supernatural beings that you believe in, this source of meaning in Tolkien's world must remain fictional. That does not drain the legendarium of all significance, any more than it makes Wagner's *Der Ring des Nibelungen*, with its Norse gods, mere story-telling, because, as Kitcher and Schacht perhaps fail to make quite clear, a world in which the supernatural significance of human life is not regarded as available can still operate with the idea of significance they pay most attention to, that in which significance comes in this world and in relation to mortal beings. For secular reasons, then, Tolkien's work becomes what Kitcher and Schacht describe *Der Ring des Nibelungen* as being, that is a moving and serious attempt to discuss the question of how life is made meaningful, always acknowledging that life is short and time is against lasting achievement.

Wagner, even although for many people his works are seemingly interminable, does not have space or time in his chosen art-form to do more than exemplify the theme in a handful of instances. Kitcher and Schacht, indeed, focus very much on one of his characters, Wotan, although they do bring in the cases of Brünnhilde and Siegfried, though they are inclined to reject the latter's relevance to the problem. Tolkien, on the other hand, appropriated vast areas of space and time for his legendarium as a whole. Wagner's work takes about fifteen hours to perform, usually on four separate evenings, probably not long enough to read *The Lord of the Rings* alone, never mind the twelve volumes of *The History of Middle-earth*. Events in *Der Ring des Nibelungen* cover just over two human generations; Wotan fathers Siegmund and Sieglinde not long after the completion of Valhalla, the central event in *Das Rheingold*, and the death of their son Siegfried marks the end of the cycle. Tolkien's legendarium (not counting the pre-history) covers around seven thousand years and, even although the life-spans of the people he writes about are much longer than what is normal for human beings, and some indeed are immortal, nevertheless there are many, many generations of history leading down to the last events he records. One consequence of this is that taken as a whole Tolkien's legends of Middle-earth cannot help but raise the question of what the worth is of the life of one of the many individuals he names in it. Kings rise and fall, dynasties flourish and decay, great heroes flash like meteors against the obscurity, innumerable named and unnamed minor characters – wives, mothers, servants, soldiers, artificers – figure briefly in the narrative and then are seen no more. In addition, there are huge armies of elves, dwarves, orcs and men, and entire populations of vast territories, who are caught up in the centuries-long wars and migrations that ebb and flow through this history. Tolkien has no truck with modern ideas of history as seen from the point of view of the ordinary and the victims. The history of Middle-earth is told almost entirely in terms of leaders and aristocrats, mostly men. Not until he invents the hobbits, by accident, according to him, and incorporates them in *The Lord of the Rings*, does Tolkien offer a viewpoint on historical events that is lowly and unassuming. Even then he makes the point that despite their ordinariness hobbits can be as heroic as elves or dwarves or men, perhaps more so, and his focus is on named hobbits of exceptional qualities, usually regarded as eccentrics by their fellow hobbits. Both the way it is presented and the sheer mass of the legendarium, then, imply the question of how life is made significant. The heroes and leaders define what this significance might be, usually in terms of war and the struggle to defend themselves and their peoples from their enemies.

Inevitably, given the mass of material, there are repetitions in the legendarium. In fact, it seems obvious that Tolkien deliberately structured the history of Middle-earth as a recurrent sequence. The same kind of event happens several times, and the same outcomes are shown. The general pattern is one of creation followed by destruction, of order imposed only to be overturned by treachery or deceit, leading to a massive phase of disorder, that will eventually be stabilised, only for the cycle to begin again. This is evident in the account of the First Age of the world, when the Ainur, descending into the created world to act as its divine powers and as such known as the Valar, create two lamps to give light to it. The rebellious Melkor, the Satan figure of Tolkien's universe, destroys the lamps, bringing darkness back. The Valar replace them with two trees whose burgeoning brings light to Middle-earth, but again Melkor sneaks in and destroys the sources of illumination. Before he did so, the elf Fëanor managed to capture some of the light of the trees in three jewels, the silmarils. When the trees are killed, Fëanor is asked by the Valar to break up the silmarils to release the light they contain, but he refuses, not knowing that in fact the jewels have just been stolen by Melkor. Fëanor then swears a terrible oath, to which his sons also bind themselves, that he will pursue the thief and never rest until the silmarils are back in his possession. This oath dooms him and his kin, and the elves who follow them, to centuries of incessant war against Melkor, and anyone else, even another elf, who happens to possess a silmaril.

Now the cycle is acted out on a continental scale, with various smaller instances within the over-arching trajectory of the wars of the elves against Melkor, whom they rename Morgoth, meaning 'dark enemy', culminating in the Last or Great Battle, when the Valar themselves intervene, destroying Morgoth's fortress and with it most of Beleriand, a huge chunk of the land-mass of Middle-earth that sinks beneath the seas, taking many of the elves and their homelands with it. Thus ends the First Age. In the next Middle-earth sees the replacement of the elves by men, and the recovery of their enemies, not led now by Morgoth but by his chief servant Sauron. He dupes men into challenging the Valar themselves, and again there is a cataclysmic upheaval. The island on which the leading human civilisation has flourished, Númenor, is like Beleriand overwhelmed by the sea, with only a few of the inhabitants still faithful to the Valar escaping to the mainland. There they find themselves confronted in due time again by Sauron, now wielding his all-powerful Ring. Eventually, a last alliance of men and elves defeats Sauron, ending the Second Age. Isildur obtains the Ring, but instead of destroying it he takes it for himself, only to be slain by orcs when it slips off his finger and reveals him as he tries to escape an ambush. The Ring itself disappears, to be acquired much later by the person who turns into Gollum because of it. The end of the Second Age is not marked by the geographical upheaval that ends the First, nor by any similarly stupendous event, although the battle at Mount Doom when Sauron is defeated is on a huge scale and the casualties suffered by the elves in particular further hasten their decline and the process of their abandonment of Middle-earth for the Undying Lands, where they draw nearer to the Valar. The ending of the Second Age, then, conforms, though not so obviously, to the pattern of destructive endings that have featured in previous cycles of events in Tolkien's history and it continues an overall process of decline, what one set of authors has called 'the Lessening of the Ages' in Tolkien: 'it is perhaps apt to picture the history of Middle-earth, not as cyclical, but as a downward spiral. The same points are passed with ancient lessons unlearned, but then rediscovered, in a constant deterioration as the world grows older' (*The Guide to Middle-earth*, page 39). The effect is enormously pessimistic.

The same pessimism is apparent in the stories of individual heroes that are embedded in the historical framework. In the two most highly developed of these, the stories of Túrin, the slayer of the dragon Glaurung, and of Beren, who, with his betrothed Lúthien, recovers one of the silmarils from Morgoth, but at terrible cost, this pessimism is very evident. Both heroes, despite their victories, are accursed figures who cause as much trouble for themselves and their friends as to their enemies, and their successes are remarkable but marred by horrible side-effects. The story of Túrin the dragon-slayer is clearly a parallel to that of Siegfried but strikingly Túrin is if anything even less attractive as a human being than Siegfried in Wagner's version. He is as headstrong and dangerously violent in his youth as Siegfried and, living longer, then brings disaster on his adult friends and family, marrying his sister without knowing it and murdering his best friend. What both these stories raise is, again, the question of what constitutes a meaningful life. Neither Túrin nor Beren are content with a life of ordinariness and comfort, both are committed to achieving something significant, and both in fact succeed in that, but their success is so surrounded with drawbacks that their life-stories force the reader to ask what was gained. Neither, it should be added, is working for a higher power. They are not acting out of belief in the will of a divinity and if one wishes to see some divine purpose behind their stories one has to import that entirely into them

Chapter Seven: The Ring and *Der Ring*

from outside. Indeed, despite the superficial resemblance of *The Silmarillion* to the Old Testament, with its beginnings in a creation myth, its stories of patriarchal elves leading mass migrations of their peoples, its chronicling of the wars of their kings against the inhabitants of the lands they settle in and its tales of heroes and heroines against a background of court-life and a constant struggle to protect the elvish kingdoms against their hostile neighbours, all told in an archaicising language and style that echoes the Bible in English, despite all this, there is next to no moral or theological discourse. Nothing resembling a priestly class or a church develops in this world. The gods of it, the Valar, withdraw from it and are ignored thereafter. They are not invoked or offered prayers (the only prayers mentioned are from the Númenoreans to Morgoth, and they accompany human sacrifice). The lessening of the ages is also a long-drawn-out *Götterdämmerung*.

To this *The Hobbit* and *The Lord of the Rings* might seem like exceptions. Here the spiral of decline seems broken. Both end with triumph and the victory of good over evil. *The Hobbit* originally, of course, was not truly a part of the legendarium any more than Tolkien's other short tales, like *Farmer Giles of Ham*, and in a story for children an upbeat ending was only to be expected. Even so, most critics have noted a darkening of the story as it passes its mid-point and increasingly so at the end, with the destruction of Laketown and the death of Thorin after a battle that is no pushover. It is true that most of this violence is kept at arm's length by the narrative, mainly by keeping to Bilbo's point of view, that of an unwarlike, physically-challenged and nervous hobbit who is not even hardy enough to be a spectator of the final conflict. Then the story wraps up with Bilbo's return home, amid general predictions that the men of the lake, the dwarves of the mountain and the elves of the wood will settle down to a peaceful life now that the dragon is dead. Taking *The Hobbit* on its own, then, it would be unconvincing to argue that it conforms to the pessimism of *The Silmarillion*. Tolkien, however, did not take *The Hobbit* on its own and deliberately joined it up to *The Lord of the Rings*. Bilbo's success and the happy outcome of the Battle of Five Armies, become the first stage in the whole process of the ending of the Third Age and the defeat of Sauron, the Lord of the Rings.

The idea of the Lessening of the Ages and the downward spiral of the history of Middle-earth has a number of aspects, some more evident than others. If the series of events through which the spiral passes after the destruction of the Trees and the theft of the silmarils is set out – the destruction of Beleriand as the Valar defeat Morgoth, the destruction of the island of Númenor when the Valar repulse the Noldor, the defeat of Sauron when Isildur seizes the Ring and the defeat of Sauron when Frodo destroys it – what can be discerned is a general diminution in scale, from the obliteration of a continent, to that of an island, to a battle and a volcanic eruption to a somewhat smaller battle and a somewhat smaller eruption. The ending of *The Lord of the Rings* is not out of line with the rest of the sequence and instead confirms the movement to ever lesser geographical and other repercussions from the defeat of the Dark One. This is not contradicted by the manner of his defeat in *The Lord of the Rings*, not by a Vala or a hero but by a hobbit, and then almost accidentally. There is a scaling down of events as time goes on, a trajectory that can be projected forward to a time like the present when heroism, magic and the glamour of Tolkien's world have given place to a plainer reality. That is where the history of Middle-earth seems to be heading, and here is where it fundamentally resembles Wagner's *Der Ring des Nibelungen*.

Those with a superficial awareness of Wagner and his *Ring* cycle often assume that it exists to glorify the strong and powerful, that it is a hymn of praise to the Northern gods and a pæan to the Aryan superman. Nietzsche, as much as Hitler, is to blame for this. Nietzsche's enthusiasm for Wagner (which he later repudiated) and therefore Wagner's apparent association with Nietzsche's most easily grasped idea, that of the superman, have led to a lazy identificaton of the Nietzschean superman with Wagner's Siegfried. In fact any careful study of *Der Ring des Nibelungen* can hardly escape the recognition that it is almost exactly the opposite of Nietzschean, as Nietzsche himself came to realise. As the title of its final part says (the first part Wagner devised), the cycle is about the decline of the gods and, with them, of their superhero, Siegfried, who never fulfils the expectations people have of him. Wagner does ask us to lament the death of Siegfried, and treat the passing of Wotan and his Valhalla with some reverence, and even regret, but by the end of *Der Ring des Nibelungen* both

Chapter Seven: The Ring and *Der Ring*

the god and his heroes are clearly obsolete and can never return. Kitcher and Schacht reflect on this in the final pages of their book:

> All the *Ring*'s great figures are tragic, doomed by the very qualities that elevate them above the rest. The order of nature can indeed be disrupted; but its disruption more readily tends toward its corruption than it is amenable to a reordering perfection, even by the greatest powers and lofty intentions to transcend and transfigure it. Even a divinity that makes bold to improve on it suffers hubris, and must fail and fall. (page 200)

The reason, of course, is that 'Alles was ist, endet'. Typically, Wagner, once he had read Schopenhauer (largely after he had written the libretto of *Der Ring des Nibelungen*), was inclined to see nothing but the pessimism in his work, though the incompatibility of this with his own drive and ambition is glaring. Nevertheless, *Der Ring des Nibelungen* is not the bombastic celebration of power the caricature performances of 'The Ride of the Valkyries' lead people to think. In fact, it is often when it seems most bombastic that it is also most cutting. The ending of *Das Rheingold*, the passage known as 'The Entrance of the Gods into Valhalla', is, in its pomp and bravado, the forerunner of the grand finales of many symphonic movements, especially those by Wagner's admirer Anton Bruckner, and of many other loud musical acclamations in the concert hall and cinema, but in its dramatic context, as Kitcher and Schacht point out, it is undercut by the refusal of Loge, the sharp-witted and sharp-tongued god of fire, to join the procession and by the wailing of the Rhinemaidens for their stolen gold, which will be (and has already been) the source of all the disasters. At the other end of the cycle, the court of the Gibichungs, presided over by the weak-willed Gunther, his pallid sister Gutrune and their shifty half-brother Hagen, is an image of hollowness and moral infirmity, for all its rousing choruses and ritual occasions, notably Hagen's organisation of the swearing of blood-brotherhood between Gunther and Siegfried. Critics of *Götterdämmerung*, following Bernard Shaw, have called the work stagy and unconvincing, a relapse by Wagner into the mode of nineteenth-century grand opera at its most artificial and conventional, not apparently noticing that that is exactly what the world of Hagen, Gunther and Gutrune should be like. As such, it is a sample of the world of men that will follow the death of Siegfried and Brünnhilde and the fall of Valhalla. In this Wagner correctly anticipates the development of the story in his sources, where, after Siegfried's death, the survivors become embroiled in bloody and treacherous tribal wars that are fictionalised versions of the struggles between the Germanic nations and the Huns as the Roman Empire in the West disintegrates and what are called the Dark Ages descend on Europe.

Despite its apparently untragic ending this too is the atmosphere of *The Lord of the Rings*. It is the story of the ending of an age. Despite the activity of its heroes and their ostensible aim of saving Middle-earth, what they are really doing is changing it as much as Sauron would, not entirely in a different direction, in as much as the outcome is the installation of an autocracy. Whatever happens to the Ring, whether it is saved or destroyed, the world will never be the same again, though few of the characters seem to recognise this, at least at first. The hobbits largely retain their bouncy optimism by being unreflective about where events are taking them. In the character of the stoical and dutiful Sam this lack of speculation is made to seem a virtue, though by the end he may have gained more insight. His master Frodo certainly has, and it leaves him depressed and unfit for the new world he has had a considerable part in bringing to pass. Many of the purely human characters are little wiser than the hobbits. Boromir, cut off in his prime, never lives to see beyond his own nationalism. His brother Faramir has intuitions but in the end will quieten these in marriage to Éowyn and identification with the inward-looking Rohirrim. Aragorn perhaps is more aware of what is happening, possibly because of his connection through marriage to Arwen with the elves. Elrond and Galadriel certainly are aware of how the Third Age is coming to an end, and with it the presence of elves in Middle-earth. Elves are already leaving before Frodo sets out from the Shire and by the time the Ring has been destroyed, and with it the power of the rings that protect Rivendell and Lothlórien, there is no place for the elves left.

Above all, Gandalf knows that an era is ending, and this puts him in the same position as Wotan in *Der Ring des Nibelungen*. Both are faced with, to use Kitcher and Schacht's phrase, finding an ending. Gandalf in fact was sent, if we follow Tolkien's comments on the role of the Istari, into Middle-earth more or less with the purpose of bringing about the end of the Third Age, the end of the threat of Sauron and of the power of the Ring and the others it rules. Again, it might look like a rescue mission, a mission to organise a resistance movement and an opposition to Sauron, but if Gandalf is any sort of wise wizard he will have realised that the outcome of his mission cannot be limited to the excision of Sauron and his minions, leaving the rest of the world intact. Once he is removed all the other factions in Middle-earth will be shifted in their positions and interrelations, new alignments will follow and a wholly new set of goals and purposes will emerge. This is not just a matter of politics. It is also a matter of ethics. Sauron, like Morgoth before him, presents a direct, personal image of evil and a definite choice for the people of Middle-earth. When they are gone, evil does not disappear with them, but takes some other form. Tolkien demonstrates this earlier in his legend cycle by the transformation of Melkor into Morgoth, and, when this figure is defeated, by the rise of his follower Sauron, who in turn undergoes transformations of both appearance and reputation (that is, how he appears to others) in the course of his career of deceit and open strife against peace and the common good. Part of Sauron's effect is to corrupt others into thinking and behaving like him, like followers of Morgoth. Finding an ending, then, for Gandalf means not just getting rid of Sauron but getting rid of him in a way that does not make those who oppose him like Sauron himself. The idea of being infected by evil is associated directly with the Ring itself but this is really only a focus for a much broader ethical concern in *The Lord of the Rings*, the struggle to act to further a purpose without succumbing to the temptations of power as represented by Sauron. Gandalf memorably refuses to take the Ring from Frodo for just this reason, because he knows that with the power of the Ring he would be as uncontrollable and oppressive as Sauron:

> 'With that power I should have power too great and terrible. And over me the Ring would gain a power still greater and more deadly.' His eyes flashed and his face was lit as by a fire within. 'Do not tempt me! For I do not wish to become like the Dark Lord himself. Yet the way of the Ring to my heart is by pity, pity for weakness and the desire of strength to do good. Do not tempt me! I dare not take it, not even to keep it safe, unused. The wish to wield it would be too great, for my strength [...]' (page 61)

Galadriel too has the same insight as she refuses Frodo's offer of the Ring, and she adds what the consequence of this refusal for her will be – that she will fade and leave Middle-earth, having lost what residue of power and significance has been left to her. Gandalf does not say so but the same applies to him. Once the Ring is gone, he too must leave Middle-earth.

The question then is, as for Wotan, how Gandalf will live and what he will leave behind him, and like Wotan he is confronted by the dilemma that the more he strives, and the more openly he strives, for ends that directly suit his purposes, the less valid and lasting will be the result. Wotan discovers that he cannot groom a hero, Siegmund, to do what he wants but cannot do himself. As his wife Fricka makes plain to him in their dialogue in the second act of *Die Walküre*, Wotan cannot pretend that Siegmund is acting freely when he has supplied the hero with a special sword and ordered his valkyrie daughter to protect him in battle, amongst other things. In the end Wotan has to step aside and let a really independent-minded hero, Siegmund's son Siegfried, do what has to be done, even although the result is not exactly what Wotan would have wanted originally, because he cannot control the headstrong boy. Tolkien, in writing *The Lord of the Rings*, seems to have had this in mind. Gandalf too needs somebody to carry out the plan to prevent the Ring falling into the wrong hands. The situation is somewhat different from that in *Der Ring des Nibelungen* because the Ring is not part of a famous dragon's hoard but possessed by a more or less innocent third party, Bilbo, unknown to the powers of evil. This means that Gandalf already has the makings of the independent hero who will dispose of the Ring, though this is partly an accident of the writing and publishing of *The Hobbit*, in which the Siegmund-like chosen hero finds the Ring, which he later freely passes to his successor; Tolkien dispenses with Wagner's genetic relationships and, while making Frodo Bilbo's adopted son and heir, avoids any sort of linking of Gandalf, Bilbo and Frodo through sexual procreation. Tolkien has to work hard to give the reader a strong impression of Frodo as independent of Gandalf while also following his advice. The somewhat elaborate arrangements to keep Frodo and Gandalf apart in the first book of *The Fellowship of the Ring* are meant to leave Frodo room to take his own decisions while at the same time Gandalf as both authority figure and informed source of knowledge about the Ring is present enough to lay the groundwork for the plot and to give Frodo and the reader what they need to know. Tolkien would later offer explanations for Gandalf's absences from the Shire, and his non-appearance at Bree to meet the hobbits as they embark on their journey with the Ring, just as he would make a virtue out of having to have Strider stand in for Gandalf on the journey from Bree to Rivendell. Underlying that substitution is the gradual displacement of Gandalf by Aragorn as the story reaches its climax.

At Bree, though, Gandalf intervenes and directs Frodo by letter. Once more Tolkien tries to disguise this intervention, by surrounding it with the fuss about the letter's not having been delivered to Frodo in the Shire and hence its belatedness. In fact, that really makes no difference, except to increase suspense and add to the anxiety attendant on Frodo's delay in starting out. From here onwards Tolkien inserts into the story a sense of pressure to meet deadlines and a race against time to accomplish the quest. The desperation to get the Ring to Mount Doom means that the characters hardly stop to reflect on what will happen after that. The destruction of the Ring, once it is decided upon by the Council of Elrond at Rivendell, is easily presented as an end in itself, and the only ending the characters are thinking about. The discovery of Gandalf's letter to Frodo at Bree initiates this increase in tempo and thus overshadows the fact that by his letter Gandalf essentially tells Frodo what to do next. A further piece of overshadowing is what accompanies the letter, the cagey first encounter with Strider, and the decision of Frodo to be guided by the Ranger seems to the reader more momentous than the fact that what he will do is follow Gandalf's instructions for the Ring to go to Rivendell.

There Gandalf himself becomes a member of the Fellowship of the Ring, collectively charged with taking the Ring to its destruction on Mount Doom. The fact that he is only one of a party of nine disguises his unique status as the only person who knows where he is going and why, and as the real instigator of the whole enterprise. The long debate at Rivendell that leads to the setting up of the Fellowship of the Ring serves as a smokescreen, too, disguising the fact that what is decided is what Gandalf in particular intends. Of course, it could be argued that he has had to persuade the others in a free debate and to that extent he is less a manipulator of the situation than a facilitator of it. The others retain the free will to decide for themselves and Gandalf can only persuade them by argument. The Rivendell council is not only a distraction from Gandalf's authority character role but also a demonstration of his restraint in using his authority. Such restraint becomes almost constraint as the Fellowship travels south and it becomes clear that at least one member of the party, Boromir, is not an unquestioning follower of its leader. Tolkien, in a way that is surely typical of his narrative style, in fact works to avoid premature isolation of Boromir from the others following Gandalf by setting up a difference of opinion between the wizard and another member of the Fellowship, the dwarf Gimli, who, apparently for personal reasons, disputes Gandalf's choice of a route across the mountains and argues instead for one underneath them, through the dwarf-made Mines of Moria. For a time it seems that Gimli is the one who challenges Gandalf, not Boromir, but, since this challenge is on the minor issue of how to complete part of the journey, and not its overall purpose, Gimli's opposition to Gandalf's judgement is not of fundamental concern. Almost ironically, however, it leads to Tolkien's most daring device for abstracting Gandalf from the leading role in the plot, when, in Moria, the party encounters the balrog, and Gandalf sacrifices himself to it so that the others can escape. Now it will seem to the reader that what Frodo, Aragorn and the rest will do is their own decision, their own choice, and not part of Gandalf's master-plan.

Gandalf's death and resurrection, and his transformation from Gandalf the Grey to Gandalf the White, is surely the most extraordinary event in *The Lord of the Rings*, not least because it seems to make so little difference, inside and outside the book. Its function as a device to realign the Fellowship's group dynamics is obvious enough. Bereft of its leader the party has to find another, and the latent struggle for power of Boromir against Aragorn and Frodo now comes into the open, leading to the division of the Breaking of the Fellowship at Amon Hen. Boromir is killed, Frodo, with Sam, sets off on a direct route to Mount Doom with the Ring, and Aragorn, assuming control of Legolas and Gimli, leads the pursuit of the other two hobbits, who have been carried off by the orcs of Saruman. It is during this pursuit that the ranger, the elf and the dwarf meet up with the resurrected Gandalf the White, who then resumes the leadership of the party. In effect he has taken no more than a detour, a kind of short-cut in the plot. While he was away the others have muddled through in much the same way as anticipated. They have become split up and lost one member, and the prosecution of the main purpose, the destruction of the Ring, has devolved to a part of the group that has gone its own way. Gandalf must now hope that Frodo and Sam do not deviate from the main aim, just as Wotan has to hope

Chapter Seven: The Ring and *Der Ring* 165

(with rather less assurance, in the end) that Siegfried will do what he should. Meanwhile, Gandalf must find a new aim for the remains of the Fellowship. Somewhat paradoxically, this involves Tolkien not in a plot development quite unlike Wagner's *Der Ring des Nibelungen* but in a variation on the last part of that work. The story moves into finding an ending at a level that is political and quasi-historical, leaving the business of the mythic ending of the age to the other half of the narrative, Frodo's half. Gandalf now takes Aragorn to court.

Gandalf's transformation from grey to white has no counterpart in Wagner. It has few counterparts in fiction at all, perhaps because its most obvious parallel is the embarrassingly blasphemous one with the death and resurrection of Jesus Christ. Gandalf's fight with the balrog in the depths of the earth seems a parallel to Christ's Harrowing of Hell. Unlike Christ, however, Gandalf returns to this world, or Middle-earth, to be more exact, and is not taken up into some heavenly sphere after a few startling appearances to his chosen followers. His first encounters with Aragorn, Legolas and Gimli in Fangorn forest look as though they will be fleeting, but after playing the revenant for a bit Gandalf puts this aside for a more down-to-earth role. Neatly, then, Tolkien slides over the implications of Gandalf's transformation and his out-of-body experience. He makes Gandalf reluctant to say what happened to him and what he has become, discouraging speculation by the others. Soon we are engaged in the hurly-burly of the War of the Ring and Gandalf becomes an active and central figure in it, as both counsellor and military commander. Despite the suggestion that White Gandalf has new powers, he in fact employs very little if any magic from now on, and less than Gandalf the Grey did. Instead he relies on force of will, diplomacy and martial skill, as he turns into a combination of international statesman and general, of Henry Kissinger and David Petraeus. There is, in short, a lessening of the wizard, a diminution in his magicality and glamour, that is part of the whole spiralling downwards of Middle-earth at the end of its Third Age. It might seem that, in contrast with the decline of Wotan from chief of the gods to the Wanderer, Gandalf's change from Gandalf the Grey to Gandalf the White is a rise in splendour and power, but the appearance is deceptive. The reality is that Gandalf moves down from a plane of activity that has supernatural aspects to one that is more mundane. In this respect, then, he is not like Christ and his death and resurrection takes him in the direction of glory only in an earthly sense, one where the rhetoric of victory and triumph are to be taken literally, in the context of battles and sieges, at Helm's Deep and Minas Tirith.

Gandalf's reverse apotheosis is confirmed by its doubling in the fate of Saruman. The defeat of that wizard is also a reverse for wizardry as such. Saruman is initially presented as the supreme wizard, Gandalf's superior and the acme of the type. That he should fail and fall is a measure of the inadequacy of that type, and this reflects on Gandalf. It is often supposed that in taking on the white colour initially associated with Saruman as the head of the order of wizards Gandalf is replacing Saruman and vindicating the order, but perhaps it is a better way of looking at this to say that in becoming white Gandalf becomes all too much like Saruman himself. Certainly, in those passages when Gandalf the White is glimpsed at the edge of Fangorn and mistaken for Saruman by members of the Fellowship the confusion between the wizards is the dominant effect. That the white wizard in the woods reveals himself as Gandalf not Saruman does not altogether erase the identification between them. The defeat of Saruman and his power as a magician stands for the diminution of Gandalf as wizard. The confrontation with Saruman in his tower after his defeat shows a wizard at bay, humiliated and made to seem ordinary and vulnerable, driven back on one remaining talent, his verbal powers of persuasion. That Saruman's humiliation takes the form of deconstructing his rhetoric runs dangerously close to undermining Gandalf, too, for he has become a rhetorician, a person who argues and persuades, as he has demonstrated at Edoras, where he awakens Théoden out of the delusion created by Grima Wormtongue, and as will be shown again in Gondor, where Gandalf tries, but fails, to persuade Denethor to resist Sauron. The reduction of Saruman's power to that of voice is an element in the sense of spiralling down towards a more ordinary kind of world as *The Lord of the Rings* goes on, and this affects the response to Gandalf as well as to Saruman.

The difference between their cases, of course, has to do with the purposes to which they are put. Saruman uses his powers of persuasion towards ends that mimic those of Sauron, that is to say, for the pursuit of personal power that cannot see beyond itself. Gandalf, on the other hand, uses his powers of persuasion for other ends, though these are no less political than Saruman's. Kitcher and Schacht give us the means to distinguish between the wizards and their aims with their ideas about finding an ending that will make a life seem meaningful. Saruman's existence would be meaningless whether or not he succeeded for in either case his power ends with him. His ambition, being self-centred, can have no significant result. Gandalf, on the other hand, looks to encourage trains of events that could have lasting consequences, long after he is no longer on the scene. For this he needs other people, and not just armies of subhumans brought into existence just to do his bidding. He needs active agents who will adopt his point of view more or less enthusiastically and join him in creating opportunities for positive change. Yet there is always the risk that things will not go as planned, that his followers will prove too weak or too confused to do what he thinks is needed, or that in the end nothing can be done. Saruman from his tower ridicules Gandalf for his faith in his assorted band of companions and so raises the bleak prospect that what Gandalf has chosen to attempt is neither worth the effort nor likely to succeed because of its reliance on beings lesser than him. Though this turns out to be less than true, it is still a powerful point to make, but just as powerful is the effect of Gandalf's rejection of Saruman's lofty pessimism and his commitment to working with those who are less than him, even if that may mean failure, or partial success only. Again Kitcher and Schacht are helpful here. It is not that a life has to be entirely successful to be meaningful but only that it should make an honest attempt to be so. We must not burden ourselves with impossible all-or-nothing criteria for success, because in the end we all fail, and 'Alles was ist, endet'. The real message of *The Lord of the Rings*, perhaps obscured from some readers by its elements of final triumph for the forces of good, lies in this insight into choosing an ending. The contrast between Saruman and Gandalf should point us towards this, not to a facile judgment on how the evil Saruman was punished while the good Gandalf was rewarded.

Looking at *The Lord of the Rings*, especially its second two volumes, *The Two Towers* and *The Return of the King*, in this way restores the balance between the story of Frodo and Sam's journey to Mordor and the other half of the narrative, the story of Gandalf and Aragorn's intervention in the war against Saruman and the war against Sauron. Too often Frodo's story has taken precedence and the significance of the actions of Gandalf and Aragorn has been reduced to mere distractions. The narrative encourages this, to be sure, by having Gandalf enunciate the strategy of diverting Sauron's attention from Frodo and Sam by engaging as noisily and vigorously as possible with his armies in pitched battles. This turns the siege of Minas Tirith into a sideshow, as military historians would put it, and it makes the war with Saruman an irritating interruption in the real campaign against the real enemy, Sauron. But if the idea of the ending of the Third Age and the sense that all the characters, not just Frodo, are, deliberately or not, engaged in finding an ending for themselves and others that will give their lives true meaning, if that is made of prime critical importance in interpreting *The Lord of the Rings*, both strands of its narrative contribute to the work's meaning. Indeed, the Gandalf/Aragorn, Rohan/Gondor strand, being more complex, might be said to contribute more to the overall effect than the simpler, more straightforward Frodo in Mordor strand.

The bias towards Frodo is probably a result of the simpler outline of his story and its introverted nature. From the point where he, with Sam, leaves the others and crosses the river to make his own way to Mordor, the narrative shape of his part of the story is clear and direct, with an obvious goal. There will be some complications. The acquisition of Gollum as a guide creates tension, as does the encounter with Faramir, but on the whole the pattern is straightforward: a hard journey, with intrusions of danger, culminating in a severe trial that resolves the issue. Though Gollum often seems like one of the hazards, his real functions are twofold. First, he acts as a dark substitute for Gandalf. He attaches himself to the Fellowship after the wizard's disappearance in Moria, becoming its unacknowledged ninth member in the journey down the river. Then he takes over the role of guide when he joins Frodo and Sam and takes them through the marches and on into Mordor. He is, after Gandalf, the greatest expert on the Ring, and on Sauron and his orcs, in the party, and without him Frodo would never have got to Mount Doom. He is as essential to the plot as Gandalf, just as Alberich is as essential to *Der Ring des Nibelungen* as Wotan. Gollum's other function is to deepen the introspection. Cleverly Tolkien has put side by side a hobbit who has just begun to feel the effects of the Ring and one who has been altered almost out of all recognition by the same Ring. Gollum's struggles with himself and his Ring obsession act as constant warnings to the reader if not to the character himself of what might happen to Frodo as Ringbearer.

Yet we can hardly not believe that Frodo sees himself in Gollum (as Sam does not) and the mixture of feelings we imagine this must cause in him becomes an important aspect of our understanding of Frodo's torment as he labours towards Mount Doom. The cheerful matter-of-factness of Sam serves as a contrast to this, adding to our imaginative sense of Frodo's mental state. On the other hand, such introspective concerns distract from large questions. Frodo's story focuses so strongly on the simple end of getting rid of the Ring that other considerations tend to be driven out of the reader's mind as much as Frodo's. Interestingly, it is Sam, with his thoughts of home and his determined refusal not to imagine not returning there, who does most to remind us that there will be something after the end of the Ring, though the way Sam is presented, as a character of comically limited sensibility, removes some seriousness from his reflections. Frodo in the end will prove lacking in Sam's resilience and his intense focus on the Ring will mean that, when it is gone, he has indeed nothing much else to live for.

Frodo's story, however, can be brought into the discussion of finding an ending stemming from Kitcher and Schacht. Judith Klinger's essay 'Hidden Paths of Time: March 13th and the Riddles of Shelob's Lair', in the second volume of the collection of essays on *Tolkien and Modernity* edited by Honegger and Weinreich (2006), is centrally concerned with the details of chronology at the end of Book 4, the chapters set in Shelob's Lair. The beginning and end of the essay, however, are about Frodo's reasons for taking ship from the Grey Havens, and, as the date in her title indicates, why his physical collapses take place on the anniversaries of his stabbing by the Ringwraith on Weathertop and of his encounter with Shelob, rather than, as we might expect, the anniversary of the destruction of the Ring. When, in his delirium, Frodo says 'It is gone for ever [...] and now all is dark and empty' (*The Lord of the Rings*, page 1024), what does he mean? Judith Klinger argues against the obvious answer, that what Frodo says is 'gone for ever' is the Ring, and instead that what he misses and longs for is an escape from the world of Middle-earth into another. During his illness on 13 March he is found clutching the white jewel Arwen gave him when she offered him her place on a journey into the west. Klinger writes:

> During the March 13th episode, Frodo is therefore 'clutching' not only an antidote that brings relief but also the prospect of travelling beyond Middle-earth. It is this connection that defines the missing reference in his 'it is gone for ever'; 'it' then refers to the westward path that Frodo perceived before he was overtaken by Shelob, to the future revealed in the Phial's light, and the 'escape' he thought was for ever out of reach when he discovered the Ring's absence in the tower. (page 204)

Frodo's journey to what Klinger calls 'a place outside the mortal continuum' (page 204) is not an easy one and he is torn between a desire to stay in the Shire, trying to recapture the past, and following the path Arwen's gift has opened for him, 'a choice,' say Klinger, 'that Frodo cannot make lightly or quickly' (page 205).

One reason for this, although I do not think Klinger brings this out clearly, is that Frodo knows he failed in Mount Doom. She says that '[a]fter his return from the Quest, Frodo certainly does not consider himself "rarefied", or equal to the company of a more "noble kind", as his final confrontation with Saruman demonstrates' (page 205), and she quotes in a footnote Frodo's speech in Chapter 8, where he prevents Sam from killing Saruman, saying '[h]e was great once, of a noble kind that we should not dare to raise our hands against' (page 1019). Frodo's protests against violence when he returns to the Shire and his refusal to put himself forward as a leader, then, are not simply a turning away from war and bloodshed but also a personal acknowledgement of lack of fitness to judge or condemn others. He has learned the lesson of Gandalf's rebuke in the second chapter of Book 1, when Frodo says that Gollum deserves death:

> Many that live deserve death. And some that die deserve life. Can you give it to them? Then do not be too eager to deal out death in judgement. For even the very wise cannot see all ends. (page 59)

The striking word here is the last one, 'ends'. Klinger's explanation of the final chapter and Frodo's passing into the west is suggestive but not altogether convincing, though she brings out a key aspect of the situation, and of *The Lord of the Rings*. Frodo's exclamation that 'It is gone for ever […] and now all is dark and empty' does, as she says, mean more than the loss of the Ring but perhaps less than the specific matter of the opportunity to sail with the elves. Frodo's more obvious and more general loss is the loss of purpose in his life with the end of his career as Ringbearer, a career that did not even give him

Chapter Seven: The Ring and *Der Ring*

the satisfaction of a successful ending. Sam may have been 'pained to notice how little honour he [Frodo] had in his own country' (page 1025) but Frodo himself may well have not wanted to be honoured for something he knew was not what it seemed. Such honouring could only remind him of his weakness at the crucial moment and make him remember how, at the point of fulfilment of the quest, he found himself wanting. But that is all now in the past and cannot be changed. It might indeed have been better if Frodo had not survived the catastrophe on Mount Doom. He had after all gone there fully expecting to die, and if he had he would not be left to reflect on what really happened there. Immediately after the Ring falls into the fire Frodo says to Sam 'Well, this is the end' (page 947), and a few pages into the next chapter, unaware that the eagles are already on their way to rescue them, Frodo tells Sam he is glad they are together '[h]ere at the end of all things' (page 950), repeating a phrase he uses at the very end of Chapter 3, 'Mount Doom'. But it is not the end of all things. Sam immediately insists he is not ready to give up yet, to which Frodo responds:

> 'Maybe not, Sam, [...] but it's like things are in the world. Hopes fail. An end comes. We have only a little time to wait now. We are lost in ruin and downfall, and there is no escape.' (page 950)

Frodo is wrong. There is an escape and he must return to the world. If there is to be an end for him it will not be the one he has expected since he left Rivendell with the Ring. It will not be a sacrificial death on the mountain. Frodo is left to make sense of a life that lacks the shape he thought it would have, with a clear ending to which he has directed himself and which would act as the fulfilment of his existence. Instead he survives into the messy world of the Shire and its politics, and while the others, Merry, Pippin and Sam, have the consolation of being able to reflect on how well they acted at the crisis of their adventures, and carry on into fulfilled lives of honour and service to the community, Frodo has to confront the fact that he was 'lost in ruin and downfall', from which there was, ironically, as he said, no escape, not in the sense that he could not survive, but in the sense that he could not forget.

Frodo is left then divided between longing for the heightened existence he had as the Ringbearer and the acknowledgment that that existence is over, 'gone for ever', leaving him in a world that is 'dark and empty' (page 1024). Middle-earth for him has become disenchanted, but his participation and commitment to its former enchanted state, and perhaps even more his realisation of how the enchantment has gone, make him unable to come to terms with what is left. The others can carry on in the new Fourth Age, the Age of Men. He cannot. He has become like the elves, unfitted and unwilling to continue an existence that lacks purpose. This means they can only live on the margins of the world, whose events they find uninteresting, and passing them by, and so logically, like the elves, Frodo must sail into the west, joining them in the other world where the actions and activities of men do not impinge. That is all the ending that he finds.

CHAPTER EIGHT

An Ending

There is one discussion of Tolkien and Wagner that is not mentioned in the opening chapter of this book. That is the essay in the second volume of *The Ring Goes Ever On: Proceedings of the Tolkien 2005 Conference* (Tolkien Society, 2008) by Michael Scott Rohan, '"Which story, I wonder?" said Gandalf..." Was Tolkien the real Ring-Thief?' (pages 147-153). This is in many ways the most knowledgeable and sensible of the shorter pieces that discuss Tolkien's possible debt to Wagner, and much of what it says is in principle close to what is said in this book, although its starting point, and more significantly the conclusion that depends on it, are quite different. A closer examination of Scott Rohan's discussion will however serve to lead to the conclusions of this book.

Scott Rohan begins, not with the question of whether Tolkien was influenced by Wagner, but with irritation at those who claim that he was over-influenced and merely copied *Der Ring des Nibelungen* in *The Lord of the Rings*. In particular Scott Rohan mentions Philip Pullman, whom he calls 'that incessant Tolkien-slagger', and A N Wilson (page 147). He accuses the latter of saying, in an article in *The Daily Telegraph*, 18 July 2005, 'that Tolkien just stole *Lord of the Rings* wholesale from Wagner's opera cycle'. He quotes Wilson's claim that Tolkien 'was hugely derivative [...] *simply taking the story of the Ring from Wagner and gutting it of its religious and sexual interest*' (page 147 – the italics here seem to be Scott Rohan's, not Wilson's). That is a little unfair as this is Wilson's only sentence about Tolkien in a brief article on *Harry Potter* (one that defends J K Rowling against her hostile critics). Wilson's other comments on *The Lord of the Rings* are much more favourable (see his book *Our Times: The Age of Elizabeth II*), though it is true he persists in seeing parallels in it with Wagner's *Ring*. In a later *Daily Telegraph* article (5 February 2007), Wilson refers to *The Lord of the Rings* as 'a narrative of immense seriousness' and says that 'although it is true that Tolkien does not write about the things that obsessed Richard Wagner, his myth is no less overwhelming'. But Scott Rohan wants to set up Wilson as a target for his complaints against those who ignorantly accuse Tolkien of stealing from Wagner. Strikingly, though, having used Wilson and others to establish the idea of the superficiality of the comparisons usually made between Tolkien and Wagner, leading inevitably to Tolkien's dismissive 'both rings were round, and there the resemblance ceases' remark, Scott Rohan suddenly turns and writes that 'you don't need to look very deep[ly] to realize that this simply isn't true' (page 147), and he then lists a number of similarities between *The Lord of the Rings* and *Der Ring des Nibelungen* pointed out by Tom Shippey in Appendix A of his book *The Road to Middle-earth*. Scott Rohan therefore has to admit that, upon examination, 'there are in fact many more and deeper similarities between the two great Rings than are usually considered' (page 148), though to see this, he says, needs somebody who has a knowledge of both. Scott Rohan's essay is important because, for once, here is a writer on Tolkien and Wagner who indeed knows both, by virtue of being a reader of Tolkien and a fantasy novelist himself and, as well, a writer on classical music.

Like this book, Scott Rohan's essay begins with some of the various lists of parallels between *The Lord of the Rings* and *Der Ring des Nibelungen*, and then produces one of its own (page 150), with twenty points of resemblance, '[s]ome specific, some general; some of incident, some of location'. Scott Rohan admits that twenty is not many, and some might be attacked, but 'to all these points some undeniable substance remains' (page 149). What is more,

> Their *cumulative* effect, the impression they create [...] is not small at all. Add these up, and you get what amounts to a very similar plot-line in each [...] And it's still more similar in detail [...] In neither case can this common element possibly have derived from the common sources [...] the story is *not* in the sources. There is *nowhere* else Tolkien can have come by it, no dark passages in which his hand rested on the enigmatic Ring. It's hard to deny the link; and yet if you admit it, all the other parallels become vastly more significant. (pages 149-151)

This leads Scott Rohan to ask how much Tolkien knew about *Der Ring des Nibelungen*. He lists the same pieces of evidence as in the first chapter of this book, concurring with the view that Tolkien's association with C S Lewis must have brought him into contact with Wagner's work. Accepting that Tolkien not only attended performances of operas from *Der Ring des Nibelungen* at Covent Garden, London, and also, with the Lewis brothers, read the librettos, Scott Rohan declares that

Chapter Eight: An Ending   175

> in my personal experience you do not travel to London to sit through *Ring* operas – with acts lasting up to two hours straight – or read through the whole thing in a go, if all you're going to get out of this is a numb backside and renewed contempt for the creator. I'd suggest that all this indicates in Tolkien a deep engagement with the *Ring* – in many respects a negative one, perhaps, but negation too can be influential. (page 152)

Yet Tolkien left, as Scott Rohan remarks, no comment on Wagner's music, though he did say he liked that of one of Wagner's immediate predecessors as a writer of opera in German, Carl Maria von Weber. Scott Rohan suggests that the connections in terms of music history and influence between Wagner and the less famous Weber 'mean it's seriously hard to like one composer, musically speaking, without having at least *some* response to the other' (page 152).

This brings him back to the question of why Tolkien denied any debt to Wagner. His answers are the political differences between them, between Wagner the revolutionary socialist and Tolkien the Catholic conservative, and the darkening of Wagner's reputation by its association with German nationalism and racialism and the Nazis and anti-Semitism. Scott Rohan then emphasises Tolkien's Englishness, though, as in Chapter 1 here, he notes the paradox that Tolkien was 'as insistently English as only someone with a slightly foreign aspect can be', but concludes nevertheless that 'Tolkien's acquaintance with Wagner was close – so close as to make some influence at least entirely possible' (page 153).

So far, then, Michael Scott Rohan's discussion of the influence of Wagner on Tolkien follows the same lines as this book, but at this point it begins to diverge. Having declared 'that rushing to deny Wagner had any influence on Tolkien is unsafe and most likely wrong, and that most of those resemblances are *not* accidental' (page 153), he goes back to the defence of Tolkien against the charge that he simply stole from Wagner, that he was a plagiarist. He does this by trying to redefine what is meant by influence and argues that the resemblances between *Der Ring des Nibelungen* and *The Lord of the Rings*, though they exist, must be seen in perspective, that is to say, in relation to the amount of difference between the two works. His first set of examples of difference are matters of scale. Wagner, he says, 'takes the sprawling, inchoate world of myth, and strips it down to bare essentials' (page 153), with very little of history, geography, space and time and only a handful of characters. 'Where Wagner only sketches,' he writes, 'Tolkien sprawls, in the best sense, as real lands and cultures do, and in many dimensions' (page 154). Scott Rohan notes, of course, that these differences are mainly consequences of the different forms of the two works, the difference between opera and prose fiction, but he claims that nevertheless

> Against such contrasts as this, the similarities we've noticed begin to look very unimportant indeed [...] Those 'similarities' are only the few faint points at which the two works briefly run alongside one another, the momentary contact of two otherwise diverging paths. (page 154)

It is interesting how 'similarities' here acquires quotation marks, to suggest they are not really similarities as they become 'the few faint points' where 'the two works briefly run alongside one another' on their 'otherwise diverging paths'. This is a different rhetoric from the quotations from page 153 of the essay given above. This rhetoric however disguises the real issue, which is not about the different scale of things in an opera compared with a novel but whether the points of comparison, however brief, are significant or not in terms of such things as characterisation, plot and theme. Scott Rohan does not, to be fair, have space to go into this, though he makes a gesture towards it by following the quotation set out above, the one with 'similarities' in inverted commas, with a three-sentence contrast between Tolkien's 'eucatastrophic, Christian' finale and Wagner's 'classically tragic' one. This seems to be a rather hasty attempt to show that in some major way Tolkien and Wagner are doing very different things, but it would take a more detailed discussion of their endings to prove this point.

From there Scott Rohan moves to an attempt to contrast the two Rings themselves, not so much in what they are in each work but in how Tolkien's comes into alignment with Wagner's. His argument here is that only after Tolkien had been through the lengthy process of developing the simple invisibility ring found by Bilbo in *The Hobbit* into the Ring as 'a malevolent entity with a will of its own' did he realise that he had coincidentally arrived at something the same as Wagner's version: '[b]y a totally separate route he'd developed the concept of the Ring to a point where that resemblance to Wagner's, supposedly crucial in the [A N] Wilson definition, had actually become almost inevitable' (page 155). For Scott Rohan the inevitability here is that of the story, which required the development of the Ring in the direction that led to an affinity with Wagner's as a kind of fiction-writing equivalent to the convergent evolution of different species into similar forms to occupy similar niches in otherwise separate ecosystems. Only afterwards does the coincidence become noticeable. The trouble with this argument to explain the convergent development of the two Rings is that it would have to apply to all the other resemblances between *The Lord of the Rings* and *Der Ring des Nibelungen*, including the rest of the twenty examples Scott Rohan himself lists. He has, again, no space to deal properly with this objection and can only remark hastily that he 'won't take time to explore them here' (page 155). He then goes back to the defence of Tolkien against Wagner on the basis that they used the same sources, though he himself has already argued that significant elements of *The Lord of the Rings* are not present in the sources but in Wagner alone, and showed near the beginning of his essay that Tolkien from the start was aware that in reading and studying the Norse mythological sources he was rivalling Wagner, and could not have forgotten that in the 1930s and 1940s.

Scott Rohan, however, wants to take issue with the idea of forgetting in relation to artistic echoes and claim, from his own experience as a writer, that it is often the case that an author unconsciously incorporates into his or her work something from elsewhere without at the moment of writing recognising it, so that, 'looking back over your writing years afterwards, you see books you read, authors you loved – or simply influenced the hell out of you – staring out at you in a way you were quite unaware of at the time' (page 155). For this reason Scott Rohan 'confidently conclude[s]' that the elements from Wagner Tolkien used 'are not as crucial or central as they might appear' (page 155). Why he is so confident of this is not clear, since the argument from unconscious coincidence does not imply anything about the nature of the elements that are unconsciously borrowed. They may be trivial or they may be highly significant. The process by which the elements got into Tolkien's work, conscious or unconscious, says nothing about their meaning. Nor does the unconsciousness of this process remove the question of legitimate or illegitimate borrowing; it merely makes the writer or artist an unreliable witness.

Any artist who creates a work with numerous points of resemblance, trivial or serious, to another work can hardly expect not to be accused of being derivative, despite how much he or she might express surprise at the resemblances. Protests of good intentions and unawareness of outcome only look naive, suggesting that the artist does not know his or her own work very well, or is ignorant of that of others working with similar material. Scott Rohan goes on to demote the influence of Wagner on Tolkien to the level of that of others, such as William Morris, H Rider Haggard and *Beowulf*, overlooking the question of how significant these actually are. In a moment we shall see how Tolkien himself tried to make them seem limited. In the case of *Beowulf* the very close resemblances, amounting almost to translation, of passages in Book 3 of *The Lord of the Rings* and passages in the Old English poem suggest a level of imitation of a source by Tolkien that itself casts doubt on Scott Rohan's theory of unconscious borrowing, since it shows Tolkien working quite deliberate references into his own text without acknowledgement. If he did that with one source he might have done the same with others. Scott Rohan ends by arguing that the idea of Tolkien the plagiarist 'vanishes […] and in his place we find the talented writer, in the normal process of transmuting what he's read and been shaped by into something entirely his own' (page 155). 'Transmuting' is an interesting choice of word for this process, as is the adjective 'talented' for the writer doing it, implying that the untalented writer may not be up to transmuting his influences. Does this mean that the difference between a plagiarist and a transmuter of his influences is a matter of success? Behind this question lies T S Eliot's notorious remark, in his 1920 essay on Philip Massinger, that '[i]mmature poets imitate; mature poets steal; bad poets deface what they take, and good poets make it into something better, or at least something different' (*Selected Essays*, page 206). Scott Rohan has taken the discussion of Tolkien's debt to Wagner into one of the thornier thickets of critical argument in the last ninety years or so, if not longer.

Part of the problem is Tolkien's own reticence about his literary sources and influences, as we can see in Tolkien's letters. Carpenter's selection contains few references to Tolkien's reading and almost all of these, except to works by C S Lewis, are very short and slight. If Tolkien did more than mention a few names and titles, and occasionally express brief words of admiration or dislike, then the *Letters* do not show this. Most of the comments Tolkien makes on books, particularly those from the age of the novel, the nineteenth and twentieth centuries, what he could be assumed to have read for pleasure, since they form no part of his professional work, leave an impression of how little they impressed him or how much he had reservations about their quality. For example, a writer of what would now be called fantasy, whose works have often been compared with Tolkien's, E R Eddison, receives several comments in the letters, more than many other writers, partly because Tolkien met him. Eddison in fact attended a meeting of the Inklings in June 1944, where he read a chapter 'from an uncompleted romance' that Tolkien describes as 'of undiminished power and felicity of expression' (*Letters*, 20 June 1944, page 84). Thirteen years later Tolkien writes another letter in which he recalls this meeting with Eddison and says he read his works, but 'long after they appeared', with 'great enjoyment for their sheer literary merit', adding that 'I still think of him as the greatest and most convincing writer of "invented worlds" that I have read'. Tolkien also writes, however, that he 'disliked his characters', 'despised what he appeared to admire' and 'thought his nomenclature slipshod and often inept'. The paragraph in the letter ends with the blunt assertion that 'he was certainly not an "influence"' (*Letters*, 24 June 1957). This looks like an exercise in closing off any suggestion of debt to another writer.

References in the letters to George MacDonald are similar. In writing about orcs to Naomi Mitchison on 25 April 1954 Tolkien says that they 'owe, I suppose, a good deal to the goblin tradition [...], especially as it appears in George MacDonald' (page 178), but five months later, in a letter of 18 September to Hugh Brogan, Tolkien modifies this in a comment on his preference for the name orcs over goblins 'since these creatures are not "goblins", not even the goblins of George MacDonald, which they do to some extent resemble' (page 185). This is like the footnote to a letter of 1968 to Michael Tolkien that says 'the episode of the "wargs" is in part derived from a scene in S R Crockett's *The Black Douglas*, probably his best romance and anyway one that deeply impressed me in school-days, though I have never looked at it again' (page 391). Crockett, then, is tantalisingly presented as a possible if partial influence on a scene in *The Lord of the Rings* but only as a distant memory of childhood reading. The academic critic is almost being dared to read anything into this. In these remarks on Eddison, MacDonald and Crockett there is a pattern of seeming to offer a comparison with his own work only to withdraw it or declare it weak and unimportant.

In the cases of writers and works briefly referred to, Tolkien's comments more often express disappointment than approval. In an early letter to Stanley Unwin, 4 March 1938, Tolkien mentions 'having read [Joseph O'Neill's] *Land Under England* with some pleasure', but immediately qualifies this by adding 'it was a weak example, and distasteful to me in many points' (page 33). Of G K Chesterton's 'Ballad of the White Horse' he writes on 3 September 1944 that 'it is not as good as I thought' (page 92) and, on the last day of the same month, of Bernard Shaw's *Arms and the Man* that it 'does not wear well' (page 94). In the first letter in Carpenter's selection, dated to 1914, Tolkien tells Edith he is trying to turn one of the stories in the Finnish *Kalevala* into something 'on the lines of [William] Morris' romances with chunks of poetry in between' (page 7) and one might expect a number of similar references to Morris in later letters, but the most substantial remark does not come until a letter of 1960 where, in arguing against reading scenes in *The Lord of the Rings* as signs of influence from either of the World Wars, Tolkien baldly states that 'they owe more to William Morris and his Huns and Romans, as in *The House of the Wulfings* or *The Roots of the Mountains*' (page 303), using Morris as just a foil to an interpretation Tolkien wishes avoided.

Tolkien's letters, then, include hints of several possible literary influences but keep them at bay and offer no substantial evidence. Instead, they as often take back whatever suggestions of influence they may seem initially to offer. The general impression is of Tolkien making minor concessions to the suggestion that his work, especially *The Lord of the Rings*, has some debts to previous writers more out of politeness than a sense of conviction, leaving largely intact the image of the work as unique and independent of modern lines of development in fiction. This is similar to his defensive response to the suggestions of the influence of Richard Wagner and *Der Ring des Nibelungen* on *The Lord of the Rings*. The tone of Tolkien's remarks as much as their content encourages his enthusiasts to think that it is really not worthwhile to go into great detail about possible parallels and borrowings. The converse of this is the idea that in fact there are no serious influences and that those who pursue what clues there are do so only out of a base intention to impugn Tolkien's originality.

Chapter Eight: An Ending

Michael Scott Rohan's article seems in its mid-section to have gone past that defensive attitude but it returns to it in its ending. The weakness of his conclusions stem not simply from the brevity of his essay but also from its starting point, its concern with the accusation that Tolkien plagiarised Wagner. The argument becomes a matter of all or nothing, since one is either a plagiarist or not. Plagiarism is not a concept that allows for degrees of guilt or innocence. Scott Rohan actually shows, though briefly and in outline, that Tolkien was in fact influenced by Wagner and owes interesting debts to him but then he comes close to throwing the proverbial baby out with the bath-water when he tries to refine and re-define these debts and influences out of existence to show Tolkien was not plagiarising. In his anxiety to defend Tolkien against critics he in fact regards as irritating and worthless Scott Rohan turns his own argument on its head and moves from showing there are connections between Wagner and Tolkien to denying they amount to anything, when what is really required is to examine those links and see what they mean.

As an aside one might ask why Michael Scott Rohan, and others, are so concerned with the accusation of plagiarism against Tolkien. It would seem that this attitude rests on a basic demand for originality, for freedom from influence by or debt to previous works, for a concept of artistic creativity that places an absolute value on innovation. This has been a fundamental aspect of modern aesthetics since it was formed in the later eighteenth century and exemplified in the work of Romantic writers, painters and composers. The idea that the truly great artist always makes something new is definitive in western culture, however problematic it is. It is a demand on artists that, if not met, can lead to their rejection by critics and the public. Nothing damns an artist more than the opinion that he or she is only copying what has been done before, and if such copying is not acknowledged or is in some way disguised or hidden from sight before being revealed, the critics and the public will feel that they have been deceived or cheated, and then the talk of plagiarism begins. Against this purist notion of originality must be set the ethos of criticism as it has developed in the prime centres of critical debate, the universities. There the fundamental operation is the identification and discussion of comparisons and influences, trends and traditions, the very opposites of the concept of individual artistic originality. The extension into the academic humanities of the pseudo-scientific approaches of the social sciences, with their search for patterns, measurable instantiations and underlying laws of behaviour, has made comparison, source-hunting and the formalisation of genres, traditions and artistic movements the normal procedures of literary criticism. Michael Scott Rohan's irritation with the way Robert Giddings, Howard Jacobson and A N Wilson automatically describe *The Lord of the Rings* in terms of something else, of other works, is a classic case of the conflict between the idea of originality and the academic practice of comparative criticism that lies unresolved among the roots of our cultural assumptions.

Tolkien's case is a fascinating one in relation to this conflict since he himself, and his works, academic and popular, straddle the divide. On the one hand, he belonged to that academic world where critical explanation rests on matters of comparison, connection and influence. For him, these were linguistic and historical. He spent his professional life tracing the development of words from their earlier to later forms, constructing chains of tradition reaching across centuries. In this context, in fact, originality is a disaster, since altogether new words are practically useless, if not meaningless. Outside the library and lecture-hall, however, Tolkien became a different man, one engaged in just the acts of neologism that as a lexicologist he had to deplore. In his private study he put together languages that had their origins in his own mind, not in manuscripts and inscriptions handed down through the ages, although paradoxically he invented along with the languages histories, geographies and sometimes even documents that corresponded to the matrices of real languages. He also invented stories and myths to go with his invented languages – indeed, the stories and myths frequently preceded them. He was not so free of the demand for evidence of influence and tradition as not to court these within his invented world and in fact also between that world and the real one. He came however to suppress those connections with the real world, at any rate when he exposed part of his myths and stories to the gaze of others. This, however, was a quite late development, and not completed in his own lifetime. Though Tolkien incorporated the academic critical ethos of tradition and influence into his other world, by keeping it largely to himself and secret from others he also preserved a kind of originality in it. Middle-earth grew in his mind alone, unexposed to critical dissection and judgement by others until *The Hobbit* in 1937, and then only in

Chapter Eight: An Ending

a minor way. Significantly, in explaining where *The Hobbit* came from, Tolkien set up a myth of original inspiration that resisted ideas of influence. The story of how he wrote down the first sentence of *The Hobbit* on a blank page of an exam script defies analysis and makes the inception of the book seem an instinctual act. The enduring popularity of this creation myth among Tolkien's readers testifies to the power of the demand for originality and innovation in modern aesthetic appreciation.

With *The Lord of the Rings* a similar effect is created by a different means. Tolkien could not claim that the novel came to him with the unconscious spontaneity of *The Hobbit*. Instead he presented it as embedded in but lifted from a rich and strange matrix of myth and history too great to be fully explicated. The prefatory material and, more, the appendices, indices and maps directed the reader's attention to an origin for *The Lord of the Rings* not in previous literature but in a mass of half-hidden writing to which only Tolkien had real access. This effect was maintained by the posthumous publication of *The Silmarillion* and intensified by the publication of much of the manuscript source material for both *The Lord of the Rings* and *The Silmarillion* in the twelve volumes of *The History of Middle-earth* edited by Christopher Tolkien. To the question of where *The Lord of the Rings* came from the obvious answer has always been that it came from Tolkien, from his mass of stories, poems, chronologies, genealogies, maps and sketches about Middle-earth – what is now called his legendarium. This is what Tolkien through his letters (or at least through the selection of them published by Carpenter) himself promotes, as he replies to questions about *The Lord of the Rings* in terms of his system, referring almost always to further elaborations of his fictional world, either written but unpublished, or to be written, or just then produced for the letter he is writing. When asked about sources and influences outside his own works, however, Tolkien is reluctant and brief in what he says, and never expands. He leaves the impression that *The Lord of the Rings* has little in common with other books, except perhaps some obscure mediæval ones, and the similarities it might have with more recent fiction are, to borrow Michael Scott Rohan's words, 'the momentary contact of [...] otherwise diverging paths' and 'very unimportant indeed' (page 154).

The concept of the independence and isolation of *The Lord of the Rings* from previous literature that Tolkien himself fosters is one that most of his readers seem very willing to share. The indifference of mainstream critics and academics to Tolkien's fiction is often the source of protests and complaints by his supporters (again Tolkien led the way) but at the same time there is a kind of glorying in this situation, too, a feeling that Tolkien's work is special and therefore different from the rest of literature. It is only to be compared with what came after *The Lord of the Rings*. The discussion of its critical neglect and the contrast of that with its popularity usually leads on to description of how it has inspired a new *genre* of fantasy fiction. To those who think of *The Lord of the Rings* in these terms the way it would be dealt with by academic critics would probably come as an unpleasant shock, because what they would do would be to open up the question of where Tolkien's fiction comes from and they would then begin that enmeshing of it with its cultural setting that it has so far largely escaped. Some of this has already begun, notably in Dimitra Fimi's book *Tolkien, Race and Cultural History: From Fairies to Hobbits* (2010), which not only shows how Tolkien's work is rooted in the Victorian passion for fairies but also how he later tried to repudiate and suppress these connections, asserting his difference from his earlier enthusiasm for fairies. The evidence for Tolkien's early delight in the sort of fairies he later rejected is not hard to find and explains his later feelings as embarrassment as much as anything. Comparable evidence of his early involvement with Wagner has not yet been found, but nevertheless it might be argued that the strength of his rejection of the comparison between the two Rings stems at least partly from a similar form of embarrassment to that of his rejection of Victorian fairies. Scott Rohan's theory that authors often recognise their reading transmuted into their writing is presented in a context of mild emotion only. He writes of Tolkien's realising there is convergence between his idea of a Ring of Power and Wagner's as 'the logical outcome of his own ideas', a 'coincidence', and something to be accepted with 'a wry smile' (page 155), but it might also have been a sore point, or the recognition might have presented itself to Tolkien as a threat to his sense of ownership of *The Lord of the Rings*, and so something better not admitted, even to himself. Though there are some good reasons for being defensive about an association with Wagner, it is still possible there are also bad reasons, and in Tolkien's case one might be a state of denial born of the anxiety of influence.

Chapter Eight: An Ending

The converse is to accept the influence of *Der Ring des Nibelungen* on *The Lord of the Rings* for what this book has tried to show it as – a way of exploring Tolkien's novel in the light of Wagner's operatic masterpiece. This is not just a matter of listing parallels or echoes but more of seeing how situations and themes are related and therefore of how both works deal with the same great ideas. In doing this Kitcher and Schacht's book *Finding an Ending*, though it is devoted to Wagner, promises an approach that can be applied to Tolkien. They claim that what *Der Ring des Nibelungen* is about is how any individual who aims to leave the world a better place has to face twin dilemmas. The first is how to effect change through other people without manipulating them so that they become mere tools, means and not ends. The second dilemma is, accepting that full and entire success is unlikely, especially in the lifespan of ordinary mortals, and so a full and successful ending is virtually impossible, how can *an* ending be brought about that at least advances the world in some way and does not leave it worse than before. In Wagner the key character who faces these dilemmas is the god Wotan. His nearest equivalent in *The Lord of the Rings* is Gandalf, who, like Wotan, is, though in a slightly lesser way, a supernatural being sent to improve the world and one who must work through others. Tolkien may have been a Christian conservative, and he may have been quite opposed to Wagner's kind of nineteenth-century revolutionary liberalism, but nevertheless his masterpiece is, like *Der Ring des Nibelungen*, centrally concerned with progressive political action, and its costs. Wagner is more brutal about these. His Wotan pays with his existence whereas Gandalf in some sense survives, though he fades away. Michael Scott Rohan is correct to say this is partly a matter of genre: a dramatic work can conform to the rules of tragedy and show, in the downfall of its hero, a paradoxical hope for the triumph of the spirit that is harder to do in a novel. On the other hand, a novel can turn tragic paradox into irony and ambiguity, showing triumph and disaster together, or closely linked, and leaving the reader with a mixture of feelings that are nearer to the muddled emotions of actual life. So the Ring is destroyed in Mount Doom, though not quite as heroically as we might expect. The king returns but displaces the wise wizard who helped him, and he cannot prevent the spoliation of the homeland of the small folk who directly and indirectly ensured his accession. The heroes, unlike Siegfried, do not die, and their women, unlike Brünnhilde, do not sacrifice themselves for love (or not entirely), but the hobbit-heroes are all changed, and three of them drift into another world, and Éowyn and Arwen, and Galadriel, all renounce some things, to become somewhat lesser figures.

What is important is that each major character lives with a sense of purpose and honestly tries to maintain it. Success is important but not all-important. It is the process, not the final outcome, that is most worthwhile, though that is not to say that the individual can ignore what his or her outcome may be. Finding an ending is important, but an ending is also part of a life and must be suited to it. It is this sense of how the characters try to shape their existence that gives both *Der Ring des Nibelungen* and *The Lord of the Rings* their power of uplifting those who experience them. It is a similar power in each case, achieved mainly by different means, the one through music and drama, the other through the techniques of the novel, but deep similarities of form and substance connect the two works and explain their similarity of appeal. *The Lord of the Rings* gives its reader images of the life well lived, with purpose and commitment, not to an abstract only, but to friends and fellows, to the commonwealth and the continuance of the community and its values. It is not another world that Gandalf and Frodo serve but their world, the one that is analogous to our own, and the message of *The Lord of the Rings* is not about the transcendence of the mundane but the defence of it against the nebulous transcendentalism of the incorporeal Sauron and his bodiless dark angels. The Ring is cursed because it promises transcendence, promises an existence outside the world in a realm of spirits without death. As such it does not offer immortality but perpetual false existence. Wagner's Ring is the same. It turns Fafner into a slothful dragon, eating, sleeping, lounging on his gold. It turns Alberich, even after he has lost it, into an obsessed maniac, like Gollum. It makes fools of Siegfried and Gunther, and even Brünnhilde. Both Rings are images of the greed for superpowers that has obsessed modern culture from at least the publication of Mary Shelley's *Frankenstein* in 1818. Both works show how this obsession affects personal life as well as politics and the fate of nations. Both offer the same alternatives in images of nature, of love and of striving to do good. Neither is blindly optimistic or without doubts about itself. We must ignore Nietzsche and Hitler, and even Wagner, and recognise that Siegfried is not the superman – or rather, he is, and that is the problem about him – just as we must ignore Tolkien's *post hoc* Christianising of *The Lord of the Rings* and decline to see Galadriel as the Virgin and Frodo as Christ. We must, however, see him, like Gandalf, as somebody struggling to do the right thing, influence the world for the better, and leave it a better place by finding an ending.

Appendix A

Der Ring des Nibelungen: a synopsis

Part 1: *Das Rheingold*

Scene 1

The scene begins in darkness, out of which emerges a low, droning sound. Gradually other, harmonising sounds are added to this, and begin to move slowly up and down the major chord (in fact that of E flat major) based on the original note. The movement of the notes becomes faster and faster, as more and more of the instruments of the orchestra join in, until they create waves of sound rippling up and down from low to high, becoming increasingly loud. At the climax voices break in, not in words but in meaningless though pleasing ululations, mimicking the undulations of the orchestral sound. By this time there should be enough light to show the three Rhinemaidens swimming about in the depths of the river Rhine and singing artlessly as they move to and fro. Their wordless song develops into banter between them about how they are keeping watch over what they refer to as 'the sleep of the gold'.

Suddenly the flow of song is interrupted by less pleasing sounds and the harsh voice of the dwarf Alberich interrupts the Rhinemaidens. He praises their beauty and declares how much he is drawn to them. Though the Rhinemaidens remind each other to be on guard against this stranger, each in turn plays with him, pretending to accept the dwarf as a lover only to cast him off in disgust as soon as he gets too close. As they tease him their litheness and agility is contrasted with his awkwardness, until his frustration turns to anger. At that moment a shaft of sunlight penetrates the depths and flashes upon the Rhinegold. Ignoring Alberich the Rhinemaidens hail the gold ecstatically, using the primitive, wordless cries they began with. The dwarf asks them what it is that so shines in the depths and they, having expressed their contempt for his ignorance, tell him about the gold, and how, if it were forged into a ring, the owner of it would win the world's wealth and boundless power. They go so far as to reveal to him that such a ring can only be made by someone who renounces love and its delights, something they believe nobody would do, least of all a lustful dwarf who has just been trying to get hold of them.

They are of course terribly wrong. Clumsily but with determination Alberich climbs up the rocks to where the gold is lodged and, pronouncing a curse on love, seizes it and carries it down into the murky depths from which he came, leaving the Rhinemaidens wailing woefully.

Scene 2

The turbulent music of Alberich's theft of the gold gives way to broader themes and the scene changes to the top of a mountain at dawn, with in the background, over the deep valley in which the Rhine flows, a splendid castle. On the mountain top, Wotan, the chief of the gods, and his wife Fricka are waking up. Wotan gazes on the castle and expresses his pride in its completion but Fricka anxiously reminds him of the contract he has entered into with the giants who built it. The payment is to be the goddess Freia, who soon rushes in seeking protection from Fasolt, one of the giants. Wotan tries to calm her and Fricka, by mentioning Loge, the tricky god of fire, on whom he relies to come up with a way of getting out of the commitment to yield Freia to the giants. Freia is not reassured and she calls on her brothers Donner and Froh to help her.

The giants Fasolt and his brother Fafner appear and demand their payment. Wotan plays for time, but the giants are insistent, though for different reasons. Fasolt wants Freia because she is so beautiful, but Fafner wants her because he knows she provides the gods with magic apples from her garden that keep them young and strong. Without her, they are doomed to age and decay. The argument soon boils over and looks like coming to blows as Donner and Froh step between the giants and their sister.

At that moment Loge appears but he refuses to get involved and infuriates Donner and Froh, and Wotan, by saying he has no alternative to the original contract with the giants. He seems to go off at a tangent in a long story about how he has travelled the world and everywhere seen how people place love and beauty before anything. Then slyly he mentions one exception – the dwarf who stole the Rhinemaidens' gold. He says he has promised to report this

Appendix A: *Der Ring des Nibelungen*: a synopsis

crime to Wotan and plead on behalf of the Rhinemaidens that the chief of the gods catch the thief and return the gold to its rightful owners. The giants are intrigued and ask Loge why the dwarf should place such a value on the gold and he explains how from it a ring of power can be forged. At this everybody begins imagining what they could do with such a thing, until Loge adds that it can only be made at the expense of love. But now that Alberich has done that it need not be done again. The Ring can be had by simply taking it from him, though in suggesting this to Wotan Loge adds that surely he would only do that in order to give the gold back to the Rhinemaidens.

Before Wotan can fully react to this, Fafner intervenes, bluntly demanding that Wotan pay for his castle with Alberich's gold instead of with Freia. In case he does not, the giants take Freia away with them as hostage. Immediately the remaining gods begin to age and grow pale. Wotan has no choice but to ask Loge to lead the way to Nibelheim, the home of the dwarfs, to find Alberich and take away his gold to ransom Freia.

Scene 3

The sound of incessant hammering on anvils rises as the scene darkens and we descend into the depths of the earth. We arrive somewhat before Wotan and Loge to find Alberich bullying his brother Mime, whom he has forced to make a magic helmet of invisibility, the Tarnhelm, so that he can spy on the other Nibelungs and make sure they are working hard for him. Mime has been pretending it is not yet finished in the hope that he can use it himself to escape Alberich's attentions, and perhaps even steal the Ring from him. But his brother is not so gullible and now seizes the Tarnhelm and demonstrates its use by making himself invisible and tormenting Mime, whom he leaves writhing in agony as he goes off to punish the other dwarfs.

Loge and Wotan appear and learn all this from Mime. Alberich returns and Mime runs off. Alberich scoffs at the gods. Though he does not trust them he thinks his new power protects him. Loge skilfully plays on the dwarf's overconfidence and eventually persuades him to demonstrate his new toy by using the Tarnhelm to change into a fearsome dragon. Alberich does so with ease and Loge pretends to be afraid of him (though Wotan merely laughs). Next, however, Loge asks if Alberich can also change himself into something really small, much more difficult than turning into something big. Alberich takes the bait and transforms himself into a toad. Immediately the gods catch him, tear off the Tarnhelm, tie him up and take him back up to the mountain-top.

Scene 4

Alberich realises he is at the mercy of Wotan and Loge and asks what they want. They demand his gold. He agrees, while quietly hoping that he can retain the Ring, with which he can soon acquire another hoard. He commands his dwarf-slaves to bring up the treasure and then asks to be freed. He also asks for the Tarnhelm back, but Loge throws it on to the pile of gold as part of his ransom. Again, Alberich privately consoles himself with the thought that, thanks to the Ring, he can soon force Mime to make another Tarnhelm for him. But Wotan has not forgotten the Ring, and demands that it too should be given up. Alberich wrangles and resists but in the end Wotan takes it from him by force. Loge releases Alberich and tells him to go, but before he leaves he pronounces his curse on the Ring and all who wear it: the master of the Ring shall be its slave, pursued by strife and trouble until he longs for death to escape it.

Donner, Froh and Fricka arrive to ask if Wotan and Loge have succeeded, and are relieved to find they have. The giants return with Freia and immediately the other gods recover something of their old selves. Fasolt, however, who has from the start been more reluctant than his brother to give up Freia, declares that he will only be satisfied if the pile of gold is large enough to hide her from his sight. Loge and Froh build up the treasure, with Fafner insisting they keep it tightly packed. When all the gold has been used Fasolt scrutinises the effect and finds he can still see a glint of Freia's hair. He points at the Tarnhelm and demands that Wotan add it to the pile. Then he takes another look. Through a small chink in the mound of gold he can still see the gleam of Freia's eyes. Fafner demands that the crack be filled but Loge tells him all the gold has been used. The giant however points out that there is one piece of it left, the gold ring on Wotan's finger, the Ring itself. Loge instantly says that that belongs to the Rhinemaidens, but Wotan says he is not about to give up to anybody what he took so much trouble to obtain. Fasolt drags Freia out from behind the stack of

Appendix A: *Der Ring des Nibelungen*: a synopsis

gold, saying that the old contract is back in force, and the gods turn on Wotan and demand that he give up the Ring, but he still refuses.

The scene has darkened, and now, surrounded by a blue light, Erda appears. She calls on Wotan to yield and escape the curse of the Ring. Wotan can only wonder who she is. Erda explains that she is the everlasting female spirit of the world, who knows all that was, all that is and all that is to be. Sensing the danger Wotan is in, she has come to warn him and make him realise that all that is must end and that a dark day dawns for the gods. As she begins to fade away Wotan tries to stop her and learn more of her wisdom. The other gods restrain him and urge him to take Erda's advice and yield the Ring to the giants. Wotan at last agrees and throws the Ring into the pile of gold.

The giants begin gathering it up but it is soon clear that Fafner is taking more than his fair share. Fasolt protests in vain. Loge however whispers to him that, provided he makes sure he takes the Ring, he can let Fafner have as much of the gold as he likes. This causes a quarrel between the brothers over the Ring that ends with Fafner killing Fasolt for it. The orchestra loudly plays the musical motif used by Alberich when he cursed the Ring to let us know that Fasolt is the curse's first victim. Fafner shoulders his sackful of treasure, including the Ring and the Tarnhelm, and leaves.

For a moment the gods are stunned by the turn of events. Wotan expresses dismay at the power of Alberich's curse but Loge jauntily congratulates him on his good luck in escaping it and seeing it fall instead on his enemies. Nevertheless Wotan continues to be anxious and declares again that he must seek out Erda to find out what she knows. Fricka however changes the subject, reminding him of the new home that is now his. Attention turns to the castle built by the giants and looming out of the mist on the opposite side of the ravine. Donner steps forward and dispels the mist and together with Froh creates a rainbow bridge across the chasm. Wotan begins to recover his self-confidence and reflects that the fortress that has cost him so much effort will at least provide some refuge from his troubles. Struck, as the stage direction puts it, by a grand new idea, Wotan picks up a sword left behind by Fafner and brandishes it towards the castle. He hails his new abode and invites his wife to join him there, naming it for the first time as Valhalla.

As the other gods prepare to cross the rainbow bridge into Valhalla, Loge hangs back. He thinks they are hurrying towards their end and has half a mind to turn back into his primal, fiery form to burn them up. Just then the voices of the Rhinemaidens, bewailing the lost Rhinegold and pleading for its return, rise up from the river below. Wotan, one foot already on the bridge to Valhalla, turns and asks what their complaint is and, when Loge reminds him of the theft of the gold, damns the Rhinemaidens for being so annoying. Loge then calls down to them that instead of the gold they can now have the brightness of the gods. The Rhinemaidens respond ominously that trust and truth live only in the deeps, while above there is nothing but falseness and cowardice, but their cries are drowned out by the thunderously grand music accompanying the entrance of the gods (except for Loge) into Valhalla.

Part 2: *Die Walküre*

Act 1

An orchestral prelude depicts a violent storm through which somebody is running. After a climactic thunderclap a man, evidently a weary fugitive, opens the door to a forest dwelling and enters, gasping that, no matter who owns this house, here he must rest. It is indeed a strange place, built around the trunk of a massive ash tree that rises from the floor and up through the roof. As the man rests beside the hearth a young woman enters. He asks for water and she fetches some. Reviving, he asks who she is but she only replies that the house and the woman in it belong to Hunding. As they talk it becomes clear that the man and woman are drawn in sadness to each other, he because he is a luckless wanderer, she as the unhappy wife of an unloving husband.

Hunding himself now returns home. His wife quickly tells him how she found the stranger and treated him as a guest. Hunding stiffly approves and tells her to make the men a meal. He is struck by the resemblance between his wife and the stranger, whom he begins to question. The man's answers are equivocal but Hunding notes the eagerness of his wife to hear them. The intruder tells a story of what he calls a life of woe. He says his father's name was Wolf, and he had a twin sister, but she and their mother disappeared when their home was

Appendix A: *Der Ring des Nibelungen*: a synopsis

attacked while he and his father were away. They became outlaws, until one day they were separated and the son was forced to make his way amongst people, with such little success that he says he now calls himself Wehwalt, meaning woeful. Hunding's wife then asks what brought him, weaponless, to them and the man explains that, after intervening to prevent a girl being forced to marry a man she did not love, there was a fight in which he killed her brothers and was pursued by her kinsmen, losing both spear and shield in the fighting. Hunding immediately announces that he himself was called on to search for the killer but came too late to help. Now he finds his enemy in his own house. He declares that by the laws of hospitality the man may shelter for the night but in the morning he must face him in battle. He orders his wife from the room and commands her to prepare his night-time drink.

The man is left alone, reflecting on his fate and the events of the day. He recalls that his father once told him that, in a time of highest need, he would find a sword with which to defend himself, and he cries out his father's name, asking 'Where is your sword?' A spurt of flame from the fire lights up the hilt of a sword buried in the trunk of the ash tree in the centre of the room, but the man hardly seems to see it. He is still dazzled by the light in the eyes of the woman he has just met. The fire dies down, the room darkens and then the girl returns. She admits that she has drugged Hunding's drink and has come to help the stranger escape. She shows him the sword in the tree and explains how, on the day she was forced to marry Hunding, an old man in a grey cloak, his hat pulled down over one eye, entered and thrust the sword into the trunk. He who could draw it out could have it, but all who tried failed to extract it, and Hunding's wife realised that it was put there for him who would rescue her from her fate. The fugitive joyfully agrees, declaring he is the man.

Just then the outside door of the house flies open and the light of the spring moon floods in. The woman exclaims 'Who went out? Who entered?' and the man replies there was no-one but the spring. The music now becomes lyrical and the man sings of the way spring conquers winter just as love has woken in them. The woman replies that he is the spring for which she has longed. As they gaze at each other she begins to see resemblances between him and her own reflection and between their voices. Abruptly she asks him his real name and that of his father, and from his answers deduces that he is a Volsung and his true name is Siegmund. At this Siegmund leaps to the tree and, with pride and defiance, pulls the sword from the trunk, naming it Nothung. He offers it to the girl as a wedding gift and asks her to escape with him into a new life. Excitedly she reveals that she is Sieglinde, his sister, and rapturously Siegmund embraces her as both bride and sister.

Act 2

The scene is rocky and mountainous. Wotan instructs Brünnhilde, the chief of the valkyries and his favourite, as well as the one after whom the opera is titled, that in the battle about to take place she must protect the fleeing Siegmund from Hunding. Whooping with exuberance she sets off, but pauses to announce to her father that she can see his wife Fricka approaching, and she looks angry. She hurries out of the way and Wotan morosely waits for Fricka's arrival. His wife has come as the guardian of marriage vows to complain on Hunding's behalf at what Siegmund and Sieglinde have done, especially as they are brother and sister, so adding incest to adultery. Wotan tries to excuse them on the grounds that they are merely overcome by the power of love. Fricka bitterly upbraids him for his disregard of moral decency, his leniency to his own offspring and his unfaithfulness to her. He tries to reply by referring to his own plans to resolve the problem of the loss of the Ring by finding a hero who can regain it but she refuses to be persuaded, asking him what a human hero can do that a god cannot. Wotan argues that the point is that the hero will act independently, since he himself cannot break his own law and take the Ring from Fafner, but Fricka counters that in that case he must not intervene to help the man, or otherwise he is just Wotan's tool. In particular, Wotan should not protect him in the fight with Hunding and should take away the sword he gave him. Reluctantly Wotan has to agree and swear that, for Fricka's honour as the goddess of marriage, Siegmund must die.

He calls back Brünnhilde. She senses that his mind is troubled and he admits to feelings of despair. Believing that, in speaking to Brünnhilde, he is only speaking to himself, so close are they, Wotan explains the history of the Ring, Alberich's curse, Erda's warning of the end of gods, Fafner's seizure of the gold, including the Ring, and his plan to recover it, using Siegmund as a proxy, since

Wotan himself cannot break his own contract and simply take the gold from the giant, who has now turned into a dragon to guard his hoard. Fricka has forced Wotan to realise that Siegmund is not the free agent Wotan thinks he needs. Wotan commands Brünnhilde to kill Siegmund and threatens her with his wrath when she shows reluctance. Then he leaves her. She sees Siegmund and Sieglinde approaching and hides herself.

The two fugitives appear and Siegmund urges Sieglinde to rest for a while, but she instead urges him to leave her and save himself. He declares that he will make a stand at this place and avenge her on Hunding. They hear the sounds of Hunding's horn and his dogs in pursuit of them and Sieglinde has a frantic vision of disaster at the climax of which she faints in Siegmund's arms. He gently lowers her to the ground and holds her close, watching over her. Then Brünnhilde returns. Solemnly she informs Siegmund that he must soon follow her to Valhalla to be one of Wotan's chosen heroes, but, when he asks her if he will meet Sieglinde there and is told he will not, Siegmund firmly rejects what Brünnhilde offers. She tells him that in that case he will die in the coming fight with Hunding. Siegmund replies that he who gave him his sword promised him victory, but Brünnhilde replies that that promise has been annulled. This, though it makes Siegmund cry shame on the sword-giver, does not change his mind. The valkyrie is so moved by Siegmund's love for Sieglinde that she promises him to protect her. He rejects this and says he will himself kill Sieglinde rather than let her fall into another's power. Immediately Brünnhilde protests that he must let her live because already she carries his child, and when he insists he will kill both the valkyrie abandons her mission and declares that she will give Siegmund the victory over Hunding and save him, Sieglinde and their child.

Again Brünnhilde rushes away and, after a moment, Siegmund also leaves, drawing his sword and heading towards the sound of Hunding's horn. Sieglinde begins to stir, nightmarishly imagining the time she and her mother were attacked while Siegmund and their father were away from home. From offstage come the voices of Siegmund and Hunding as they seek each other. Sieglinde, awake again, sees the two men in a flash of lightning from the storm that is breaking. She hurries to intervene but can only watch the fight, over which Brünnhilde presides, encouraging Siegmund. Then suddenly Wotan appears and intervenes with his spear. Siegmund's sword Nothung shatters on Wotan's spear-shaft and Hunding kills him. Sieglinde collapses again but Brünnhilde rushes to her and carries her away, leaving Wotan gazing down from a rock on Hunding as he stands over Siegmund's body. With a contemptuous gesture Wotan kills Hunding, sarcastically telling him to go and kneel before Fricka and tell her Wotan has avenged her honour, while he will follow Brünnhilde and punish her disobedience.

Act 3

The final act of *Die Walküre* opens with what is now Wagner's best-known piece of music, 'The Ride of the Valkyries'. Brünnhilde's eight sisters, Gerhilde, Ortlinde, Waltraute, Schwertleite, Helmwige, Siegrune, Grimgerde and Rossweisse, gather on a rocky mountaintop, each bearing on her flying horse a slain warrior destined for Valhalla. They exchange greetings and banter about the heroes they carry. When they are all together they see Brünnhilde approaching on her horse and soon realise she is bringing not a man but a woman. They are shocked to discover that their sister is being pursued by their father Wotan, who is very close behind. Brünnhilde has only a few moments to tell the others what she has done, who Sieglinde is and ask for their help, but they fear Wotan too much to agree. Despairing, Sieglinde tells Brünnhilde that all she wants is to die like Siegmund, but the valkyrie insists she must live for the sake of her unborn child. This changes Sieglinde's mind and now she pleads for help to escape. Quickly Brünnhilde finds out from her sisters that to the east lies the forest where Fafner, in dragon form, hides with his gold. There Wotan is reluctant to go. She shows Sieglinde the way and, in parting, gives her the fragments of Siegmund's sword to keep for his son, whom she names as Siegfried. Sieglinde responds to this with excited rhapsody (singing a line of melody that will only re-appear at the very end of *Götterdämmerung*, the last opera) before hurrying away, moments before Wotan's angry voice is heard. The other valkyries gather around Brünnhilde to conceal her as he strides on to the mountaintop.

Their attempt to hide their sister is in vain. Wotan chides them for their weakness and spells out to them Brünnhilde's disobedience. When he accuses her of being too much of a coward to face him she steps forward. He bitterly contrasts

Appendix A: *Der Ring des Nibelungen*: a synopsis

what she was to him with what she has become, now she has set up her own will against his, and as a result he banishes her from Valhalla and her life as a valkyrie. Instead he will put her to sleep on this mountain and whichever mortal man wakes her will make her his. The other valkyries cry out against such a shameful punishment but angrily Wotan threatens them with the same if they do not depart immediately, and they fly away with wild cries of dismay.

Left alone with her father, Brünnhilde quietly asks if what she did was really so terrible that he should so humiliate her. This begins a long dialogue between them in which Wotan tries to assert that, after Fricka's intervention and his change of orders to her, Brünnhilde should have obeyed him, while she argues that in disobeying him she in fact carried out his secret wish. As they talk, and Brünnhilde dwells more and more on the tragic nobility of the Volsung twins, Wotan's own feelings for them return and his mood changes from wrath to sadness as he contemplates the failure of his own plans. He refuses, however, to alter the sentence on Brünnhilde, but she pleads with him that, if she must become the wife of the first mortal man to find her on the mountain, she might be protected by a circle of fire that only a true hero will be able to penetrate. Roused by her spirit, Wotan consents to this request. He takes a sad farewell of his favourite child, kisses away her godhead and puts her to sleep. Then he summons Loge in his fiery form and commands him to surround the rocky summit and, before sadly departing, he raises his spear and declares that no man who fears its point will pass through the flames. He does this, however, to the musical phrase that designates Siegfried, so foretelling who the hero will be who will awaken the sleeping valkyrie.

Part 3: *Siegfried*

Act 1

The opera begins with a low, dark and winding theme, that later will be associated with Fafner the dragon, but it becomes clear that at this point what is being represented are the brooding thoughts of the dwarf Mime as he sits in the cave where his smithy is, trying to work out how he can take the Ring from the dragon. He knows he cannot face Fafner himself, but he has, somehow, become the guardian of the young Siegfried, and he has the fragments of Nothung, the sword of Siegfried's father Siegmund, which Mime knows is the only sword that will kill Fafner. Nevertheless, despite all his skill, he cannot forge the sword anew. All the other swords Mime makes for Siegfried the boy smashes to pieces.

Just then Siegfried himself returns from the forest with a wild bear to chase Mime. The boy laughs uproariously at the dwarf's fright and only calls the animal off when Mime tells Siegfried he has made him another new sword. This, however, Siegfried as usual easily breaks. He derides Mime's efforts and the dwarf whines about the boy's ingratitude and goes over, not apparently for the first time, all that he has done in bringing him up. Siegfried shows no sympathy, wondering why it is he keeps returning to Mime's cave when he feels more at home in the forest. Mime tries to persuade him this is because he really loves him, but Siegfried then asks why it is that, whereas the forest animals that live together resemble each other, he and the dwarf are so different. Where did Mime get him from, since he has no wife? Mime claims that he is both father and mother to Siegfried but the boy rejects this as a lie, seizes the dwarf and forces him to tell him who his parents were. Mime tells how he found a woman in the forest and helped her give birth to a boy she named Siegfried before she died. Siegfried demands to know the woman's name and Mime grudgingly tells him it was Sieglinde. Then he asks his father's name but Mime says all he knows is that he was killed. Siegfried wanting proof of all this, Mime produces the fragments of the sword Nothung. The boy immediately insists that Mime must forge his father's sword for him as soon as possible, and then he will run off into the world and never see Mime again.

Siegfried rushes out, leaving Mime with his old problem of how to forge the sword. As he racks his brains for a way out of his troubles, a stranger arrives, a man wearing a long blue cloak and a wide-brimmed hat that covers one eye, and using a spear as a staff, who calls himself the Wanderer, although musical phrases from the orchestra make clear that he is in fact Wotan in disguise. Despite Mime's inhospitable attitude, the Wanderer settles himself by the hearth and offers to engage the dwarf in a contest of knowledge, with the loser forfeiting his head. Mime thinks it smart to ask three questions to which he knows the answers: who lives under the earth, who lives on its surface and who lives among the clouds. The Wanderer has no trouble answering, respectively, the Nibelungs, the giants and the gods, in the process recapping the story of the Ring so far.

Then he asks the dwarf his three questions. First he asks which family of men Wotan treated badly though they were dearest to him. Mime smugly replies that they are the Volsungs, Siegmund (he remembers the name now) and Sieglinde, and their son Siegfried. The Wanderer's second question is which sword Siegfried must use to kill Fafner and gain the Ring. Feeling very pleased with his insight, Mime correctly answers that the sword is Nothung. Next the Wanderer asks the question that Mime should have asked *him*: who will forge the fragments of Nothung? Mime cannot answer. The Wanderer tells him that only he who has never known fear can re-forge the sword. He leaves Mime's head as forfeit to him without fear and disappears into the forest, leaving the dwarf prostrate with anxiety again.

Siegfried returns, demanding to know what progress Mime has made. The dwarf tries to distract him by teaching him the meaning of fear, but without success. His attempt to make Siegfried fearful by telling him about the dragon Fafner only rouses the boy's desire to go to his lair. In the end Mime decides that, given that re-making the sword is beyond him, perhaps somebody who does not know fear may be able to do it. Nothing loath, Siegfried takes the pieces of Nothung and begins boisterously filing them down, melting them, moulding them and then hammering and sharpening the new blade, singing lustily. Meanwhile, Mime pretends to be making some broth for the boy. In fact he is mixing up a drink to put Siegfried to sleep after he has killed Fafner, so that Mime can kill him with his own sword and take the Ring for himself. Siegfried, despite his crude methods, finishes the sword and, lifting it up, cries 'See how Siegfried's sword can slice!' and cuts through the anvil.

Act 2

It is night in the depths of the forest, near the mouth of a cave, over which Alberich keeps watch, because this is the lair of Fafner. There is a gleam of light and the Wanderer arrives. Alberich has no doubt who he is. The dwarf jeers at Wotan because he cannot take the Ring from Fafner without breaking the contract he made with him and so undermining the system of laws the god has built. Wotan warns the Nibelung that a hero comes who will kill Fafner and free the treasure. Perhaps, says Wotan, if Alberich warns Fafner the dragon will give him what he wants. The god wakes the sleeping monster and Alberich tells him a hero is coming, but Fafner merely says he is hungry. He refuses to yield up the Ring. The Wanderer laughs and says he hopes Alberich will have better luck with his brother Mime. Then he departs, Alberich hides and day breaks.

Mime leads Siegfried, wearing the sword, into the clearing in front of the cave and tells him about Fafner in horrifying detail. The boy is unimpressed and only anxious to get rid of the dwarf. Once he is alone, Siegfried stretches out under the trees. The orchestra creates a sound-picture of the forest morning while Siegfried muses on his parents, sadly wondering if all mothers die when giving birth to sons. His attention is taken by the song of a bird and he wishes he could understand what it means. He goes to the stream, cuts a reed and tries to make a pipe from it so that he can imitate the birdsong. The results are crude and, dissatisfied, he decides instead to play the bird a tune on his hunting horn. Perhaps its sound will bring him a friend. But the sound of his horn rouses Fafner and the dragon crawls out of the cave. They fight and Siegfried kills him, thrusting Nothung deep into his heart. With his dying words Fafner warns Siegfried that he who brought him there is plotting his downfall.

When Siegfried pulls his sword out of the dragon's carcass some of its blood gets on his hand. The blood stings and instinctively he puts his hand to his mouth to suck it off. As a result he finds he can understand the bird. It sings to him that he now owns the Nibelung Hoard and can take the Tarnhelm and the Ring. Siegfried thanks the bird and climbs down into the cave. When he is out of sight Mime and Alberich creep in from opposite sides of the clearing and, meeting each other, quarrel violently over who should have the Ring. Neither will let the other have anything, but both run off when Siegfried re-appears. He has the Ring and the Tarnhelm, though he does not know what they are for, and he is more concerned that he has still not learnt fear. The bird sings again, warning Siegfried not to trust Mime, who now approaches with the potion he prepared earlier. In a wheedling tone he offers this to the boy but, because of the dragon's blood, Siegfried can perceive the dwarf's real meaning in his words,

Appendix A: *Der Ring des Nibelungen*: a synopsis

which spell out Mime's murderous intentions, until Siegfried, disgusted, strikes him dead with his sword. From his hiding place Alberich laughs.

Siegfried throws Mime's body into the cave and rolls the dead dragon in front of its mouth. It is now noon and he takes a rest under the tree where the bird sings. He longs for a companion and the bird sings to him of a wonderful woman, Brünnhilde, who lies asleep on a rocky crag surrounded by fire, waiting for somebody who knows no fear to come to waken her as his bride. Eagerly Siegfried jumps up and asks the bird to lead him to the place.

Act 3

A stormy prelude brings us to the foot of the mountain where Brünnhilde rests. Wotan the Wanderer appears and loudly calls up Erda from her slumbers under the earth. Sleepy and reluctant, she is compelled to answer his summons, but when Wotan demands she share her knowledge of what must happen she tries to evade him by saying first the Norns, who spin and weave the web of fate, or else the valkyrie she herself bore him can answer instead. The more Wotan presses her with his questions, the more confused she becomes. In the end he turns prophet himself, predicting the end of her and all the gods, but the main thing he wants to tell her is that the end of the gods is something he accepts and is glad of. He will leave the world to the young hero who will wake Brünnhilde and make her his bride. He sends Erda back down to endless sleep.

Siegfried arrives, following the bird, but it is driven off by ravens, Wotan's birds. Siegfried notices the Wanderer and begins asking him about the way to Brünnhilde, but Wotan answers in counter-questions and riddles that make the boy more and more impatient. This amuses Wotan, but his laughter annoys Siegfried and he becomes less respectful. The discussion turns into an argument, with Siegfried accusing the old man of standing in his way and Wotan demanding the youngster show respect for the guardian of the mountain. At last he brandishes his spear and tells Siegfried that it once shattered the sword he carries and can do so again. Instantly, Siegfried concludes that the Wanderer is his father's enemy and strikes out with Nothung. This time it is Wotan's spear that is broken. Sadly he picks up the pieces and retires into the darkness, saying he cannot stop Siegfried from going on. The fire around the mountain top burns brighter and brighter but this merely exhilarates the hero, who sounds his horn and plunges fearlessly into the flames.

When Siegfried emerges on the summit he enters the scene as it was at the end of *Die Walküre*. He gazes around in wonder and soon notices what he takes to be a man in armour, lying asleep under his shield. He goes over and lifts it off. Then he removes the figure's helmet and is struck by the abundance of hair beneath it. Next, to allow the warrior freedom to breathe, he loosens the breast-plate, cutting the straps with his sword, pulls the armour away and instantly jumps back in a fright, exclaiming 'That is no man!' The sight of a woman teaches him the fear he did not know before, but after frenzied debate with himself he plucks up courage to awaken her with a kiss.

The woman slowly rouses, hailing the light of day, the world and her awakener Siegfried. He is both amazed and enthralled by her as she explains and answers his questions with the wisdom of her greater knowledge and experience. His feelings for her become more insistent just as she looks around and sees her horse Grane, put to sleep with her, and her shield and her armour and realises that her old, semi-divine existence is gone. For a moment she tries to resist the change and demand that Siegfried treat her with the reverence she was used to, but he overbears this with his ardour, she accepts her fate and the two come together as lovers, and the act and the opera end with them both declaiming they are each other's for ever, one and all, in shining love and laughing death.

Part 4: *Götterdämmerung*

Prologue

It is again night on the mountain crag where the previous opera ended. The fire lower down the slopes still burns. The three Norns, tall, female figures in long robes, sing disconsolately of how they used to weave the rope of fate attached to the World Ash Tree. One day Wotan came and drank from the spring that welled up at the foot of the tree and so gained its wisdom, but he also broke off a branch to make a spear. This so damaged the tree that it died and the Norns abandoned it. Wotan's spear became the instrument of his attempt to impose

Appendix A: *Der Ring des Nibelungen*: a synopsis

law and order on the world and on its shaft were carved runes recording pacts and agreements. Now the spear has been shattered by Siegfried and Wotan has sent his heroes to chop down the old ash tree and carry the wood to Valhalla. There it has been piled up around the great hall, where Wotan and his heroes wait for the end, when Loge will come and burn down Valhalla. The future, however, is not clear to the Norns. They refer to Alberich, his theft of the gold and his curse on the Ring, but they do not know what will happen next. The strands are tangled and fraying and, when they try to pull it tight, the rope breaks. Their knowledge is ended and they sink down into the earth to return to their mother, Erda.

Dawn breaks, and Siegfried and Brünnhilde emerge from the cave where they have spent the night. She has given him all the divine knowledge and protection left to her but now she must let him venture into the world to fulfil his heroic destiny. They sing of their love for each other and, before he leaves, Siegfried gives Brünnhilde the Ring as a token of his constancy. She in turn gives him her horse Grane, though he is no longer able to fly. Siegfried rides off down the mountain and through the fire, that still burns to protect Brünnhilde, and she watches his progress down the valley, hearing his horn-calls as he rides towards the Rhine.

Act 1

In the great hall of the Gibichung tribe their leader, Gunther, and his sister, Gutrune, sit on their thrones discussing Gunther's reputation with their half-brother Hagen, son of Alberich. Hagen tells Gunther that it is time he was married and he knows of the ideal bride, a woman called Brünnhilde who lives on a mountain surrounded by fire. Gunther asks who has the courage to go through the flames and Hagen tells him only Siegfried can do this, but he will win Brünnhilde for Gunther if first he is won over by Gutrune. Gunther thinks this is unlikely but Hagen reminds him of the drugged drink he has that will make Siegfried forget all other women for the sake of the one in front of him. Gunther instantly accepts this plan but wonders where they will find Siegfried. At that moment his horn-call is heard outside as he sails down the Rhine. Hagen immediately invites him in.

Siegfried enters and is greeted with enthusiasm by the others. He reacts with a mixture of eagerness and brashness. Gutrune soon brings him a drinking horn, filled of course with the love-potion. Ironically, Siegfried, before he drinks, toasts Brünnhilde as his true love but after he drinks he has eyes only for Gutrune, although he has to ask Gunther her name. A moment later he asks Gunther to let him marry his sister. Even Gutrune is embarrassed by the speed of this but Siegfried hurries on to ask if Gunther himself has a wife and soon Hagen's scheme to use Siegfried to win Brünnhilde for Gunther in return for marrying Gutrune has been agreed, with Siegfried himself suggesting he can use the Tarnhelm to trick Brünnhilde into mistaking him for Gunther. Gunther and Siegfried seal the bargain by swearing blood-brotherhood (when Siegfried asks Hagen why he does not join in the latter excuses himself on the grounds that his blood is not pure and noble enough) and then they set out, leaving Hagen on guard. He settles down to keep watch, gloating on how Siegfried will bring him the Ring and then he will lord it over them all.

Back on the mountain, Brünnhilde sits gazing fondly at the self-same Ring. There is a roll of thunder and her valkyrie sister Waltraute flies down. After fending off Brünnhilde's hopeful inquiries about a change of mind by her father or that Waltraute has come to join her, Waltraute tells her sister what has happened in Valhalla and how Wotan has gathered all the heroes and the eight valkyries together in the hall, surrounded by kindling, and does nothing but wait for the end. Waltraute, however, overheard him muttering that, if Brünnhilde gave the Ring back to the Rhinemaidens, the gods and the world would be saved. She has come to implore Brünnhilde to return the Ring to the Rhine. Brünnhilde flatly refuses to throw away the pledge of Siegfried's love. Waltraute departs, foretelling the end of them all.

After the valkyrie leaves, the fire around the mountain blazes up. Brünnhilde hears a horn-call and jumps to the conclusion that Siegfried is returning, but the figure who emerges from the flame is a stranger. Muttering the word 'betrayed', Brünnhilde asks who he is. He says he is the man who will make her his wife and names himself Gunther. He moves to take her into the cave and she holds out the Ring to drive him back, but the disguised Siegfried takes it from her by force. Defeated, Brünnhilde has to enter the cave. Before he does so, Siegfried draws his sword and declares that, to be true to his brother Gunther, he will lay Nothung between himself and Brünnhilde to keep them apart.

Act 2

It is night on the shore of the Rhine by the Gibichung palace. Moonlight shows Hagen sitting with his father Alberich crouched in the darkness in front of him. Only half-awake, Hagen listens as Alberich urges him to make sure he gets hold of the Ring from the naive Siegfried. When Alberich presses Hagen to swear to do this, his son answers that he has sworn it for himself. Alberich fades from sight as the night ends.

Suddenly Siegfried appears. He has used the Tarnhelm to transport himself back, in his own shape, leaving Gunther and Brünnhilde to follow by more natural means. He asks for Gutrune and Hagen calls her out. Siegfried reports the success of his mission to them. Gutrune asks Hagen to summon the Gibichungs to welcome Gunther and his bride while she goes to arrange the wedding. Siegfried is delighted to go with her.

Hagen loudly rouses the tribe as though they are about to be attacked and then surprises them with the truth, that Gunther is returning with his bride, Brünnhilde. They all give the pair a rousing welcome as they arrive by boat down the river, but as soon as Brünnhilde lands and sees Siegfried with Gutrune her actions become so strange the onlookers think she is mad. When Siegfried tells her she is married to Gunther as he is to Gutrune she calls him a liar. Then she notices the Ring on his hand and asks how it got there, since she saw it taken from her by Gunther. Neither Siegfried nor Gunther can give a convincing explanation of this. All Siegfried remembers is taking the Ring from the dragon's lair. Hagen now seizes his chance and says if the Ring Brünnhilde gave Gunther is now on Siegfried's hand he must have got it by trickery. Brünnhilde, too shocked and angry to realise what is happening, vehemently denounces Siegfried's treachery, and the word is echoed by Gutrune and the people watching. Brünnhilde then goes further and claims that she is married not to Gunther but to Siegfried, since he it was who slept with her. Siegfried tries to protest that, though he spent the night with her, his sword lay between them, but Brünnhilde asserts that all that night Nothung hung in its sheath on the wall. By this time there is uproar. Siegfried cries out for a weapon upon which he can swear an oath that he has been loyal to Gunther. Hagen quickly offers the point of his spear and the oath is sworn, but immediately Brünnhilde seizes the spear and swears a counter-oath that Siegfried has sworn falsely. Siegfried, however, convinced of his innocence, now turns on his charm and persuades everybody that they should go on with the wedding preparations. He puts his arm round Gutrune and leads her into the palace, followed by all except Gunther, Hagen and Brünnhilde.

As her anger cools, Brünnhilde begins to ask herself what has happened, especially to Siegfried. Hagen offers to help her, introducing the idea of revenge, but when he says he can avenge her on Siegfried she laughs at the notion that he could defeat the hero. For one thing, she herself has cast spells on his body to protect him. Hagen asks if any weapon can harm Siegfried and Brünnhilde tells him that, knowing he would never act like a coward, she put no magic protection on his back.

Hagen now turns to Gunther, who has been moping at the side, bewailing his bad fortune. Brünnhilde scoffs at his weakness but Hagen rouses him by saying that the only thing that will help him now is the death of Siegfried. Gunther, typically, is aghast and reminds Hagen of the oath of blood-brotherhood between him and Siegfried, but Hagen argues that Siegfried has broken the oath by cheating Gunther. Brünnhilde agrees, saying she has been cheated, too. Hagen whispers to Gunther that when Siegfried is dead he will have the Ring and the power it gives, but Gunther sighs for the pain the hero's death will give his sister. Hearing her name makes Brünnhilde realise that it is Gutrune who has bewitched Siegfried. Hagen, however, takes Gunther's point and proposes that they murder Siegfried out of Gutrune's sight during a hunting party, and pretend he was killed by a wild boar. With these details settled Gunther, Brünnhilde and Hagen end the act with a trio expressing their resolve that Siegfried must die, but while Gunther and Brünnhilde call on the gods to hear their oath of vengeance, Hagen calls on his father Alberich to prepare to be master of the Ring once more.

Act 3

In broad daylight by a wild and rocky shore the Rhinemaidens swim in the river, still lamenting the loss of their gold. They can hear the sound of a horn and know that a hero is coming to them. They dive out of sight just as Siegfried appears, having become separated from the rest of the hunting party. The Rhinemaidens swim up to the surface again and speak to him, at first teasing him, then bringing the talk round to his Ring, until they ask him to give it to them. For a moment he almost agrees, but when the girls become serious and try to warn him that if he does not give them back the Ring he will die, just as Fafner did, Siegfried refuses to yield to what he thinks are threats. The Rhinemaidens leave him, calling him a fool for not knowing what he has done in throwing away a wonderfully good thing (they mean Brünnhilde) and insisting on keeping something that will kill him. Siegfried shrugs and expresses to himself callow pride in his knowledge of how to deal with women.

Hagen appears, followed by the other hunters, including Gunther, and the party settles down for a meal. Hagen provides Siegfried with something to drink, which he tries to share with Gunther, who is gloomy with foreboding. Hagen asks Siegfried if it is true that he can understand the language of birdsong and, to cheer Gunther up, Siegfried tells the story of his life. He narrates his upbringing by Mime, the making of the sword, the slaying of the dragon and how the wood-bird told him to fetch the Ring and the Tarnhelm from Fafner's cave. Then he tells how the bird warned him against Mime, and so he killed him. Hagen laughs at this. Some then ask Siegfried what the bird told him next and Hagen, before Siegfried replies, gives him another drink, into which he has put the antidote to the potion of forgetfulness Gutrune gave him. Siegfried is therefore able to go on to say how the bird told him about Brünnhilde, asleep on the fire-encircled rock waiting to be woken, and how he passed through the flames and claimed her as his own.

At this Gunther starts to his feet. Hagen, to distract Siegfried, asks him if he understands the two ravens that have just flown up over his head and, as Siegfried turns to look, Hagen stabs him in the back with his spear, crying that the birds speak to him of revenge. Appalled, the other Gibichungs, including even Gunther, ask Hagen what he has done. He calmly replies that he has punished a false oath, takes up his spear and leaves the scene. Siegfried revives a little and speaks of his first meeting with Brünnhilde in a distracted way, as though reliving the memory, until, at the climax, imagining her offering him a greeting, he dies. Gunther orders his men to carry Siegfried's body away on his shield, while the orchestra plays a funeral march that recapitulates themes associated with the Volsung family, Siegmund and Siegfried himself, rising to a great climax, after which the music dies away in allusions to Brünnhilde, her love for Siegfried, the Ring and at length the sweet if pallid music linked to Gutrune.

Darkness has fallen as we return to the Gibichung palace. Gutrune appears, unable to sleep and worrying about what has happened. Hagen enters to tell her the hunters are returning with their spoils and when Gutrune says she has not heard Siegfried's horn he tells her the hero can no longer blow it. As the procession carrying Siegfried's body approaches Hagen tells Gutrune they are bringing the victim of a wild boar, her dead husband. She throws herself on the body. Gunther tries to comfort her but she accuses him of murder. He in turn blames Hagen, who defiantly accepts the guilt and steps forward to claim the Ring as his reward. When Gunther tries to stop him Hagen draws his sword, they fight and Gunther falls. Hagen grabs Siegfried's hand to take the Ring but as he does so the dead hand rises up. Everyone freezes in horror, except Brünnhilde, who now enters and takes over.

Brushing aside Gutrune, Brünnhilde orders that a funeral pyre be built for Siegfried on the bank of the Rhine and that his horse should be brought. She sings Siegfried's praises and complains to the gods about their treatment of him and her, but now she knows what the gods require and she ends by wishing them peace. She then takes the Ring as her legacy and announces she will return it to the Rhinemaidens, who will find it among the ashes after she has burnt herself to death with Siegfried. She takes a torch to light the pyre and tells the ravens to fly home to Valhalla and let them know what she has done. As they go they will pass her rock and so they can send Loge to Valhalla, too. She hurls the torch into the logs and, as the flames rise, she takes to her horse and rides triumphantly into the fire with a final greeting for Siegfried.

Appendix A: *Der Ring des Nibelungen*: a synopsis

The pyre flares up and sets fire to the palace, forcing the people back, before it dies down, leaving a pall of smoke. Then the Rhine rises and floods in, bringing the three Rhinemaidens. At the sight of them Hagen throws off his armour and plunges into the waves shouting 'Get back from the Ring!' but two of the Rhinemaidens catch him and drag him down into the water, while the third retrieves the Ring and holds it aloft. In the distance a red glow is seen that grows brighter until it becomes a vision of Wotan and his heroes seated in Valhalla as it succumbs to the fire. The orchestra reprises the themes of Valhalla and Siegfried, mingled with those of the Rhinemaidens' singing and the theme first used when Sieglinde learned that she bore a son, and this is the music, raised to a high pitch of serenity, that closes the opera, and the whole cycle.

Appendix B

The Legend of Sigurd and Gudrún

At least since the publication of Humphrey Carpenter's selection of Tolkien's letters in 1981 it had been known that Tolkien had written his own version of the saga of the Volsungs, brought together from the poems in Old Norse that tell the story of Siegfried, Brünnhilde and Gutrune, to give the characters Wagner's versions of their names, and on which, amongst other things, *Der Ring des Nibelungen* is based. As already noted in Chapter 6, in the postscript to a letter of 29 March 1967 to W H Auden Tolkien wrote that 'I hope to send you, if I can lay my hands on it (I hope it isn't lost), a thing I did many years ago when trying to learn the art of writing alliterative poetry: an attempt to unify the lays about the Völsungs from the Elder Edda, written in the old eight-line fornyrðislag stanza' (*Letters*, page 379). An endnote to this passage quotes from another letter to Auden of 29 January 1969, not included in Carpenter's collection, where Tolkien in similar terms refers to his poem as 'an attempt to organise the Edda material dealing with Sigurd and Gunnar' (page 452), here using the accepted English versions of the Old Norse equivalents of the names Siegfried and Gunther. It was this information that prompted Tom Shippey in 2003 to give a conference paper, subsequently published in his collection *Roots and Branches* (2007) under the title 'The Problem of the Rings: Tolkien and Wagner' (pages 97-114), already referred to in the first chapter of this book, in which he imagines how Tolkien might have tried to solve one of the problems in the plot of the story of the Volsungs, caused partly by the loss of a crucial set of pages from the only surviving copy of its fullest source, what Tolkien calls *The Elder Edda*, and others *The Poetic Edda*.

The publication in 2009 by Christopher Tolkien of an edition of his father's Eddic poems under the title *The Legend of Sigurd and Gudrún* has now made them available to all, and presumably allows Professor Shippey to decide whether or not Tolkien's version solves the problem he discusses in his essay. That is not however a matter that concerns us here. This is not a book about Tolkien's knowledge and use of the sources Wagner used, or how his version of them compares with Wagner's, but rather it is about how he was influenced by the Wagnerian work that resulted. Nor is it a comparison of *Der Ring des Nibelungen* with *The Legend of Sigurd and Gudrún* (for that please see Renée Vink's forthcoming book *Wagner and Tolkien: Mythmakers*, from Walking Tree Publishers). Nevertheless, readers of a book about Tolkien and Wagner might reasonably expect at least a reference to *The Legend of Sigurd and Gudrún*, if only to explain why it is not a major concern here.

The only real point that, in the context of this book, seems worth making arises from the final passage in Christopher Tolkien's foreword to *The Legend of Sigurd and Gudrún*, which requires to be quoted at some length:

> It will be seen that there is no reference in this book to the operas of Richard Wagner that are known by the general title of *Der Ring des Nibelungen*, or *The Ring*.
>
> For his work Wagner drew primarily on Old Norse literature. His chief sources, known to him in translation, were the lays of the *Poetic Edda* and the *Saga of the Völsungs*, as they were my father's also. [...]
>
> But Wagner's treatment of the Old Norse forms of the legend was less an 'interpretation' of the ancient literature than a new and transformative impulse, taking up elements of the old Northern conception and placing them in new relations, adapting, altering and inventing on a grand scale, according to his own taste and creative intentions. Thus the libretti of *Der Ring des Nibelungen*, though raised indeed on old foundations, must be seen less as a continuation or development of the long-enduring heroic legend than as a new and independent work of art, to which in spirit and purpose *Völsungakviða en nýja* and *Guðrúnarkviða en nýja* [the titles of the two poems in *The Legend of Sigurd and Gudrún*] bear little relation. (page 10)

This is a remarkable statement both in tone and content. It must have taken Tolkien many weeks, if not months or years, to write the two linked poems in *The Legend of Sigurd and Gudrún*. In his letters to Auden Tolkien refers to these as exercises in alliterative verse but they are surely much more than that. The first poem, 'The New Lay of the Völsungs', runs to 339 stanzas in a prologue and nine sections, and the second, 'The New Lay of Gudrún', has 166 stanzas without a break. That makes a total of 565 stanzas, each, with a few exceptions, of eight lines, or, technically, half-lines, though the edition prints each as a separate line. This is a considerable amount of work, that survives, according to the section on 'The Text of the Poems' in the introduction to the

Appendix B: *The Legend of Sigurd and Gudrún*

printed text, in the form of 'a fair copy' (page 40), that is, a deliberately careful consummation of the creative process, itself bound to take up much time and effort. It is hard to believe that while engaged on all this Tolkien never reflected on the relationship of what he was doing with what Wagner had done with the same material in *Der Ring des Nibelungen*. Shippey's speculations in his 2003 paper may or may not be relevant to the text he did not then have but the *idea* of his essay, that Tolkien's version of the saga of the Volsungs is part of the tradition of interpretation and re-interpretation of the Norse story to which Wagner's opera cycle belongs, and that Tolkien must have been aware of this, is still the case. *The Legend of Sigurd and Gudrún*, therefore, is a part, small but significant, of the evidence for Tolkien's engagement with Wagner, and, if we accept Christopher Tolkien's 'intuition' in his foreword that it should be dated 'later rather than earlier in his years at Oxford before the Second War, perhaps to the earlier 1930s' (page 5), then it fits the period of other evidence of that engagement.

Christopher Tolkien's attempt, quoted above, to head off speculation about a Wagnerian connection with the poems in *The Legend of Sigurd and Gudrún* seems at least mistaken, if not misleading. It appears indeed to follow his father's own attempts to reject comparison between his work and Wagner, as though there were a family fear of Wagner and his influence. In this case the denial is surely not only unconvincing but unlikely to produce its intended effect. Those who have never heard of *Der Ring des Nibelungen* or of its possible influence on Tolkien will have it brought to their notice, and may well give it some thought, and those who suspect an influence from Wagner on Tolkien will be reminded of the possibility, and look out for resemblances between *Der Ring des Nibelungen* and *The Legend of Sigurd and Gudrún*, and *The Lord of the Rings*. Both Rings are round, after all.

Bibliography

Anderson, Douglas A, *The Annotated Hobbit* (London: HarperCollinsPublishers, 2003).

Anonymous, 'Dutiful Daughters', review of Simone de Beauvoir, *A Very Easy Death*, in *TLS*, 5 May 1966, page 382.

de Beauvoir, Simone, *All Men Are Mortal*, translated by Leonard M Friedman and Euan Cameron (London: Virago, 1995).

---, *Une Mort Très Douce* (Paris: Gallimard, 1964), edited by Ray Davison (London: Methuen Educational, 1986); translated by Patrick O'Brian as *A Very Easy Death* (London: Andre Deutsch and Weidenfeld and Nicolson, 1966).

Birzer, Bradley J, '"Both rings were round, and there the resemblance Ceases": Tolkien, Wagner, Nationalism and Modernity' (Wilmington, Delaware: Intercollegiate Studies Institute, 2003: available online at http://www.isi.org/lectures/lectures.aspx: accessed 8 August 2011).

Carpenter, Humphrey, *J R R Tolkien: A Biography* (London: George Allen & Unwin, 1977).

---, *The Inklings: C S Lewis, J R R Tolkien, Charles Williams and their Friends* (London: George Allen & Unwin, 1978).

Chance (Nitzsche), Jane, *Tolkien's Art* (London and Basingstoke: Macmillan, 1979).

--- (editor), *Tolkien the Medievalist* (London and New York: Routledge, 2003).

Chism, Christine, 'Middle-earth, the Middle Ages and the Aryan nation: myth and history in World War II' in *Tolkien the Medievalist*, edited by Jane Chance (London and New York: Routledge, 2003), pages 63-92.

Colley, Linda, *Britons: Forging the Nation, 1707-1837* (New Haven: Yale UP, 1992).

Curry, Patrick, *Defending Middle-earth: Tolkien, Myth and Modernity* (Edinburgh: Floris, 1997).

Drout, Michael D C (editor), *J R R Tolkien Encyclopedia: Scholarship and Critical Assessment* (Oxford and New York: Routledge, 2007).

Eliot, T S, 'Philip Massinger' in *Selected Essays* (London: Faber and Faber, third edition, 1951), pages 205-220.

Fimi, Dimitra, *Tolkien, Race and Cultural History* (Basingstoke and New York: Palgrave Macmillan, 2010).

Flieger, Verlyn, *A Question of Time: J R R Tolkien's Road to Faërie* (Kent, Ohio: Kent State University Press, 1997).

Forster, E M, *Aspects of the Novel* (London: Edward Arnold, 1927; Harmondsworth: Penguin Books, 1962).

Goldman, David P ('Spengler'), 'The "Ring" and the remnants of the West' in *Asia Times Online*, 11 January 2003 (available online at http://www.atimes.com/atimes/Front_Page/EA11Aa02.html: accessed 8 August 2011).

--- ('Spengler'), 'Tolkien's *Ring*: When immortality is not enough' in *Asia Times Online*, 5 January 2004 (available online at http://www.atimes.com/atimes/Front_Page/FA05Aa01.html: accessed 8 August 2011).

Hammond, Wayne G, and Christina Scull, *The Lord of the Rings: A Reader's Companion* (London: HarperCollinsPublishers, 2005).

Harvey, David, 'One Ring to Rule Them All: A Study of the History, Symbolism and Meaning of the One Ring in J R R Tolkien's Middle-earth' (http://www.tolkienonline.de/etep/ring_toc.html: accessed 8 August 2011).

Haymes, Edward R, 'The Two Rings: J R R Tolkien's and Richard Wagner's' (lecture given in New York, 14 January 2004: available online at http://de-vagaesemhybrazil.blogspot.com/2008/12/two-rings-tolkien-and-wagner-dc-before.html: accessed 8 August 2011).

Hilton, James, *Lost Horizon* (London: Macmillan, 1933).

Izzard, John, *Release: J R R Tolkien*, BBC television programme, first broadcast 30 March 1968 (available online at http://www.bbc.co.uk/archive/writers/12237.shtml: accessed 1 December 2011

Kitcher, Philip and Richard Schacht, *Finding an Ending: Reflections on Wagner's Ring* (Oxford: Oxford University Press, 2004).

Klinger, Judith, 'Hidden Paths of Time: March 13th and the Riddles of Shelob's Lair' in *Tolkien and Modernity 2*, edited by Thomas Honegger and Frank Weinreich (Zurich and Berne: Walking Tree Publishers, 2006), pages 143-209.

Kocher, Paul, *Master of Middle-earth: The Achievement of J R R Tolkien* (Harmondsworth: Penguin Books, 1974).

Lowson, Iain, Peter MacKenzie and Keith Marshall, *The Guide to Middle Earth* (London: Reynolds & Hearn, 2001).

Macpherson, James, *The Poems of Ossian and Related Works*, edited by Howard Gaskill (Edinburgh: Edinburgh University Press, 1996).

Ricks, Christopher, 'Prophets', review of Roger Sale, *Modern Heroism*, and Frank Kermode, *D H Lawrence*, in *The New York Review of Books*, vol. 20, nos. 21 and 22, 24 January 1974, page 44.

Rosebury, Brian, *Tolkien: A Cultural Phenomenon* (New York and Basingstoke: Palgrave Macmillan, 2003).

Ross, Alex, 'The Ring and the Rings: Wagner vs. Tolkien' in *The New Yorker*, 22 December 2003 (available online at http://www.newyorker.com/archive/2003/12/22/031222crat_atlarge?currentPage=1#ixzz0uWWEbKTn: accessed 8 August 2011).

Russell, Anna, '"The Ring of the Nibelungs" – An Analysis' in *Anna Russell Sings! Again?* (Columbia Masterworks ML4594/ML4733, 1953).

Scott Rohan, Michael, '"'Which story, I wonder?' said Gandalf..." Was Tolkien the real Ring-Thief?' in *The Ring Goes Ever On: Proceedings of the Tolkien 2005 Conference*, edited by Sarah Wells (Coventry: The Tolkien Society, 2008), volume 2, pages 147-153.

Scruton, Roger, *An Intelligent Person's Guide to Modern Culture* (London: Duckworth, 1998: new edition, South Bend, Ill.: St Augustine's Press, 2000).

Scull, Christina and Wayne G Hammond, *The J R R Tolkien Companion and Guide* (Boston and New York: Houghton Mifflin, 2 volumes, 2006).

Shaw, Bernard, *Back to Methuselah* (1921; Harmondsworth: Penguin Books, 1961).

---, *Man and Superman* (1903; Harmondsworth: Penguin Books, 1967).

---, *The Perfect Wagnerite* (London: Constable, 1898).

Shippey, Thomas A, *J R R Tolkien: Author of the Century* (Boston and New York: Houghton Mifflin, 2000).

---, *Roots and Branches: Selected Papers on Tolkien* (Zurich and Berne: Walking Tree Publishers, 2007).

---, *The Road to Middle-earth* (London: George Allen & Unwin, 1982; revised edition, London: HarperCollinsPublishers, 2005).

Tolkien, J R R, *The History of Middle-earth*, edited by Christopher Tolkien (London, George Allen & Unwin and HarperCollinsPublishers, 12 volumes, 1983-96).

---, *The Hobbit* (London, George Allen & Unwin, 1937).

--- *The Legend of Sigurd and Gudrún* (London: HarperCollinsPublishers, 2009).

---, *The Letters of J R R Tolkien*, edited by Humphrey Carpenter, with Christopher Tolkien (London: George Allen & Unwin, 1981).

--- *The Lord of the Rings* (London: George Allen & Unwin, 1954-55; fiftieth anniversary edition, London: HarperCollinsPublishers, 2005).

---, *The Monsters and the Critics and Other Essays*, edited by Christopher Tolkien (London: George Allen & Unwin, 1983).

---, *The Silmarillion*, edited by Christopher Tolkien (London: George Allen & Unwin, 1977).

---, *Tree and Leaf* (London: George Allen & Unwin, 1964; second edition, 1988).

---, *Unfinished Tales of Númenor and Middle-earth*, edited by Christopher Tolkien (London, George Allen & Unwin, 1980).

Twain, Mark, 'The £1,000,000 Bank-Note' in *The £1,000,000 Bank-Note and Other New Stories* (New York: Charles L Webster, 1893; New York: Oxford University Press, 2010).

Vink, Renée, 'Immortality and the death of love: J R R Tolkien and Simone de Beauvoir' in *The Ring Goes Ever On: Proceedings of the Tolkien 2005 Conference*, edited by Sarah Wells (Coventry: The Tolkien Society, 2008), volume 2, pages 117-127.

Wagner, Richard, *Der Ring des Nibelungen*, with translation by William Mann (London: The Friends of Covent Garden, 1964).

Wilson, A N, 'Why I believe in Harry Potter' in *The Daily Telegraph*, 18 July 2005 (available online at http://www.telegraph.co.uk/culture/books/3645158/Why-I-believe-in-Harry-Potter.html: accessed 8 August 2011).

---, 'World of Books', in *The Daily Telegraph*, 5 February 2007 (available online at http://www.telegraph.co.uk/comment/personal-view/3637131/World-of-books.html: accessed 8 August 2011).

---, *Our Times: The Age of Elizabeth II* (London: Hutchinson, 2008).

Index

£1,000,000 Bank-Note 37

A
Ainulindalë 150f
Ainur 150-153, 155
Alberich 4f, 29f, 32, 36f, 39f, 42-46, 48, 54, 61f, 134-136, 146-148, 150, 152, 168, 186
Amon Hen 37, 164
Andreth 77
Anglo-Saxon 9f, 21, 31, 52
Annotated Hobbit 97
Anti-Semitism 175
Aragorn 4f, 29, 47, 49f, 59, 62, 92f, 106, 114, 123, 126-134, 160, 163-165, 167f
Arcadia 95
Arkenstone 92f, 100
Arms and the Man 180
Arthur 58, 115
Arthurian legends 31
Arwen 29, 49-51, 129, 131-133, 160, 169f, 186
Aryan 23, 158
Asia Times Online 20, 29
Aspects of the Novel 87
Athrabeth Finrod ah Andreth 77
Atlantis 11
Auden, W H 132, 213f
Avalon 58

B
Back to Methuselah 84
'Ballad of the White Horse' 180
Bard 100
Battle of Five Armies 157
Bayreuth 14, 84
Beauvoir, Simone de 67-69, 78f, 83f
Beleriand 155, 158
Beorn 90, 92
Beowulf 1, 8, 13, 25, 53, 178
Beren 50, 131f, 156
Bible 151, 157

Bilbo 2, 4, 29, 36, 37, 42-44, 46, 52, 74, 84, 89, 92-107, 110, 112f, 120, 130, 136, 157, 162, 176
Birmingham 75
Birzer, Bradley J 7f, 10f, 14-17, 20, 29, 53
Bismarck, Otto von 11
Black Douglas 179
Black Riders 95, 115
Bombadil, Tom 89
Bonapartism 39
Borodin, Alexander P 14
Boromir 38, 44, 125, 160, 164
'"Both rings were round, and there the resemblance [c]eases": Tolkien, Wagner, Nationalism, and Modernity' 7
Boughton, Rutland 14
Bree 89, 131, 162f
Brewer, Derek 24
Britons: Forging the nation, 1707-1837 12
Brogan, Hugh 179
Bruckner, Anton 159
Brünnhilde, Brynhild 4, 17, 19, 26, 29, 33, 36f, 45, 48-51, 53f, 56, 59, 61f, 127, 129, 131-133, 143, 153, 159, 185f, 213

C

Čapek, Karel 84
Capra, Frank 84
Caractacus 14
Carpenter, Humphrey 1, 24, 117, 178, 180, 183, 213
Celtic 12, 14, 31, 58
Chance, Jane 23
Charles V 80
Chaucer, Geoffrey 22
Chesterton, G K 180
Chism, Christine 23f, 38, 46
Churchill, Winston 16
Cirith Ungol 91
Colley, Linda 12
Comus 6
Crockett, S R 179
Curry, Patrick 1

D

Dalberg-Acton, John E E Lord 8
Dale 94, 100

Dark Ages 13, 66, 160
Das Rheingold 2, 5, 26, 32-34, 40, 42, 48, 51, 54f, 145, 149, 151f, 154, 159
Davison, Ray 79, 83
Deagol 29, 45, 136
Defending Middle-earth 1
Denethor 40, 125, 129f, 133, 166
Der Fliegende Holländer 52
Der Ring des Nibelungen 1-3, 5, 7, 17f, 20, 24-27, 29f, 32-34, 37, 39f, 42f, 46, 49, 51-55, 60-63, 84, 123-126, 129, 132-134, 136f, 139f, 142f, 144-150, 152-154, 158-160, 162, 165, 168, 173-175, 177, 180, 185f, 213-215
Dernhelm 62f
Die Walküre 25f, 33, 49, 51, 54f, 60, 62, 162
Dream of Gerontius 14
Drout, Michael D C 1
Dvořák, Antonín 4

E

Edda or Eddaic poems 25, 31, 132, 213
Eddison, E R 179
Edoras 34, 91, 115, 128, 166
Elendil 47
Elgar, Sir Edward 14
Eliot, T S 21, 178
Elrond 49, 89, 160, 163
Elvenking 100
Enlightenment 81, 140
Entrance of the Gods into Valhalla 159
Éowyn 51, 61f, 128f, 131-133, 160, 186
Erda 5, 33, 36, 44, 51, 54, 125, 136, 148-150
Eru 150
Essai sur les mœurs et l'esprit des nations 16
Eucatastrophe, eucatastrophic 77, 176

F

Fafner 4f, 29, 31f, 36, 39, 41, 44-46, 54, 130, 134, 148, 186
Falstaff 142
Fangorn (forest) 91, 165f
Faramir 4f, 91, 133, 160, 168
Farmer Giles of Ham 157
Fasolt 5, 29, 31f, 39, 41, 45, 148
Fëanor 115
Fellowship of the Ring 115, 117, 120f, 127, 162
Fimi, Dimitra 58, 61f, 66, 71, 184

Finding an Ending: Reflections on Wagner's 'Ring' 139, 185
Finnegans Wake 142
Finrod 77
First World War, World War I, Great War 5, 38f, 69, 75, 78, 85, 151
Flieger, Verlyn 10, 67
Forster, E M 87
Fosca, Raymond 79-84
Franciscans 114
Franco, Francisco 16
Frankenstein 186
Freia 5, 31-33, 39-41, 51, 136, 148
French Revolution 81
Fricka 26, 48, 51, 162
Frodo 4, 37, 42, 44, 61, 74, 84, 89, 92-96, 106f, 115f, 120, 123, 125, 134-136, 143, 158, 160-165, 167-172, 186f

G
Gaelic 12
Galadriel 4f, 51, 115f, 149, 160f, 186f
Gandalf 4f, 42, 58-60, 74, 87-90, 92, 95-107, 109-131, 133-137, 139, 160-168, 170, 173, 185-187
Garden of Eden 16, 152
Genesis 42, 152
Gibichung 17, 37, 45, 60f, 128f, 133f, 159
Giddings, Robert 182
Gimli 93, 164f
Glaurung 156
'Goblin Feet' 58
Götterdämmerung 1, 17, 26, 44f, 51, 53, 58, 60f, 63, 126, 128f, 134, 145, 157, 159
Goldberry 51
Goldman, David P ('Spengler') 20f, 24, 29, 33, 35, 42f, 52f, 58, 61, 63
Gollum 2, 4, 29f, 43-46, 52, 61, 90, 95, 110, 120, 134-137, 143, 155, 168-170, 186
Gondor 62, 92f, 115f, 120, 127f, 130, 133f, 143, 166, 168
Grail Legend 31
Grey Havens 58, 169
Grieg, Edvard 14
Grima Wormtongue 116, 128f, 133 166
Guide to Middle-earth 156
Gulliver's Travels 71
Gunther, Gunnar 37, 45, 49, 62, 128f, 133, 159, 186, 213
Gutrune, Gudrún 37, 51, 128, 131-133, 159, 213

H

Hagen 17, 30, 37, 44f, 51, 61, 128f, 132-134, 159
Haggard, H Rider 22, 178
Hammond, Wayne G 2
Harrowing of Hell 165
Harvey, David 7
Haymes, Edward R 18-21, 23f, 43
Helm's Deep 91f, 129f, 166
'Hidden Paths of Time: March 13th and the Riddles of Shelob's Lair' 169
Hilton, James 84
History of Middle-earth 77, 120, 154, 183
History of the Hobbit 97, 120
Hitler, Adolf 5, 23f, 38f, 53, 158, 186
Hobbit 2, 4, 11, 22, 27, 35, 37, 42-46, 52f, 60, 67, 76f, 83f, 86f, 89-98, 100f, 103-107, 109-112, 114-116, 120-124, 126, 130f, 142, 150, 157, 162, 176, 182f
Hobbiton 34, 120
Holst, Gustav 14
Holy Grail 31
Holy Roman Empire 8, 16
Holy Scripture 152
Honegger, Thomas 169
House of the Wulfings 180
Hunding 48
Huns 160, 180

I

Icelandic 3, 18, 25, 32, 47, 53, 132
Ilúvatar 150-153
Immortal Hour 14
'Immortality and the Death of Love: J R R Tolkien and Simone de Beauvoir' 68
Inklings 7, 24f, 179
Intelligent Person's Guide to Modern Culture 17
Invisible Man 43
Isengard 91
Isildur 4, 45, 47, 61, 120, 127, 155, 158
Islands of the west, Isle of the West 58, 84
Istari 117-121, 160
Izzard, John 67

J

Jackson, Sir Barry 84
Jackson, Peter 19, 21, 49, 66, 129
Jacobson, Howard 182

Janáček, Leoš 84
Jesus Christ 165, 187
J R R Tolkien: Author of the Century 2, 22
J R R Tolkien Companion and Guide 2
J R R Tolkien Encyclopedia 1
Johnson, Samuel 13
Joyce, James 142

K
Kalevala 180
King of Dale 100
Kissinger, Henry 165
Kitcher, Philip 139-145, 147-150, 153, 159f, 166f, 169, 185
Klinger, Judith 169f
Klingsor 31
Kocher, Paul 1
Kolbitars 25

L
Lake Town, Laketown 91, 93f, 157
Land Under England 180
Lands of the West 58
Lang, Andrew 78
'Leaf by Niggle' 76f
Legend of Sigurd and Gudrún 3, 132, 213-215
Legolas 93, 164f
Leipzig 38
Leitmotif 148
Letters of J R R Tolkien 1, 117
Lewis, Clive Staples 7, 9, 18, 24-26, 35f, 43, 66f, 151, 174, 178
Lewis, Warren 25f
Loge 4, 32f, 40f, 55, 60, 148f, 159
Lohengrin 52
Loki 32
Lone Ranger 113
Lonely Mountain 91, 93, 96, 99, 102, 112, 120
Lord of the Rings 1-4, 8, 10f, 17, 19-23, 26f, 29, 33, 35-39, 41f, 44, 46f, 50-53, 56, 58, 60-63, 65, 67f, 70, 75, 77, 83f, 86f, 89-97, 99, 103f, 106f, 109-111, 114-126, 129-135, 137, 139-145, 149f, 153f, 157f, 160-162, 164, 166-170, 173-175, 177-180, 182-187, 215
Lost Road 10
Lost Tales 77
Lothlórien 41, 90, 115, 135f, 160

Lúthien 50, 131f, 156

M
Macbeth 3, 6
MacDonald, George 22, 179
Macpherson, James 13f
Malvern drama festival 84
Man and Superman 85
Massinger, Philip 178
Master of Middle-Earth 1
Melkor 42, 118, 150f, 155, 161
Merry 90, 93f, 171
Meyerbeer, Giacomo 18
'Middle-earth, the Middle Ages and the Aryan nation: myth and history in World War II' 23
Milton, John 6
Mim 4
Mime 2, 4, 29, 36, 44, 46-48, 52, 54, 134, 146
Minas Tirith 34, 62, 91, 115, 128-130, 133, 166, 168
Mirkwood 90, 92, 105, 120
Misty Mountains 36, 60
Mitchison, Naomi 179
Montreal 80
Mordor 60, 93, 106, 115, 120, 135f, 167f
Morgoth 32, 39, 41, 50, 118, 155-158, 161
Moria 59, 99, 106, 117f, 124f, 130, 135f, 164, 168
Morris, William 22, 178, 180
Mort très douce 68, 79
Mount Doom 30, 60, 126, 134, 136, 156, 163f, 168-171, 185
Murray SJ, Robert 117
'Music of the Ainur' 150
Mussorgsky, Modest P 14

N
Napoleon 38
'Nationality' 8
Nazgûl (Black Riders) 92, 133
Nazis 5, 23, 35, 175
Necromancer 106, 120
New Lay of Gudrún 214
New Lay of the Völsungs 214
New York Review of Books 14, 75
New Yorker 19

Newman, John Henry 14
Nibelungenlied 1f
Nietzsche, Friedrich 8f, 158, 186
Nitzsche, Jane Chance 1
Noldor 158
Norns 51, 145f
Norse 1, 3, 32, 45, 62, 153, 177, 215
Nothung 47
Notion Club Papers 10
Númenor, Númenoreans 11, 155, 157f

O
O'Brian, Patrick 68
O'Neill, Joseph 180
Obama, Barack 15
Odin 32, 62
'Of the Rings of Power and the Third Age' 119f
'Of Túrin Turambar' 4
Old English 25, 178
Old Norse 3, 213f
Old Testament 152, 157
'On Fairy-stories' 17, 43, 76-78
'One Ring to Rule Them All: A Study of the History, Symbolism and Meaning of the One Ring in J R R Tolkien's Middle-earth' 7
Ossian 13f, 75
Our Times: The Age of Elizabeth II 173
Oxford 11, 24f, 75, 215

P
Pacific 80
Paris 78, 81f
Parsifal 17, 31, 52, 128
Paths of the Dead 130
Pearl 1
Petraeus, David 165
Phial of Galadriel 115, 170
Pippin 90, 93f, 171
Plimmer, Charlotte and Denis 8
Poetic Edda 52, 213f
'Problem of the Rings: Tolkien and Wagner' 2f, 213
Pullman, Philip 173

Q

Quenta Silmarillion 4
'Quest of Erebor' 97
Question of Time: J. R. R. Tolkien's Road to Faërie 10

R

Racialism 175
Radagast 114, 118, 119
Ratcliffe, Michael 68f
Rateliff, John D 97, 120
Reader's Companion to 'The Lord of the Rings' 2
Return of the King 16, 115, 117, 126, 167
Rheingold, Rhinegold 48, 60, 146
Rhine 30, 34, 37, 40, 42, 54, 60f, 134, 145, 147
Rhinemaidens 4, 30, 36f, 40-42, 45, 60f, 145-148, 152, 159
Ricks, Christopher 14, 75
Riddle contest 2, 52, 146
Ride of the Valkyries 159
Riders of Rohan 92
Rienzi 39
Rimsky-Korsakov, Nikolai A 14
'"Ring" and the remnants of the West' 20
Ring Goes Ever On: Proceedings of the Tolkien 2005 Conference 68, 173
Ringwraith 37, 169
Rivendell 41, 89, 115, 120, 127, 135, 160, 163, 171
Road to Middle-earth 2, 174
Robin Hood 127
Rohan 92f, 115f, 127-129, 133f, 168
Rohan, Michael Scott 173-178, 181-185
Rohirrim 128, 160
Roosevelt, Theodore 16
Roots and Branches 3, 76, 213
Roots of the Mountains 180
Rosebury, Brian 2
Ross, Alex 19-21, 24, 30f
Round Table 113
Rowling, J K 173
Russell, Anna 49

S

Saga of the Völsungs 214
Sam 37, 44, 93f, 106, 127, 135, 160, 164, 167-171
Sartre, Jean Paul 78

Saruman 38, 40, 93, 114, 116, 118-120, 128, 137, 164, 166-168, 170
Satan, Satanic 15, 32, 118, 152, 155
Sauron 4, 29-34, 37-48, 60f, 93, 97, 106, 114, 116-120, 127, 129f, 155-158, 160f, 166-168, 186
Schacht, Richard 139-145, 148-150, 153, 159f, 166f, 169, 185
Schopenhauer, Arthur 17, 142, 159
Science fiction 22, 43
Scouring of the Shire 130, 142
Scruton, Roger 17
Scull, Christina 2
Sea-Bell 23
Second (World) War, World War II 5, 15, 78, 215
Shakespeare, William 6, 22, 142
Shaw, Bernard 84f, 159, 180
Shelley, Mary 186
Shelob 92, 115, 136, 169f
Shippey, Tom 2-7, 18, 21f, 31, 65-67, 76, 174, 213, 215
Shire 8, 16, 42, 44, 92, 95f, 112, 114, 120, 130, 142, 160, 162f, 170f
Siegfried, Sigurd 4f, 17, 19, 21, 23, 26, 29, 36f, 44f, 47-56, 58f, 61f, 123, 126f, 128-134, 143, 153f, 156, 158f, 162, 165, 185f, 213
Siegfried 2, 4, 26, 44, 47, 51, 54, 60, 126, 134, 146
Sieglinde 48-51, 127, 154
Siegmund 26, 48-51, 56, 125, 127, 154, 162
Silmarillion 4, 22f, 31, 39, 42, 50, 56, 73, 86, 103, 119f, 123, 150, 157, 183
Sir Gawain and the Green Knight 1
Smaug 92f, 99, 102-104, 106, 112, 114
Smeagol 29, 45f, 135
Smetana, Bedřich 14
Socrates 140
Spengler (David P Goldman) 20f, 24, 29, 33, 35, 42f, 52f, 58, 61, 63
St Andrews 76
Stalin, Josef 16
Straight, Michael 117, 119
Strider 89, 127, 131, 163
Struldbruggs 71
Suffield, J R R 9
Suffield, Mabel 9, 75, 151
Superman 99, 105, 158, 186
Swift, Jonathan 71

T
Tannhäuser 17, 31, 52
Tarnhelm 4, 36, 62

Tea Club Barrovian Society 75, 77
Théoden 92, 116, 125, 128-130, 133, 166
Third Reich 23, 53
Thor 32
Thorin 92f, 96f, 99f, 103-106, 112, 157
Thror 103, 113
Thror's map 103-105, 112
Time Machine 43
Tolkien: A Cultural Phenomenon 2
Tolkien and Modernity 169
Tolkien, Arthur R 12, 75, 151
Tolkien, Christopher 10, 12, 15, 22, 50, 66, 119f, 151, 183, 213-215
Tolkien, Edith 50, 151, 180
Tolkien, J R R 1-26, 29-32, 34-47, 49-54, 56-63, 65-79, 83-87, 89, 94-99, 103-107, 109-112, 114f, 117-134, 139-142, 145, 149-158, 160-165, 168, 173f, 175-185, 187, 213-215
Tolkien, Michael 5, 9, 179
Tolkien, Priscilla 24
Tolkien, Race and Cultural History: From Fairies to Hobbits 58, 61, 66, 71, 184
Tolkien the Medievalist 23
'Tolkien's Academic Reputation Now' 76
Tolkien's Art 1
'Tolkien's Ring and Der Ring des Nibelungen' 7
Tous les hommes sont mortels (*All Men Are Mortal*) 79, 84
Tree and Leaf 76
Treebeard 90
Tristan und Isolde 52
Túrin 4, 156
Twilight of the Gods 16
Two Towers 115, 117, 120, 167
Twilight of the Gods 16

U
Ulysses 142
Undying Lands 84, 156
Unfinished Tales 97, 119
Unwin, Rayner 1
Unwin, Stanley 59, 180

V
Valar 118, 155-158
Valhalla 5, 17, 20, 29-32, 34, 36, 39f, 48, 53f, 58, 62, 147, 149, 154, 158f
Vaughan Williams, Ralph 14

Věc Makropolus (The Makropulos Affair) 84
Very Easy Death 68, 84
Vink, Renée 68, 214
Virgin (Mary) 52, 187
Völsungasaga 1, 31
Völsungs, Volsungs 213-215
Voltaire 16

W

Wagner and Tolkien: Mythmakers 214
Wagner festivals 84
Wagner, Richard 1-11, 12-26, 29-40, 42-49, 51-56, 58-63, 85, 122f, 125-135, 139, 140-143, 145, 150-153, 158f, 162, 165, 173-178, 180f, 184-186, 213-215
Waldman, Milton 10f, 75
Waltraute 36, 51, 54
Wanderer 2, 46, 59, 114, 126, 165
War of the Ring 165
Warrack, John 68f
Weathertop 89, 169
Weber, Carl Maria von 68f, 175
Weinreich, Frank 169
Wells, H G 22, 43
Welsh 12f
'"Which story, I wonder?' said Gandalf…" Was Tolkien the real Ring-Thief?' 173
Wild West stories 113
Wilde, Oscar 78
Wilson, A N 173f, 176, 182
World Ash Tree 55, 145-147
World Wars 5, 19, 180
Wotan 4f, 17, 19, 26, 29, 31-34, 36f, 39-44, 46, 48-52, 54-56, 58-60, 122-127, 133-137, 139, 143, 146-150, 153f, 158, 160, 162, 164f, 168, 185

Y

Yggdrasil 145-147

Walking Tree Publishers

Walking Tree Publishers was founded in 1997 as a forum for publication of material (books, videos, CDs, etc.) related to Tolkien and Middle-earth studies. Manuscripts and project proposals can be submitted to the board of editors (please include an SAE):

Walking Tree Publishers
CH-3052 Zollikofen
Switzerland
e-mail: info@walking-tree.org
http://www.walking-tree.org

Cormarë Series

The *Cormarë Series* has been the first series of studies dedicated exclusively to the exploration of Tolkien's work. Its focus is on papers and studies from a wide range of scholarly approaches. The series comprises monographs, thematic collections of essays, conference volumes, and reprints of important yet no longer (easily) accessible papers by leading scholars in the field. Manuscripts and project proposals are evaluated by members of an independent board of advisors who support the series editors in their endeavour to provide the readers with qualitatively superior yet accessible studies on Tolkien and his work.

News from the Shire and Beyond. Studies on Tolkien
Peter Buchs and Thomas Honegger (eds.), Zurich and Berne 2004, Reprint, First edition 1997 (Cormarë Series 1), ISBN 978-3-9521424-5-5

Root and Branch. Approaches Towards Understanding Tolkien
Thomas Honegger (ed.), Zurich and Berne 2005, Reprint, First edition 1999 (Cormarë Series 2), ISBN 978-3-905703-01-6

Richard Sturch, *Four Christian Fantasists. A Study of the Fantastic Writings of George MacDonald, Charles Williams, C.S. Lewis and J.R.R. Tolkien*
Zurich and Berne 2007, Reprint, First edition 2001 (Cormarë Series 3), ISBN 978-3-905703-04-7

Tolkien in Translation
Thomas Honegger (ed.), Zurich and Jena 2011, Reprint, First edition 2003 (Cormarë Series 4), ISBN 978-3-905703-15-3

Mark T. Hooker, *Tolkien Through Russian Eyes*
Zurich and Berne 2003 (Cormarë Series 5), ISBN 978-3-9521424-7-9

Translating Tolkien: Text and Film
Thomas Honegger (ed.), Zurich and Jena 2011, Reprint, First edition 2004 (Cormarë Series 6), ISBN 978-3-905703-16-0

Christopher Garbowski, *Recovery and Transcendence for the Contemporary Mythmaker. The Spiritual Dimension in the Works of J.R.R. Tolkien*
Zurich and Berne 2004, Reprint, First Edition by Marie Curie Sklodowska, University Press, Lublin 2000, (Cormarë Series 7), ISBN 978-3-9521424-8-6

Reconsidering Tolkien
Thomas Honegger (ed.), Zurich and Berne 2005 (Cormarë Series 8),
ISBN 978-3-905703-00-9

Tolkien and Modernity 1
Frank Weinreich and Thomas Honegger (eds.), Zurich and Berne 2006 (Cormarë Series 9), ISBN 978-3-905703-02-3

Tolkien and Modernity 2
Thomas Honegger and Frank Weinreich (eds.), Zurich and Berne 2006 (Cormarë Series 10), ISBN 978-3-905703-03-0

Tom Shippey, *Roots and Branches. Selected Papers on Tolkien by Tom Shippey*
Zurich and Berne 2007 (Cormarë Series 11), ISBN 978-3-905703-05-4

Ross Smith, *Inside Language. Linguistic and Aesthetic Theory in Tolkien*
Zurich and Berne 2011, Reprint, First edition 2007 (Cormarë Series 12),
ISBN 978-3-905703-20-7

How We Became Middle-earth. A Collection of Essays on The Lord of the Rings
Adam Lam and Nataliya Oryshchuk (eds.), Zurich and Berne 2007 (Cormarë Series 13), ISBN 978-3-905703-07-8

Myth and Magic. Art According to the Inklings
Eduardo Segura and Thomas Honegger (eds.), Zurich and Berne 2007 (Cormarë Series 14), ISBN 978-3-905703-08-5

The Silmarillion - Thirty Years On
Allan Turner (ed.), Zurich and Berne 2007 (Cormarë Series 15),
ISBN 978-3-905703-10-8

Martin Simonson, *The Lord of the Rings and the Western Narrative Tradition*
Zurich and Jena 2008 (Cormarë Series 16), ISBN 978-3-905703-09-2

Tolkien's Shorter Works. Proceedings of the 4th Seminar of the Deutsche Tolkien Gesellschaft & Walking Tree Publishers Decennial Conference
Margaret Hiley and Frank Weinreich (eds.), Zurich and Jena 2008 (Cormarë Series 17), ISBN 978-3-905703-11-5

Tolkien's The Lord of the Rings: Sources of Inspiration
Stratford Caldecott and Thomas Honegger (eds.), Zurich and Jena 2008 (Cormarë Series 18), ISBN 978-3-905703-12-2

J.S. Ryan, *Tolkien's View: Windows into his World*
Zurich and Jena 2009 (Cormarë Series 19), ISBN 978-3-905703-13-9

Music in Middle-earth
Heidi Steimel and Friedhelm Schneidewind (eds.), Zurich and Jena 2010 (Cormarë Series 20), ISBN 978-3-905703-14-6

Liam Campbell, *The Ecological Augury in the Works of JRR Tolkien*
Zurich and Jena 2011 (Cormarë Series 21), ISBN 978-3-905703-18-4

Margaret Hiley, *The Loss and the Silence. Aspects of Modernism in the Works of C.S. Lewis, J.R.R. Tolkien and Charles Williams*
Zurich and Jena 2011 (Cormarë Series 22), ISBN 978-3-905703-19-1

Rainer Nagel, *Hobbit Place-names. A Linguistic Excursion through the Shire*
Zurich and Jena 2012 (Cormarë Series 23), ISBN 978-3-905703-22-1

Christopher MacLachlan, *Tolkien and Wagner: The Ring and Der Ring*
Zurich and Jena 2012 (Cormarë Series 24), ISBN 978-3-905703-21-4

Renée Vink, *Wagner and Tolkien: Mythmakers*
Zurich and Jena, forthcoming (Cormarë Series 25)

J.S. Ryan, *In the Nameless Wood* (working title)
Zurich and Jena, forthcoming

The Broken Scythe. Death and Immortality in the Works of J.R.R. Tolkien
Roberto Arduini and Claudio Antonio Testi (eds.), Zurich and Jena, forthcoming

Constructions of Authorship in and around the Works of J.R.R. Tolkien
Judith Klinger (ed.), Zurich and Jena, forthcoming

Tolkien's Poetry
Julian Morton Eilmann and Allan Turner (eds.), Zurich and Jena, forthcoming

Beowulf and the Dragon

The original Old English text of the 'Dragon Episode' of *Beowulf* is set in an authentic font and printed and bound in hardback creating a high quality art book. The text is illustrated by Anke Eissmann and accompanied by John Porter's translation. The introduction is by Tom Shippey. Limited first edition of 500 copies. 84 pages.
Selected pages can be previewed on:
www.walking-tree.org/beowulf
Beowulf and the Dragon
Zurich and Jena 2009, ISBN 978-3-905703-17-7

Tales of Yore Series

The *Tales of Yore Series* grew out of the desire to share Kay Woollard's whimsical stories and drawings with a wider audience. The series aims at providing a platform for qualitatively superior fiction with a clear link to Tolkien's world.

Kay Woollard, *The Terror of Tatty Walk. A Frightener*
CD and Booklet, Zurich and Berne 2000, ISBN 978-3-9521424-2-4

Kay Woollard, *Wilmot's Very Strange Stone or What came of building "snobbits"*
CD and booklet, Zurich and Berne 2001, ISBN 978-3-9521424-4-8

www.ingramcontent.com/pod-product-compliance
Lightning Source LLC
Chambersburg PA
CBHW070732160426
43192CB00009B/1411